ADVANCE PRAISE FOR *TEACHING PARTICULARS*

"*Teaching Particulars* is an exemplary series of literary conversations by a master teacher on a great variety of important, life-shaping books. The guidance is unfailingly humane, the essays thoughtfully presented by someone who cares as much for the written word as she does about her classroom and her subject matter. Her commentary on Hecht's 'Rites and Ceremonies,' the poet's complex response to Eliot's 'The Waste Land,' ranks among the very best anywhere, as is true for her reading of Hecht's 'Devotions of a Painter,' which has the further advantage of illuminating that work in light of Elizabeth Bishop's profound meditation on painting in her 'Poem.' Reading *Teaching Particulars* makes me wish that all of my students could have had Helaine Smith as their teacher." —Jonathan F. S. Post, Distinguished Professor of English and former Chair of the Department, UCLA

"There's simply nothing else like *Teaching Particulars*, a book packed with so much wisdom and practical advice about teaching literature that every instructor of grades 6 to 12—and of college classes, too—will want to get a copy right now. Even if you're not a teacher, I highly recommend it. The love of books pulses through every page Helaine Smith writes, and her passion is infectious. She opens our eyes to the pleasures of reading in a way that few critics can, and she does it all in a book whose style is both elegant and friendly." —David Mikics, John and Rebecca Moores Professor of English, University of Houston, and author of *Slow Reading in a Hurried Age*

"Helaine Smith's *Teaching Particulars* is not only a rich resource for teachers, but, as a collaborative adventure, also a medium for the reader to enjoy being Smith's student. Her pairing of Coleridge's 'This Lime Tree Bower, My Prison' with Hopkins's 'Pied Beauty' is inspired, her chapter on 'My Last Duchess' is a lesson in how to manage adult questions for young readers, and by the time they and we come to *Pride and Prejudice*, we and they are primed to test every masterful word of Austen's layered conversation. *Teaching Particulars* is a bounteous resource for all teachers, as well as a pleasure just to curl up with and read away." —Susan J. Wolfson, Professor of English, Princeton University and past President, Association of Literary Critics, Scholars, and Writers

HELAINE L. SMITH

Teaching Particulars

Literary Conversations in Grades 6–12

PAUL DRY BOOKS
Philadelphia 2015

First Paul Dry Books Edition, 2015

Paul Dry Books, Inc.
Philadelphia, Pennsylvania
www.pauldrybooks.com

For a list of text permissions, see page 247, which constitutes
an extension of this copyright page.

Cover photograph by Nathan Blaney

Printed in the United States of America

Library of Congress Cataloging-in-Publication Data

Smith, Helaine L.
  Teaching particulars : literary conversations in grades 6–12 /
Helaine L. Smith.
     pages cm
   ISBN 978-1-58988-091-7 (paperback)
 1. Literature—Study and teaching. I. Title.
  PN59.S58 2015
  807—dc23

                                               2014047031

For Elise Partridge
poet, teacher, and friend

Contents

GRADE 10

GRADE 12

GRADE 12 SPECIAL TOPICS

Acknowledgments

To my Brearley and Hunter students for their constant engagement with all that we studied together; to Jonathan Post, who so generously corresponded with me about my draft of "Rites and Ceremonies"; to Jee Leong Koh and Stephen Cox, for reading portions of this text; to the Association of Literary Scholars, Critics, and Writers, for its support over many years; to John Corenswet, for his scrupulous and patient editing; to Paul Dry, publisher, reader, and friend, for proposing this project, shaping its direction, and offering advice, humor, and encouragement along the way; and to my husband, Stuart A. Smith, for his wisdom, wit, and love.

Introduction

This book is about studying great literature in grades 6–12 by looking closely at the "particulars" of each text and finding there the keys that unlock meaning. The poems, short stories, novels, plays, and essays discussed in these pages are complex enough to repay the most probing study, profound enough to be treasured all one's life.

This book is also about "particulars" of teaching—about the sorts of questions that guide but do not limit students, the capacities that students have, and the pleasure they take in discovering those capacities and encountering emotional and aesthetic beauty firsthand.

Once a visitor asked my class of eleven-year-olds what they did in sixth-grade English. A hand went up and a small, high, and emphatic voice answered, "We think!" And then about six or seven other students echoed, "Yes." "That's it!" "We think." I don't know what the visitor took that to mean, but I do know that all students love to "think," to find that they have developed the skills to ask the right questions about a text and that they know where and how to look for the answers. That's what this book is about: classes in which we learn what questions to pose and what directions to go in. There's no pleasure, not for student and not for teacher, in examining material so as to arrive at a single, predetermined, "right" answer. What makes teaching and learning a pleasure is a sense of shared discovery. Good questions at each grade level need to be open-ended, but not directionless. Students are most at ease when they feel held, but by the loosest of ties, like Frost's "silken tent."

When I was in high school I had an English teacher who, for every class discussion and every writing exercise, asked one question, and one question only: How do character, plot, and setting reveal theme? His approach was deadening. A good teacher's job is to hold each piece of great literature in trust for her or his students, to catch its music, and to hand it on as one would any object of beauty—unchipped, untarnished, its surface bright and clear. And so the questions one asks cannot be formulaic; instead, they must be "particular." Each great work of literature tells, if we let it, what sort of inquiry suits it—although as teachers we arrive at that ideal place, if at all, only through trial and error.

While there are differences in what students at each grade level respond to, there is virtually no difference in *how* one teaches great literature to sixes or to twelves. The only difference is the pace at which one goes. For younger students, I break all questions down into component parts; their answers tend to be correspondingly brief. With older students, often I need only broach a topic or urge on a discussion. The older ones can do much because they have been trained for years to look at "particulars." And so my voice is often almost entirely absent in the later chapters, just a nudge here and an approving nod, smile, or word there, as these skilled older students develop ideas and arguments, raise possibilities, tack in new directions, and constantly seek to understand the artistry of each text and each author.

In every grade and for every text we discuss, the questions are really always the same question: *Why is this or that in the text? What if it weren't? What if, instead of this, the author had written that?* (and here I offer examples of weak alternatives). The assumption behind each question is that everything a great author does is deliberate rather than accidental. While that is not quite an accurate view of the creative process, it is the necessary starting point for close analysis. Great poems, plays, essays, and stories are so finely calibrated that we can inquire about virtually everything in them. A text that can't sustain that sort of scrutiny is not a very good text. Of course, one can go too far, but students are excellent critics of this sort of thing.

I try to master whatever text I'm teaching, but when I'm puzzled about something, I admit my uncertainty to my students and we soldier on together. Because, like most teachers, only after I've taught something many times do I begin to grasp what is most important about it and to move expeditiously through it, each of these chapters reflects many years of teaching the same text. Such rereading is, however, a pleasure rather than a chore, because with great texts each rereading yields new "particulars" and new understanding.

Every text discussed in these pages can also be taught to older students, but not to younger ones. The same is not true in the other direction. There is, for example, no way that *Hamlet* (Chapter 28) can be taught as a tragedy of cognition in any grade below eleven. To do so would be to strip a great text of its subtlety and beauty because students are simply too young to follow with patience all that it offers. The aim of close reading, of teaching the "particulars," is never to be reductive.

What students can do at a particular age is, to a fairly large extent, a function of the degree of personal identification that they need to feel with what they're reading. For young students—sixth and seventh graders—texts in which some of a character's feelings are familiar or in which there are clear demarcations between good and evil, justice and injustice, or sincerity and hypocrisy work well.

My slightly older students—eighth and ninth graders—are capable of both understanding the emotions of a variety of characters and appreciating literary technique. They tend to be suddenly and strongly aware of natural beauty and the natural world, and poems such as "This Lime-Tree Bower My Prison" and "Pied Beauty" tap into those energies. A number of Shakespeare's sonnets work well in ninth grade—those that reflect experience with which the student can identify and offer, at the same time, significant aesthetic and intellectual challenge. "Goodfriday, 1613, Riding Westward" strikes the same balance—its emotion perhaps less familiar to students, but discernible nonetheless, and its extended intellectual argument appealing to a new-found capability for abstraction. Social conscience seems to flower around tenth grade, making students particularly responsive to texts that assist them to see the world through others' eyes—from the perspective of a house slave in Rita Dove's poem or a believer in Christian salvation in Flannery O'Connor's stories.

Older students—eleventh and twelfth graders—can respond to texts where emotional identification is not key, but where thoughts about art itself, about memory and mutability, about pain and fraught relationships, about death, and even about delight in frivolous things are dominant.

Welcome to our classes.

Teaching Particulars

1

Genesis

*In which we begin to think about what each word
and phrase of a great text implies.*

GRADE 6

The Seven Days of Creation

The account of the Seven Days of Creation in the 1611 King James
translation of the Bible is just over 860 words; in the original Hebrew, it is just over 460. In both languages, it is a marvel of compression and profound simplicity.

My sixth-grade students come from religious homes of all sorts
and all levels of observance and from non-religious homes, and my
first job is to assure everyone that we are not teaching religion or
instilling belief. What we are doing is learning to read literature
closely by using a text in which every detail has significance, a text
that also gives us essential information for approaching other Western texts with understanding.

After a brief introduction I ask my class to imagine, just for our
immediate purpose, not that God dictated these words to Moses on
Mt. Sinai, but that someone long ago looked at the physical world
and set down with extraordinary compactness, in prose both simple
and majestic, the nature of that world. I ask them to imagine, for our
immediate purpose, that this someone took nothing for granted, and
that this someone was very intelligent and recorded as God's work
the miraculous reality of what he saw.

As we look at the account of the Seven Days of Creation, we find
that that someone, or those someones, looked at the light that lights

1

up the world each morning and asked, What if there were no light? and realized what an extraordinary thing it is that there is light.

That that someone saw that the night turned into day and into night and into day again, and so on. And saw that in our universe there is a thing we call time.

That that someone imagined something before "the beginning," since God must somehow antedate the physical world if He is there to create it. I ask my class to try to imagine a moment before creation, before time. We sit very still and very silently and time doesn't seem to pass—it doesn't seem to exist. So God is perhaps imagined by that someone as existing in a world without time, in a kind of eternal present, since God makes time only when He divides the light from the darkness, creating change.

That that someone thought about the phenomenon of rain and, in looking upward at the sky from which rain fell, saw only a clear vault, and, at times, stars and sun and moon in that vault, and posited that the clear vault was solid and that beyond it were waters, just as there were waters on earth. And, in the story of Noah, that the "windows" of that vault were opened and the contained and always-present waters poured down. While we talk of these things, I ask my class to put aside what we all know about clouds and condensation in the atmosphere and instead to imagine whether, without such knowledge, such an explanation is not, indeed, a description of what we see.

That that someone saw seas and dry land and asked, What if there weren't seas and dry land? What if it all were the same—all water, or all earth and water mixed as mud and ooze—nothing stable and solid?

That that someone looked at all the plants and herbs and fruit trees of the world, and at all the seeds, and said, What if there were no seeds? How miraculous it is that there are seeds, and that from seeds spring plants and herbs and fruit trees exactly like the ones the seeds come from! How orderly is this physical world, and how chaotic it would be if monkeys could grow from banana trees!

That that someone looked at all the animal life on earth—at fish in the sea, birds in the air, beasts on the earth, insects that crawl—and asked, How can I define what all these things have in common? Not by saying they have "breath," because who can see an insect breathe? or a lion breathe?—but what we do see is that these things move, and so movement is a way of defining what lives but is not a plant.

And that that someone, in completing this magisterial account of the physical universe in so few words, with such miraculous concision, included in this account a definition of God as a benign creative force, the maker of this world we know and see.

That this God conceives of what has not ever been. I say to my students, *If I ask you to imagine a color you have never seen before, can you?*

"No," they say, a bit shocked after closing their eyes and trying very hard to see a new color, "we can't."

But, I say, *if I asked you to imagine a form that you have never seen, you could do that, couldn't you?*

"Yes, of course, look at what I've drawn on my notebook!" And together we figure out why—they would be putting together in new ways forms they had already seen. That is the difference between what this text says God can do and what we can do—we can create, but not out of nothing.

That this God "saw the light, that it was good," "good" being a word that is repeated again and again in the account of the Days of Creation. I ask, *If a teacher writes "good" on something you have done, what is that teacher saying?* Eventually we get to the answer— the teacher is saying that what you have done is what the teacher intended for you to do, so that when God "saw that it was good" that means that the result of God's action exactly matches God's intention, and that, for each day and each thing God does, that is the case. And so, according to this someone, whatever God conceives of immediately comes into being and is precisely as God wished it to be.

We notice that on the sixth day God refers back to what has been created on the third day—all that grows on the earth shall be "meat" (food) for man and beast. And we realize that the account of the six days, which we have read as one good idea followed by another and another, was actually a larger plan, its end in sight from the beginning, with man as the pinnacle of creation, because in God's mind it was for man that those growing things were made.

We learn gradually to trust the text to tell us all that we need to know, and thus, when that someone says that God will make man "in His image," we agree that, while we've heard nothing about

God's physical form, we have discovered a great deal about God's non-physical "self": God plans, God imagines and creates, God evaluates and judges, God prefers what is good over what is not good, God is satisfied and pleased, God expresses his thoughts and takes actions—and all these things man can do, in addition to doing what animals can do, which is to "move." And this, as far as we can guess, may be what is meant by "in His image."

On the seventh day nothing is created. *Why, then, I ask, might our someone have included a seventh day?*

The immediate answer is always "Maybe God was tired and wanted to take a nap." Together we recall the work God has done in the preceding days, which turns out to be simply conceiving of something and instantaneously calling it into being—not sweaty labor.

So, if God isn't tired, why this seventh day? What, I ask, could have occurred on this seventh day that did occur on all of the preceding six?

"God could have made something."

And therefore . . . ?

"And therefore, since there is another day in which something could be made if anything needed to be made, nothing more needs to be made."

Bravo.

And so we conclude that the inclusion of a seventh day tells us that the work of creation is complete. We have learned to trust the text, to imagine an authorial mind behind the text, whether belonging to our useful "someone" or to God Himself, and to probe. The account of the days of creation, despite the divergence of that account from what science has taught us, is realistic—a description, brilliant, intuitive, and concise, of the visible realities of the physical world.

The Garden of Eden

The story of the Garden of Eden is a very different sort of narrative from the Creation narrative. The truths it tells are as profound, but they are truths about human nature and the human condition rather than truths of the natural world. The method of telling those truths is the method of fiction writers. There are magic trees, talking animals, fruit that brings knowledge and produces death—elements that appear sometimes in simple folk tales. But the Garden story is not a simple folk tale. It is a brilliantly conceived presentation of what it is to be human.

My students always begin with a plaintive "Why did Eve have to eat the fruit?" accompanied by "Why did God put those trees in the garden if Adam and Eve weren't supposed to eat of them?"

Eve had to eat the fruit, I answer, because death is our reality. Like the Creation story, the Garden of Eden story describes reality—our physical and mental states. The story doesn't create the fact of death; the fact of death, the necessary end of life, creates the story. If we can find other truths about human beings in the story, then this is a good thesis. Let's see what we find.

My students focus first on what is overtly stated. It's true, they say, that when women give birth, it's painful—and that's in the story. It's true that, in order to eat, one must farm, and farming is hard and sweaty work—and that's in the story. It's true that men hate snakes—and that's in the story. And it's true that we die.

We look next at the emotional and psychological responses of Adam and Eve, and we find something tremendously significant— that the Garden story defines humans as self-conscious beings. We know that as we grow up we become conscious of our bodies, in a way that as toddlers we are not, and in becoming self-defining, we become capable of embarrassment and shame. So it is with Adam and Eve. They realize that they are naked and they "are ashamed." This is not, we agree, something that animals feel. It is distinctively human, and as remarkable a way of defining humanness as motion was a way of defining living beings in the Seven Days of Creation.

We look next at sin, not in terms of man's relation to God, but in terms of man's relation to man, and we find something else just as definitive. When asked by God, "Hast thou eaten of the tree whereof I commanded thee that thou shouldest not eat?" Adam answers, "The woman whom thou gavest to be with me, she gave me of the tree, and I did eat." Like Adam, we try to avoid blame and, in so doing, may betray, shift blame to, or desert even those closest and dearest to us. Adam, someone notices, goes so far as to blame both Eve and God.

It's interesting, I say, that this first sin involves not something as unusual as murder—most of us, I tell my students to their giggles, will not go on to murder someone, but all of us, myself included, have tried to pass the blame for something we've done onto someone else when we feared the consequences, or have stood silent and watched someone blamed for something we've also done and are ashamed of, or have gossiped about someone to make ourselves appear interesting. We try to learn not to betray others, but we do betray them, at least at first. The sin of murder, I say, Cain's sin, comes in a later story, and is far more unusual. The sin we see here, a mundane betrayal when things get tough, is everybody's sin, just as shame and embarrassment are everybody's reaction. How wise this "someone" is, we decide.

Why, I conclude, *do you suppose that God punishes the serpent first? Is it because the serpent's sin is the least important—after all, he has not eaten of the tree—or because the serpent's sin is greatest?*

"Well," one student offers, "my mother always yells at me first because I'm oldest and should, she says, 'know better.'"

A hand goes up. "Then maybe God thinks what the serpent did is even worse than what Eve and Adam did."

How is what the serpent does different from what Adam and Eve do?

"He knows the consequences, but they don't."

"He's not putting himself in danger."

"He's not gaining anything from what he does."

"Except the pleasure of seeing someone else get hurt."

"Adam and Eve don't want to hurt anyone; they just want to better themselves."

Then, I say, *the act of leading others to self-destruction while one-self remaining out of danger is perhaps the greatest evil of all.* It is, I recall to myself, like what Deuteronomy enjoins—placing a stone in the path of a blind man.

Reading Genesis through a narrative lens rather than through a religious one means that we consider only what the text actually contains. Thus, we do not talk of "original sin" or of Satan. In training students to make inferences that are purely literary, we prepare them to read closely and with precision, and to trust to their own logic and experience to guide them.

.■ 2 ■.

The Wonderful Tar-Baby Story

JOEL CHANDLER HARRIS ("UNCLE REMUS")

*In which we discover, to our delight, that we know
more than we think we know.*

GRADE 6

While Joel Chandler Harris's "The Wonderful Tar-Baby Story" is
not great literature, it is a fine introduction for young students who
are learning how to read a text. It teaches that literature need not be
grim to be good—it can be very funny. It also teaches that what we
hear when we read should not be flat, but dramatic—the more dramatic, the better. It introduces metaphor, puns, irony, and the con-
cept of structure—a lot for a little story. It's one of the first pieces
we tackle in sixth grade.

The story is not long, and so we read all of it aloud in class. Br'er
Fox is mixing tar and turpentine to create a "Tar-Baby," which he
sets in the road, and then waits behind the bushes for Br'er Rabbit to come along, "lippity-clippity, clippity-lippity." I ask someone to
drum out "lippity-clippity" on a desk—my class loves any opportu-
nity to make noise—and then we talk about how the words sound
like the rhythm of Br'er Rabbit's steps.

A lesson in dramatic reading comes next, in the sentence, "Br'er
Fox he lay low." *What*, I ask, *must "lay low" mean?*

We define it and then we dramatize it by dropping our voices
almost an octave—not easy, but very funny for sixth graders with
small, high voices. Everyone giggles. Br'er Rabbit greets the Tar-

Baby with "Mawnin' . . . Nice weather this mawnin'," and receives no reply. He then says, "How does your symptoms seem to segash-uate?" I ask the class what he's saying and they assume "segash-uate" must be "a big word" they just don't know. I tell them that I've never seen it before either. It's a word Br'er Rabbit makes up, but the context suggests its meaning. "Symptoms" turns out to be a clue, and that—plus the fact that when we see someone we normally say, "Hello. How are you?"—tell us that that's what Br'er Rabbit is say-ing. I ask, *What does Br'er Rabbit's creating such a "fancy" phrase indicate about his character? How does he regards himself, and how does he want others to regard him?*

"As very smart."

"As sort of uncommon and elegant."

Excellent, I reply. Meanwhile, the phrase "he lay low" punctuates every bit of the story's action and makes us begin to feel the story-teller's rhythms, especially as our attention is drawn to it because whoever is reading tries to lower her voice to bassoon level. When Br'er Rabbit finally becomes enraged at the Tar-Baby's indifference to his courtesies, he "draw back with his fist, he did, and blip he took her side of the head." We stop at "blip."

Isn't that good! I say. *It's so fast and crisp and explosive! Much bet-ter than, for instance, "bang" would be.* They agree, and we've had a mini-lesson in onomatopoeia. This time I write "onomatopoeia" on the board.

We go on, because now the story's getting really exciting. Just after "blip he took her side of the head," Harris writes, "Right there's where he broke his molasses jug."

"What molasses jug?" someone asks. A few wild guesses follow about the meaning of the line, and if we seem to be getting no closer to the answer, I ask what molasses is. Someone explains.

And what happens if a ceramic jug full of molasses drops on the ground and breaks?

"Yuk," is the answer I'm offered.

Can we scoop up the molasses?

"No, because it sticks to everything."

So breaking a molasses jug is doing something that . . . ?

"That can't be fixed or corrected."

"Something final."

Great, I say.

So, why does Harris write, "Right there's where he broke his molasses jug?"

And they tell me, "It's when we see that the trick works."

"It's when we know what the outcome will be."

I write the words "turning point" and "metaphor" on the board, explaining the former as a point after which the ending becomes inevitable and the latter as one thing that stands for another.

We read on. In retaliation for the Tar-Baby's not releasing his hand, Br'er Rabbit punches the Tar-Baby with his other hand, then with his foot, then with the other foot, and finally with his head, a wonderful example of story-building by similar, successive actions. And when Br'er Rabbit is stuck to the Tar-Baby in five places, "Br'er Fox he sauntered forth."

What's "sauntered"? I ask.

Someone thinks she knows, can't quite put it into words, but agrees to get up and saunter around the room for us. Three others, convinced they are superior saunterers, join her, and soon everyone is sauntering, in a complete collapse of classroom decorum. I get everyone to sit down again, and we define the word as "to walk as if you're very important," "to sway or strut when you walk as if to show that everyone should look at you," and "to throw your shoulders right and left as you walk to occupy as much space as possible."

We return to the story and somebody laughs at what Br'er Fox says next, "Howdy, Br'er Rabbit . . . you look sorter stuck up this mawnin'." A momentary silence, and then someone else calls out, "Oh, I get it!"

Why is that line funny? I ask.

"Because," they shout exuberantly, "he's really 'stuck up' to the Tar-Baby, and that's because he's been so 'stuck up' in dealing with the Tar-Baby." I ask for a definition.

"'Stuck up' means, you know, stuck up." My student juts out her chin, closes her eyes, and raises her body.

Appreciative of whatever I can get, I say, *Exactly, and when you're doing that, what sort of message are you sending?*

"That I'm the best; that I'm better than someone else."

So what does "stuck up" mean?

"Feeling superior!"

"Being snotty."

"Being arrogant."

Definitions are important, not just for building vocabulary, but because the experience of trying to define a term forces the mind into logical paths and requires making distinctions and thinking with specificity. We learn that, with a little effort, we can make explicit what we know, or put another way, we learn that we know more than we think we know. From "stuck up" we've also learned how much fun a pun can be. I write "pun" on the board, and next to it the words "literal" and "figurative."

The sophisticated wordplay that comes next in the story is, we decide, another pun. Br'er Fox seems to be proffering a kindly and hospitable invitation to dinner when he says, "I expect you'll take dinner with me this time, Br'er Rabbit." *What is he saying?* I ask.

Everyone understands that "He's really telling Br'er Rabbit that Br'er Rabbit is about to be his dinner!" We decide at this point that things look very bleak for Br'er Rabbit. The trick, whose purpose we did not initially know, has worked perfectly, Br'er Rabbit is caught, and Br'er Fox is about to enjoy a sweet revenge. But the story is only half over.

Br'er Fox, much like the rest of us, can't leave well enough alone. Instead, he launches into a long self-justification in which he sets out prior offenses of Br'er Rabbit and describes exactly how Br'er Rabbit's self-importance and vanity have resulted in his being caught that "mawnin'." Br'er Fox concludes with, "I'm going to barbecue you this day sure."

Br'er Rabbit, the character who has been tricked, then turns the tables and becomes the trickster, and we begin to see the story as constructed of two parts. What Br'er Rabbit does, for he has no weapons and no physical resources to aid in his escape, is use his wits. We read the second part of the story together, and then someone says we can call Br'er Rabbit's method "reverse psychology."

"He pretends that the one thing that can save him—being thrown in the brier-patch—is the thing he fears most."

"Br'er Rabbit understands that Br'er Fox's wish to cause him the most pain possible is greater than any other wish that Br'er Fox has, including wanting to kill and eat him. So Br'er Rabbit begs Br'er Fox to follow through with each method of execution that Br'er Fox proposes—roasting, hanging, drowning, and skinning—anything, so long as Br'er Rabbit is not thrown 'in the brier-patch.'"

Excellent.

The patterns of Br'er Rabbit's speech are fun—"Hang me just as high as you please," "Drown me just as deep as you please"—and someone notes that these repetitions are a little like the repeated phrase "he lay low" from earlier in the story, and also like the series of repeated punches that Br'er Rabbit throws.

The story ends with Br'er Fox flinging Br'er Rabbit into the brier-patch and Br'er Rabbit, a moment later, calling to Br'er Fox from the top of a distant hill, "Bred and born in a brier-patch, Br'er Fox—bred and born in a brier-patch!" He has eluded his foe with nothing more than his wits. The story ends with another comparison, this one a simile—"and with that he skip out just as lively as a cricket in the embers." We talk for a minute about crickets, I explain that crickets are not hurt in a fireplace full of hot embers, and we agree that the story ends with another "homey" comparison.

I ask what we can say about how the story is shaped, and am told that "It has two parts, each involving a trick."

Great. And what makes each trick work?

"The trickster uses psychology. He knows something about the character of his victim. Br'er Fox can anticipate the lengths to which Br'er Rabbit's vanity will take him, and Br'er Rabbit understands Br'er Fox's eagerness for revenge, even if that revenge doesn't let Br'er Fox eat Br'er Rabbit."

Then I ask a different question: *Do we prefer one character to another?*

"I like Br'er Rabbit better."

"Me, too!"

But, I continue, *if each character is tricked at one point and is a trickster at another, what explains our preference?*

"Br'er Rabbit doesn't want to harm anyone, he just wants to be free."

"I think we like Br'er Rabbit because we like to watch people get out of tough spots."

"I like Br'er Rabbit because the second part of the story is a little scary and when he escapes I'm not scared anymore." We've covered a lot of ground in this initial excursion into the fairly subtle topic of the placement of reader sympathy.

I assign the class a story to write of two or three pages, with two parts, in which what happens in the second half either repeats or inverts what happens in the first half. The hero must be an "unlikely" hero—someone not particularly impressive or brave, who triumphs either by wit or by accident. If there is a metaphor that can be included in the story, all the better. We've had our first lesson in looking at structure, metaphor, puns, and irony, and an even more important lesson in not assuming that just because we don't know something we're dumb. We've learned that many things can be defined if we try. And we've learned not to skip over words that we don't know, words like "sassy," "symptoms," "respectable," "presently," "saunter," and "kindle." Later, when we have time, I'll give a vocabulary quiz that will consist of using these words in a story, with enough details to make the meaning of each word clear, on a topic to be determined—perhaps "My favorite holiday" or "Lunch in the cafeteria"—a story that can be true or full of lies, so long as the words are used correctly.

We have begun lightly, and will try to maintain moments of lightness throughout the year, as students become ever more serious readers of text.

▪■ 3 ▪■

The Odyssey

HOMER

In which we find that tiny details contain
clues to character.

GRADE 6

I remember the topic my eleventh-grade teacher assigned for *The Odyssey*: "What makes *The Odyssey* a classic?" I didn't know what made anything a classic, let alone what made *The Odyssey* one. Doc Campbell set demanding and specific questions that required close study of *Macbeth* and *Huckleberry Finn*, but his broad question about *The Odyssey* stumped me. So, as a teacher I try to break things down for my students. (We read *The Odyssey* slowly, but in its entirety, in grade six.) These three examples from *The Odyssey* suggest how, through a series of questions, students can be led to an understanding of the text and the artistry behind it. I begin by assuming deliberate authorial intent and ask myself and my students, again and again, "Why did the author include this or that detail?"

Book 11. Anticleia and Odysseus in the Underworld

In Book 11 Odysseus descends to the Underworld where he encounters his mother, Anticleia. He has been absent from Ithaca for 13 years and asks her for news of home. His questions fall into five general categories, which we try to identify. Grouping things into categories is hard for students. It requires insight and confidence. The more students worry about omitting something, the more categories they are likely to come up with. My question is purposeful

13

also because the ability to subsume ideas under broad headings is a skill necessary for writing well-organized essays. We finally settle on (1) how did you die? (2) how is my father? (3) how is my son? (4) how is my kingdom? and (5) how is my wife? We number those items lightly in our texts, turn to Anticleia's reply, and discover that she is answering Odysseus's questions in reverse order.

I write *hysteron proteron* on the board, explain that it means "last, first" in Greek, and then we practice using *hysteron proteron* for a few minutes in everyday conversation. Someone makes up three or four questions: "What time did you get up this morning? Were you late getting to school? Did you get your math homework done?" Someone else answers in reverse order. "Yes, I got my math homework done. I arrived on time. I woke up at 6:30." Students enjoy mastering sophisticated literary terms, but this is just the beginning—we are laying the groundwork for the close reading to come.

Upon which of the five topics does Anticleia linger?
"On Laertes, her husband, Odysseus's father."
And what sorts of things preoccupy her?
"Domestic things, household things."
"That he's not sleeping on clean sheets."
"That his clothes aren't mended."
"That sometimes he sleeps in the dirt."
So, what kind of wife does she seem to have been? It's a large question, but simple now. They answer and we drop down a few lines to find corroborating evidence in Anticleia's farewell to her son: "But now quickly make for the light! And bear in mind all you have learnt here, so that one day you can tell your wife." *How does this last exhortation, to report to Penelope, reinforce what we've just seen? What does Anticleia assume about husbands and wives? What do her words tell us about her own marriage?*
"That she and Laertes probably talked about lots of things together."
"That he probably confided everything in her,"
"That she thinks of marriage as a relationship of great closeness between husband and wife."
Reminding ourselves of the *hysteron proteron* pattern, we complicate Homer's design. *Why might Homer have used* hysteron proteron *here? Why might he have chosen to have Anticleia speak of her own death last?*

"Perhaps *hysteron proteron* shows she hesitates to make her son feel guilty. She thinks hearing that she died of a broken heart might do that, so she puts it off."

Good.

"Maybe she's modest and considers other news more important than news about herself."

Nice.

"But maybe what she most wants to stay in his mind is how urgent his homecoming is."

Excellent.

Without my talking formally about the difference between ascertainable fact and inference, they've made the distinction with "perhaps" and "maybe." I don't know whether Homer, in his genius, used such rhetorical patterns as *hysteron proteron* simply for the beauty and orderliness he found in them, or for characterization as well. I like to think for both, but it doesn't matter at this point. What I want to do is train my students to go beyond literary labels—which they of course have to master—and consider the dramatic and contextual importance of details as small as these. Put simply, I want them to ask why this or that detail is in the text.

Book 13. Odysseus's Lie

Immediately after he arrives on Ithaca with gifts of Phaeacian treasure, Odysseus encounters a shepherd to whom he lies about his identity and his history. Readers, including my students, are eager to skip over the lie to get to the action, but I don't let them. I ask, *Why does Odysseus tell this lie? Is he being clever or just having some idle fun?* I know these questions are too broad for them, as they would have been for me in Doc Campbell's class, but I want to plant these possibilities in their minds.

Then we break these questions down into manageable units: *What does he have with him?*

"Treasure."

What might he fear?

"That the shepherd and perhaps the shepherd's friends will steal it?"

Good, and what is the essence of his lie?

"That he killed someone who tried to take his booty."

So what's he doing?

"Warning the shepherd!"
Yes, and why make his victim a prince?
"To show he's not scared of anyone?"
Good, and why make his victim so fast a runner?
"To show he can overcome the strongest, fastest man."
Why does he say he killed Orsilochus in ambush?
"To show he's clever."
"To show he's patient."
"Sneaky."
"To show he'll wait quietly for as long as it takes."
"To show he studies the habits of his opponent."
And why does he say the sky was "pitch-black" that night?
"Perhaps to suggest the gods were on his side and sent clouds to cover the moon and stars?"
So what's his message to the shepherd?
"Better not touch my stuff."
And what does he say he did for the Phoenicians who took him aboard?
"'Made them a suitable payment from his booty.'"
Why does he include this second big lie?
"To tell the shepherd if you help me stow this stuff and keep it a secret, I'll give you something."
How clever is Odysseus?
"Very!" emphatically, from everyone in the class. After close reading, Odysseus's cleverness becomes, not a term that students are told to associate with Odysseus, but a truth they have uncovered themselves. All that I have done is turn into specific form the repeated question "Why is this detail here?"

Book 4. Helen's Entrance

Like Odysseus's lie to the shepherd, Helen's entrance into the great hall where Menelaus is entertaining his visitors, Telemachus and Peisistratus, is something one might understandably pass over. It is also the beginning of Homer's characterization of Helen. The poet seems to have put to himself the question, What was Helen like? What could have made her so devastating to men? Was it simply, as Marlowe claimed centuries later, her "face" that launched those "thousand ships"? Homer introduces Helen to us as a woman of supreme confidence, quick with a range of moods, who loves being the focus of everyone's attention, and who knows how to shower attention on all the men around her. Menelaus sees in Telemachus a resemblance to Odysseus but hesitates, out of courtesy, to mention it. Helen enters. *In Book 1 when Penelope comes down the staircase to the great hall to address her Suitors, what does she have with her?*

"Just her ladies."

And Helen here in Book 4?

"Three attendants and lots of stuff."

What kind of "stuff"?

"Beautiful stuff."

Be more specific.

"'A rug of the softest wool.'"

"A 'silver work-basket.'"

"'A golden spindle.'"

"'Fine-spun yarn.'"

Of?

"Of 'dark wool.'"

How do these things make her look?

"Glamorous but domestic."

"Like she's a good housewife about to weave something."

And does she?

"No."

So what is the purpose of these things?

"They're like props to make her look like a devoted and contented wife."

Excellent. And why does she want to look that way?

"To dispel her husband's memory of her infidelity?"

So what is Homer telling us about Helen, even before she speaks?

"That she's conscious of her audience."

"And of how she wants to present herself."

What about the end of this passage? Why does Homer say that she "at once asked her husband about everything"? Does she wait and listen to the conversation that's going on?

"No. She jumps right in."

And is the "admiration" in which she is "lost" admiration for Telemachus's "likeness" to his father or for Telemachus's own youthful beauty?

We don't know, but we laugh and conclude that in Homer's portrait we have a woman who is impulsive—we agree that that really

fits her history—assertive, supremely confident, and brilliantly flir-
tatious. Her compliments to men are seductive.

Then Helen turns to the entire company—her husband, chiefly,
but also to the other Greeks—to castigate herself, "shameless creature that I was!" We talk a bit about how one behaves if one feels
truly ashamed—perhaps not quite in this way. And we go on to the
story she tells of Odysseus and to its counterweight, Menelaus's
story of the wooden horse, both really about Helen, both examples
of a husband and a wife broaching topics in public that are impossible to speak of in private.

We do this kind of close reading in sixth-grade. As students grow
older, questions need not be broken down into units quite so small,
and answers become far more expansive. But the process from grade
six through grade twelve is exactly the same: in all cases we select
texts of beauty and complexity, texts that when examined closely
yield riches as great as Odysseus's treasure.

.▪ 4 ▪.

My Last Duchess

ROBERT BROWNING

*In which we see the connection between
the whole and its parts.*

GRADE 7

My Last Duchess

That's my last Duchess painted on the wall,
Looking as if she were alive. I call
That piece a wonder, now: Fra Pandolf's hands
Worked busily a day, and there she stands.
Will't please you sit and look at her? I said
"Fra Pandolf" by design, for never read
Strangers like you that pictured countenance,
The depth and passion of its earnest glance,
But to myself they turned (since none puts by
10 The curtain I have drawn for you, but I)
And seemed as they would ask me, if they durst,
How such a glance came there; so, not the first
Are you to turn and ask thus. Sir, 'twas not
Her husband's presence only, called that spot
Of joy into the Duchess' cheek: perhaps
Fra Pandolf chanced to say, "Her mantle laps
Over my lady's wrist too much," or "Paint
Must never hope to reproduce the faint
Half-flush that dies along her throat": such stuff
20 Was courtesy, she thought, and cause enough
For calling up that spot of joy. She had

A heart—how shall I say?—too soon made glad,
Too easily impressed; she liked whate'er
She looked on, and her looks went everywhere.
Sir, 'twas all one! My favour at her breast,
The dropping of the daylight in the West,
The bough of cherries some officious fool
Broke in the orchard for her, the white mule
She rode with round the terrace—all and each
30 Would draw from her alike the approving speech,
Or blush, at least. She thanked men,—good! but thanked
Somehow—I know not how—as if she ranked
My gift of a nine-hundred-years-old name
With anybody's gift. Who'd stoop to blame
This sort of trifling? Even had you skill
In speech—(which I have not)—to make your will
Quite clear to such an one, and say, "Just this
Or that in you disgusts me; here you miss,
Or there exceed the mark"—and if she let
40 Herself be lessoned so, nor plainly set
Her wits to yours, forsooth, and made excuse,
—E'en then would be some stooping; and I choose
Never to stoop. Oh sir, she smiled, no doubt,
Whene'er I passed her; but who passed without
Much the same smile? This grew; I gave commands;
Then all smiles stopped together. There she stands
As if alive. Will't please you rise? We'll meet
The company below, then. I repeat,
The Count your master's known munificence
50 Is ample warrant that no just pretence*   *claim
Of mine for dowry will be disallowed;
Though his fair daughter's self, as I avowed
At starting, is my object. Nay, we'll go
Together down, sir. Notice Neptune, though,
Taming a sea-horse, thought a rarity,
Which Claus of Innsbruck cast in bronze for me.

We approach Robert Browning's dramatic monologue "My Last Duchess" in a way that appeals to seventh graders—as a murder mystery. What has happened? Who has died? Who ordered her death?

We talk about the elliptical and wry confession of murder ("This grew; I gave commands;/Then all smiles stopped together."), and we consider what the ellipsis contained in "commands" reflects about the speaker—perhaps an aristocratic disinclination to do more than allude to things that others of one's circle are expected to understand, or perhaps a nobleman's view that anything other than understatement is inelegant. The emissary's shock is also presented elliptically. He must be reminded to "rise" and to accompany the Duke down the stairs ("Nay, we'll go/Together down, sir"). The Duke does not read the emissary's response as shock, and blithely shifts the topic to another work of art.

I ask *why*, and am told that it must be because he assumes that no one would find fault with what he has done.

Browning deliberately waits, we note, until this moment (lines 49–53) to reveal the identity of the stranger and the purpose of the visit—the visitor is arranging, on behalf of the Count his master, dowry for the marriage of the widowed Duke and the Count's daughter. Our shock at the murder is compounded by future murderous possibilities opened up by the anticipated betrothal.

The natural course of discussion is from action to character, and we begin with the character, not of the Duchess, but of the Duke. While clues to his character are everywhere, we start at the poem's end:

> Notice Neptune, though,
> Taming a sea-horse, thought a rarity,
> Which Claus of Innsbruck cast in bronze for me.

After a confession of murder, the Duke casually directs his auditor's attention from the portrait of "my last Duchess" to another work of art in the ducal palace—a bronze sculpture prominently placed at the grand staircase and valued by the Duke for its "rarity."

Why, I ask, do you suppose the Duke mentions its "rarity"?

"He's drawing attention to the fact that he and only he possesses it."

Good. And the statue itself—what does it depict?

"Neptune, god of the sea, 'taming a sea-horse.'"

What sort of creature is a sea horse?

"A gentle, frolicking creature."

So what is Neptune doing?

"Subduing the natural and harmless movements of a gentle creature."

"Controlling it."

We note that the Duke not only draws attention to this sculpture but also has commissioned it. I ask *why.*

"He likes to tame things."

And when he can't? We leave this last question for a moment. Instead I continue, *Why is this particular image in the poem? Is the Duchess in some way like the sea-horse? For example, is she strongly associated with nature?*

"Well, she loves sunsets, and the white mule, and boughs of cherries."

And does she behave naturally?

"She smiles a lot and blushes."

So what sort of person is this Duke?

"Someone uncomfortable with natural impulses?"

"Someone who feels showing happiness is not aristocratic?"

"Someone who wishes exclusive possession of people and things."

"Someone with a violent temper—a nature he, ironically, can't control—who wants to appear calm."

We go back to the sea horse. *What happens when the Duke can't tame things?*

"He kills them."

"And," someone adds, "turns them into art that he can tame and control with a curtain."

Excellent. The class has seen the power of a single image.

Still working backward from the end of the poem, and still focusing on the Duke's character, we look at how the Duke negotiates the dowry.

> I repeat,
> The Count your master's known munificence
> Is ample warrant that no just pretence
> Of mine for dowry will be disallowed;
> Though his fair daughter's self, as I avowed
> At starting, is my object.

Particular words stand out in this negotiation, words like "pretence" and "object." "Object," given that the "sea-horse" is also an object and that the Duchess has been turned into a portrait, is a rather chilling word here. Students understand "pretence" to mean "false show," but Browning uses an earlier, archaic meaning, derived not from the Latin *praetensa* ("false show") but from the Norman-French *pretensse* ("the assertion of a right or title; the putting forth of a claim"), and the choice of a more rarified word, one that might easily be misconstrued by someone with less breeding and less background than the Duke, or with less claim to a "nine-hundred-years-old name" than he, is itself a window into his character and his aesthetic of exclusivity.

Does he say, explicitly, that he requires a dowry?

"No," students concede. "He speaks as if the negotiation is completed before it has begun."

"His way of asking is to compliment the Count for the Count's expected generosity."

That, I suggest, *is a form of aristocratic etiquette.*

"He doesn't actually ask for anything. As he says earlier, he is not someone who likes to ask. Instead, he likes to assume that he is understood."

In addition to what the Duke's manner of negotiation and description of Neptune's statue tell us, we have a further clue to character in the very form of the poem itself—a dramatic monologue in which the speaker shapes things according to his will. We talk briefly about what a dramatic monologue is, about how it differs from a soliloquy, and about what kind of person engages in a monologue of this length and type.

A further picture of the Duke emerges as we begin to look at the behavior of his "last Duchess." Had she been guilty of infidelity, the meaning of the poem would be radically different. We decide to look for the most damning lines we can find about her, and come up with, "she liked whate'er/She looked on, and her looks went everywhere." And then we look at the climactic phrase that immediately follows and merits, from the Duke, an exclamation point: "Sir, 'twas all one!" The Duke's complaint, and the Duchess's enormous sin, is that she has treated everyone, the Duke and their servants, with equal "courtesy" and warmth. Three times in the poem the Duke juxtaposes her response to him against similar responses to others. The parallels are unbearable; they "disgust" him. If there is sexual jealousy here, it is of an extremely distorted sort, prompted neither by present nor anticipated acts of infidelity but by some deep-seated fear of responsiveness and by his need for absolute control and possession.

It's time to look at the poem through the lens of style. *Tell me, without looking down at the poem*—which we have now read through at least two times—*whether it rhymes.*

No one can say with any certainty. And then we look, and discover not only that it does rhyme but also that it employs the tightest rhyme scheme possible—the couplet—28 of them, in fact. We don't hear the rhyme because of something called "enjambment" and something else called "mid-line caesurae," which override the rhymes.

And then I ask *whether we can say, if we stretch our analysis to the breaking point, that these enjambed and rhymed lines somehow reflect the Duke's character? After all, this is his monologue.*

Someone says that maybe the underlying rhyme reflects his underlying control.

Someone else says that maybe the enjambed lines imitate the way his grievances spill over and don't stop.

And finally someone adds that maybe the muting of rhyme through enjambment reflects an aristocratic dislike of the obvious. We've perhaps taken our analysis to the limit, but it has helped us see how all the parts of a great poem hang together.

.∎ 5 .∎

Great Expectations

CHARLES DICKENS AND DAVID LEAN

*In which we find, to our regret, that films can't do
all the things novels can.*

GRADE 7

Dickens's novel is divided into three sections. The first ends with
Pip's setting out for London to become a "gentleman," the second
with his discovery that his benefactor is the convict Magwitch
rather than the eccentric Miss Havisham, and the third with his re-
union with Joe and Biddy, his meeting little Pip, and his final encounter with Estella. Director David Lean's 1946 *Great Expectations*
is a masterpiece of cinematography and attempts great fidelity to
the text. Seeing it is a treat for students, many of whom have never
watched a black-and-white film before. My rule and that of my col-
leagues is that we watch film adaptations after, rather than before,
reading the text.

Because there is much to talk about, I pause the film at the moment corresponding to the end of section one. Lean's *Great Expectations* compresses Dickens's length into two hours and necessarily
omits much, but captures, beautifully, many things. Paying attention to both text and video, and closely comparing them with our
books open we see that a good film can enhance the experience of
reading a novel, and that a great novel can do things beyond what a
film can do.

We begin by talking about what we've just seen—the part up to
the point where, dressed in a new suit and a foppish bow, Pip sets

off on the carriage ride to London. *For the time being, I say, let's call Magwitch "the convict," since that's how Pip speaks of him at this point in the novel. What did the film help you see?*

"The marshes and the churchyard. Especially the marshes. I can picture a churchyard pretty well, but the opening scene, with all the streaks across the sky and the thin horizontal bands of the marshes and the river, was great. I didn't think I'd like something in black and white, but this was beautiful. The 'lines' of the landscape were just like those that Pip speaks of when he says,

> the dark flat wilderness beyond the churchyard . . . was the
> marshes; and . . . the low leaden line beyond was the river;
> and . . . the distant savage lair from which the wind was rushing
> was the sea . . .

What I missed, though, was the last item in this series, where Pip says, 'and . . . the small bundle of shivers growing afraid of it all and beginning to cry was Pip.' But that's not something a film can show."
Excellent.

Another hand goes up. "The exchange between Pip and the convict was really good. Lean used the text, but there was one detail I wish had been included. Pip, who is naturally timid and very frightened, tells the convict his name softly, and the convict responds, 'Once more . . . Give it mouth!' That was so funny, because it was as if, in the middle of desperate escape, the convict stops to give the little boy an elocution lesson. It shows, as much as anything else in the scene, that the convict is not unkind—he's even fatherly, although Pip is terrified of him. And that's funny, too."

"This is another small criticism, but the film cut back the number of times the convict repeated 'wittles' and 'a file.' He still repeated it, but the number of repetitions in the text was important—it showed that the convict was aware of how little Pip was, and that the convict knew that little children tend to forget things."

"There was something else the film omitted. When the convict threatens Pip with the ferocious 'young man,' the convict's supposed accomplice, what the convict says is,

> A boy may lock his door, may be warm in bed, may tuck himself
> up, may draw the clothes over his head, and may think himself
> comfortable and safe, but that young man . . .

The film left out the part about tucking himself in and drawing the bedclothes over his head, and I thought those details were the best part. They were vivid and specific. When I read the passage I thought that's just what I did when I was little. I thought my blankets could protect me from witches and tigers. Part of what I liked so much about the opening chapter was Dickens's awareness of how children think."

Another hand goes up. "Seeing the tombstone, inscribed 'PHILLIP PIRRIP' and beneath that, 'Late of this Parish' and 'also GEORGIANA' and beneath that 'wife of the above,' really helped, even though we had talked about it in class, but I missed Pip's saying of his parents,

> my first fancies regarding what they were like were unreasonably derived from their tombstones. The shape of the letters on my father's gave me an odd idea that he was a square, stout, dark man, with curly black hair. From the character and turn of the inscription, "Also Georgiana Wife of the Above," I drew the childish conclusion that my mother was freckled and sickly."

Why did you miss that?

"Because Pip's conclusions are so naive and silly—and made me think of when I'd done the same thing myself, formed an impression of someone from a completely irrelevant detail, or imagined someone as a sound or a color. That passage made me sympathize with Pip right away because he made me laugh and because he laughs at himself as he looks back at his 'first fancies.'"

"I really liked the way he takes from the tombstone the impression that his mother's name is 'Also Georgiana,' and tells that to the convict. What Dickens does, I think, is to set up a joke or an image and then come back to it in a shortened way that is very funny."

Good. But I have a question—why doesn't the film show these things to us?

"Because the story is told in first person—from Pip's point of view. When we read, we know his thoughts. But if the movie consisted of voice-overs rather than action, it would be boring. The camera would have to stay too long on a single image like the tombstone."

What about the characters? Did they look the way you had pictured them?

"I thought of Joe as bigger, and as having light hair and blue eyes. But even if he had blue eyes, the camera couldn't have included Dickens's description of Joe's eyes as 'a very undecided blue.' I remembered that phrase because it characterized Joe's own gentle, malleable nature. But I thought all the other characters looked just right."

Someone raises a small objection: "I didn't actually picture Mrs. Joe—just the bib of her apron and how she 'sawed' and 'hewed' loaves of bread. The film showed that she was harsh and ill-tempered, but anyone could be that way. What Dickens did was to make her ill-nature special by focusing on her apron with its pins and needles that sometime came off into the bread she 'hewed.' In the film she was harsh, but in the novel her harshness was also funny."

How about some of the other characters?—in this chapter or in others.

"I thought Herbert Pocket looked just right, and I loved his fight in the garden with Pip. I thought that was terrific—even funnier than in the book, with Herbert bouncing all around before each inept blow. I think Miss Havisham should have been gaunter, but what she wore and the cobwebs over everything were just right."

Were there any settings other than Satis House and the churchyard that you liked? I ask the class.

"When the soldiers were marching across the marshes to find the convict, the silhouetting was beautiful—both of the line of soldiers with their muskets, and the close-up silhouette of Pip and Joe."

I agree that the camera is used beautifully and promise the class that we'll see something as handsome later on when the camera silhouettes the London skyline in the rain. Then I continue, *David Lean omits some larger things in section one. Did you miss any of them? Anything about Joe, perhaps, or anyone else?*

"I missed the scene in which Joe has received 'five-and-twenty' guineas from Miss Havisham for Pip's indenture. Mrs. Joe is angry not to have been invited to Satis House along with Joe, and Joe, instead of keeping the money, which is his due for Pip's instruction at the forge, tells Mrs. Joe that he was 'partick'ler' instructed to convey Miss Havisham's 'compliments' and her wish that 'the state of [her] 'elth would have—allowed . . . having the pleasure of ladies' company.' Joe adds that Miss Havisham instructed him to give Pip's money 'into the hands of his sister, Mrs. J. Gargery.' Miss Havisham, of course, said no such thing. There are other scenes that David Lean includes to show how little Joe cares for money and how deferential he is to his wife, but this was my favorite, and I missed its being there."

"I missed something else: the whisper scenes between Joe and Pip. There's one in which Joe whispers 'hulks' in answer to Pip's question about where the guns are being fired from, and Pip mouths 'sulks?' and points to Mrs. Joe. It's a little thing but part of the fun of Dickens's writing."

"I thought it was bad to omit Orlick and just have Mrs. Joe die, rather than become an invalid unable to speak. We suspect Orlick of the vicious attack on her, and that adds suspense, and there's something else lost, too. We never get to see Mrs. Joe asking forgiveness."

Good.

"I agree. Mrs. Joe doesn't know that it was Orlick who struck her—he struck from behind—but her summoning him by drawing what she thinks is a hammer on a tablet signifies that, weakened and ill, she remembers that she was cruel and wishes to make amends. It's ironic because it's Orlick who should be seeking forgiveness, but the need to be forgiven is something Dickens stresses again and again. Pip is ashamed for having looked down on Biddy and Joe and Magwitch, and Estella needs forgiveness for having been unkind."

Good.

"I guess it's hard to show irony on film, but Orlick is also an ironic contrast to the convict. We see the goodness in the convict when he tries to protect Pip by saying it was he who stole the pork pie and the liquor, and later we find that he hasn't done anything as awful as Orlick has, but, unlike Orlick, he's caught and tried and convicted—twice."

"There's something else that's wrong about eliminating Mrs. Joe rather than making her an invalid. Biddy comes to Joe's house to care for Mrs. Joe. In the film there's no justification for Biddy's coming to live with Joe and Pip. In fact, it's improper and reflects badly on both herself and Joe. Dickens never would have done that."

"I have a confession."

Yes?

"When Mrs. Joe, who screams and shouts all the time, can no longer speak, I was sort of pleased. It seemed a just punishment. But when she dies, it seems too harsh."

Someone voices the opposite objection to Mrs. Joe's death: "Actually, her death in the film didn't seem at all harsh to me. It just seemed completely random, and Dickens uses every detail in his novel in one way or another."

"There's something else about Biddy. David Lean makes her too old. She needs to be closer to Pip's age and we need to see that she's really a little in love with him, and that he doesn't notice. The film made it obvious that she was going to marry Joe eventually and had no other romantic feelings. Dickens makes her more complex than David Lean does."

Why are her feelings for Pip important?

"Because both she and Joe never stop loving Pip and overlooking his poor judgment and his neglect. And because she, like Pip, but in a smaller way, loves someone she can't have."

"When the movie has Biddy and Joe see Pip off as he goes by coach to London, and when Pip hugs them both, that bothered me, because Pip's leave-taking is much sadder and more complicated."

Let's talk about that leave-taking. What doesn't the film include? Who'd like to begin?

"Basically, once Pip meets Estella, he grows ashamed of his and Joe's 'commonness.' When his fortune suddenly changes and he finds himself with a benefactor who plans to 'make' him 'a gentleman,' Pip can't resist feeling that Joe is beneath him. The irony, as we said in class, is that Joe is truly a 'gentleman,' however unlearned and unsophisticated. Pip can't help what he feels and at the same time feels ashamed for feeling that way. The film doesn't show any of this."

"In chapter 18, Joe looks at Pip's 'untasted supper as if he thought of the time when we used to compare slices.' Neither this scene nor the earlier scene to which it refers is in the film, and I thought that was too bad, because this reminder of Pip's innocent self is touching and sad."

"Could I read the passage from chapter 19 about what goes through Pip's mind as he strolls out 'to finish off the marshes at once'?"

Certainly. But before you do, what's ironic about his doing so— though we don't know it at the time?

"The irony is that 'the marshes' and the convict are exactly what Pip is not shaking off—they are the source of his 'expectations.'"

Excellent. And what did you want to read?

"The part where he's so condescending. The film omits this, but I think it's important to what Dickens is saying about pride and humility and being sensitive to the feelings of others. Not only does Pip imagine someday

> bestowing a dinner of roast beef and plum pudding, a pint of ale, and a gallon of condescension upon everybody in the village,

but he also tells both Biddy and Joe that he will 'never forget' them. That's just awful!

> 'You may be sure, dear Joe,' I went on, after we had shaken hands, 'that I shall never forget you.'

That's what you say to someone you hardly know. Joe has brought him up, found 'room for him at the forge,' protected him from Mrs. Joe, loved him and loves him still, and released him from his indenture for no remuneration at all, and the best Pip can do is tell Joe that he, Pip, in his high state, will *remember* Joe?!"

"He says the same condescending thing to Biddy, to 'raise her spirits,' as if his thinking of her from time to time is some great gift. And then he makes it even worse. He urges her to encourage Joe to improve 'his learning and his manners' because otherwise Pip won't be able to raise Joe up. Biddy ignores Pip's insult to herself, but can't ignore his insult to Joe. And when she tells Pip, 'And don't you think he knows that?' and speaks of Joe's 'dignity,' Pip accuses Biddy of having a 'bad' and 'envious' nature."

"But Pip's feelings are so mixed at this time. He goes off to London without apology or reconciliation, but sad at heart. I wish the film had included that. Unlike a comment by Dickens or a private thought of Pip's, that's something that a film can show. There's a lot of dialogue that the director could have used."

You're right, but there is something at the very end of chapter 19 that a film director can't include. As the coach ride begins, Pip weeps and thinks that he might turn back at the next change of horses for one more evening to have "a better parting." He doesn't dismount. Instead, Pip says,

> We changed again, and yet again, and it was now too late and too far to go back, and I went on. And the mists had all solemnly risen now, and the world lay spread before me.

I think, I continue, *Dickens is alluding to the end of a very great and long poem by John Milton called "Paradise Lost," which describes the expulsion of Adam and Eve from the Garden of Eden. Its final lines are these:*

> The World was all before them, where to choose
> Thir place of rest, and Providence thir guide:
> They hand in hand, with wand'ring steps and slow,
> Through Eden took thir solitary way.

I'm just guessing, I tell my students, *but Dickens's phrase, "and the world lay spread before me," sounds to me like a deliberate echo of Milton's, "The World was all before them." Can anyone think why Dickens may have done that?*

"In a sense," someone says, "that's what the novel is about—when Pip leaves Joe and Biddy, he is, like Adam and Eve, leaving Eden and innocence forever."

Someone else adds, "I really like the movie, but I think now I like the book even more."

.■ 6 .■

The Cask of Amontillado

EDGAR ALLAN POE

*In which we talk about sources
of sympathy and suspense.*

GRADE 8

When I tell my class that we are going to read a short story by Edgar
Allan Poe, they are thrilled because they love nothing better than
being terrified by the supernatural. But instead of the bizarreness of
"The Black Cat" or "The Raven" or "The Masque of the Red Death,"
they find themselves in the presence of an apparently rational man
who recounts every detail of the revenge he undertakes.

"The Cask of Amontillado" is, I remind my students, *a "first-person"
narrative, a form in which one of the characters, in this case the protagonist, tells the story.* A member of a once-great and now declining aristocratic family, Montresor recounts to an unnamed "you"
every detail of how he "avenged" himself upon Fortunato. He begins this way:

> The thousand injuries of Fortunato I had borne as I best could;
> but when he ventured upon insult, I vowed revenge. You, who so
> well know the nature of my soul, will not suppose, however, that
> I gave utterance to a threat. *At length* I would be avenged; this
> was a point definitively settled—but the very definitiveness with
> which it was resolved precluded the idea of risk. I must not only

punish, but punish with impunity. A wrong is unredressed when retribution overtakes its redresser. It is equally unredressed when the avenger fails to make himself felt as such to him who has done the wrong.

And Montresor, we find, has done both—he has "punished with impunity" and he has made "himself felt" as the avenger "to him who has done the wrong."

Montresor lures Fortunato into the catacombs beneath Montresor's palazzo on the night of Carnival, pretending that he seeks Fortunato's opinion about a just-purchased "cask of Amontillado." As the two men proceed through the catacombs, Montresor offers Fortunato, who has a bad cough, glass after glass of rare wine, until he and Fortunato reach a niche where the Amontillado supposedly is stored. Montresor thrusts his drunken companion into the niche, chains him, and then immediately walls up the niche with the building stone and mortar he has set out beforehand, using a trowel he has carried with him and jokingly shown to Fortunato along the way. His crime is never discovered.

While not Poe's goriest story, "The Cask of Amontillado" is scary and full of suspense, but we're not sure what the source of that suspense is. "After all," someone says, "we know from the beginning who the victim and the killer are. In Sherlock Holmes and Agatha Christie stories, you don't find that out until the very end."

This story, I gently suggest, *is as much a character study of a brilliant murderer as it is of anything else.* I am temporarily ignored, while the class thinks about the topic of suspense.

"Maybe," someone suggests, "the suspense comes from our knowing that something terrible is going to happen to Fortunato but not knowing how or when."

"Or maybe it comes from watching the victim ignore chance after chance to save himself."

Could we, I ask, *recognize danger if we were in Fortunato's place?*

"No, because Montresor is so friendly and concerned—is 'solicitous' the right word?"

Yes.

"—about Fortunato's cough."

"And maybe because Fortunato is not conscious of having wronged Montresor."

Should he be? Do we see Fortunato insult Montresor in the time they are together?

"No."

"Absolutely not."

We decide that if Fortunato were conscious of having offended Montresor, of having turned Montresor into a mortal enemy, Fortunato would not accompany Montresor into the catacombs. Logic further tells us that if Fortunato were guilty of "injuries" and "insult," there would be additional examples of such behavior in the time he and Montresor spend together in the catacombs in pursuit of the Amontillado.

"But," my class insists, "there are none."

I say, *Where a normal person hears nothing insulting, someone as proud of his rank and intelligence as Montresor may hear many insults. Let's look very hard.*

"This is just a guess but there's a moment in the catacombs where Fortunato forgets Montresor's coat of arms and family motto. I guess that could be an insult if you're obsessed with your family's honor."

Good.

Another hand goes up. "Fortunato says that Montresor isn't a Mason. Maybe that's an insult."

I explain, *Montresor, in all likelihood, would regard being a Mason as beneath his dignity. The Masons were, and still are, a secret society to which members of the middle class, not the nobility, belonged—but if we look closely at what Fortunato says, we might find something in that conversation which Montresor might regard as an insult.* We read their exchange.

> "You do not comprehend?" he said.
>
> "Not I," I replied.
>
> "Then you are not of the brotherhood."
>
> "How?"
>
> "You are not of the masons."
>
> "Yes, yes," I said, "yes, yes."
>
> "You? Impossible! A mason?"
>
> "A mason," I replied.
>
> "A sign," he said.
>
> "It is this," I answered, producing a trowel from beneath the folds of my roquelaire.

"You jest," he exclaimed, recoiling a few paces. "But let us proceed to the Amontillado."

"I think," someone says, "it's the 'You? Impossible! A mason?' part that Montresor takes as an insult."

Good.

Her friend agrees. "Fortunato is merely registering his surprise, but his words sound to Montresor as if he's accusing Montresor of lying. And to accuse a nobleman of lying is about as insulting as you can get."

Someone adds, "I think the very same thing happens at the beginning of the story. When Montresor says he has purchased a pipe of Amontillado, Fortunato replies, 'Impossible.' There Fortunato is not so much calling Montresor a liar as saying that Montresor is not as discriminating as Fortunato is, not as expert in vintages."

"And he's calling Montresor gullible."

And is it an insult to call a nobleman gullible or to claim that your connoisseurship, and thus your breeding, exceed his?

Enthusiastic nods.

Does one kill for offenses like these?

"Of course not."

So what kind of protagonist do we have?

"A nasty one. I thought we were supposed to like the protagonist."

We think back to other things they've read, *Jane Eyre*, for example, or *Great Expectations*, and agree that usually we like or sympathize with the protagonist. Here we don't. It's one of the distinctive features of this tale.

So what sort of person is Montresor?

"He's someone who exaggerates and magnifies the wrongs done to him."

What exaggerations do you have in mind?

"At the very beginning, he speaks of 'the thousand injuries of Fortunato.'"

Good. And how does he view himself?

"As virtuous. When he says he 'had borne' those injuries until Fortunato 'ventured upon insult,' he's actually commending himself for his patience and forbearance."

Excellent.

"He feels neither remorse nor guilt for what he's done, and doesn't think anyone of discernment or rank will condemn him."

"That," someone says, "sounds just like the Duke in 'My Last Duchess.'"

Excellent. And how do we know he feels no guilt?

"Because he seems to relish telling every detail of the murder to the person referred to as 'You, who so well know the nature of my soul,' in the opening paragraph."

"Another quality of Montresor's is that he's very proud."

Yes. Of what in particular?

"Of his lineage."

"And of his intelligence, and particularly of his ability to manipulate and outwit others. He's sort of a master psychologist. For example, he tells his servants to be sure to remain in the palazzo while he's away, thereby assuring their absence, and he lures Fortunato to the catacombs by telling Fortunato, who regards himself as a connoisseur of wines, that he's on his way to seek Luchesi's advice about the pipe of Amontillado he's just purchased and stored there."

"Both things you've mentioned show that Montresor is also very cynical about people."

Excellent.

"And he's so proud of his intelligence that he keeps on dropping hints to Fortunato that he knows Fortunato won't pick up on. For instance, when Fortunato, coughing, insists on going further into the catacombs, saying that he 'won't die of a cough,' Montresor says, 'True—true.'"

"And Montresor shows Fortunato the trowel, which actually is the murder weapon. He walls Fortunato up with it."

"Montresor is someone who likes to play with his victim—it's like a cat-and-mouse game for him."

"He likes that his words have double meanings that Fortunato, who is not as smart as he is, cannot grasp."

"He's so proud of his wit that he can't resist a final joke at Fortunato's expense, even 50 years after Fortunato's death. When he says *'In pace requiescat,'* I think he's not saying, 'In peace may it, the soul of the dead man, rest,' but 'In peace may it, the pile of bones hiding the death crypt, rest.' In other words, he's praying for himself, for his deed not to be discovered, and not for Forunato. And of course he's mocking the service of the dead at the same time. He's really cynical. And he thinks he's so clever."

Is he?

"Yes, and maybe that's what makes the story so scary—this killer can outsmart everybody."

So, I ask again, do we like this protagonist? Do we like his intelligence?

A hearty "No!"

"I like his intelligence, but not him."

Is he mad?

"I don't know. I think of the mad in books and movies as being like Mrs. Rochester in *Jane Eyre*, violent, disheveled, screaming. Montresor is perfectly calm, absolutely logical, restrained, methodical, self-controlled, and brilliant. Maybe that's what makes 'The Cask of Amontillado' so scary."

"I think that another thing that makes 'The Cask of Amontillado' scary is that it's a story in which evil, not good, prevails."

Excellent.

Let's talk about Fortunato. If Montresor is the protagonist, is Fortunato the antagonist?

"Yes and no," I'm told. "He's the antagonist according to Montresor, but he doesn't see himself as the antagonist—he thinks they're friends."

Good, I say. We are beginning to see the variety that can exist in the nature and function of both protagonist and antagonist.

What might we—and Montresor—imagine goes on in Fortunato's mind when he's walled up?

My class stops for a moment, and then continues, "He has to be recalling that he himself insisted that they enter the catacombs and continue traveling through it. So he has to regard himself as a fool, and has to feel the bitter joke of his costume of motley with 'cap and bells.'"

"I think that he also realizes, at the same moment, that there was no Amontillado at all, that it was just a trick of Montresor's that he fell for, and that he, and not Montresor, was the gullible one."

"And he would probably remember other clues that he missed,

like Montresor's motto, *Nemo me impune lacessit*, 'No one injures me with impunity.'"

"Maybe Fortunato also reflects on his name and how ironic it is to be called 'Fortunato.' This man, whom Montresor resents for being one of the class of men who have amassed a 'fortune' that seems to displace the power once held by the aristocrats, is made by Montresor the least 'fortunate' of men."

"If Montresor understands that Fortunato is probably thinking those things, and he well may understand that, then it's likely that Montresor is delighted that Fortunato is tortured by his own stupidity. That's a kind of psychological revenge, in addition to the revenge of murder itself."

Excellent. Ascribing this moment of recognition to Fortunato is, of course, guesswork on our part.

A hand goes up. "Maybe another reason we don't like Montresor is that he has no such moment."

Excellent possibility. In almost all stories, such moments, if they are present, belong to the protagonist rather than to the antagonist, and tend to move our sympathy in that direction.

"I think it's really interesting that what we are calling 'revenge' is what Montresor calls 'punishment,' 'retribution,' and the 'redressing' of a 'wrong.' His language defines what he's doing as an act of justice. And that suggests, if not madness, at least a mind that sees things only as in terms favorable to himself."

Excellent.

Another hand goes up. "At the end of the story, as he describes the actual walling up of Fortunato, Montresor again uses words to neutralize the evil of what he's doing by minimizing the humanity of Fortunato."

Such as . . . ?

"Such as calling what he's doing a 'task' and a 'labor,' not a murder. And referring to Fortunato not as a person but as 'the chained form' and 'him who clamored'."

Great.

And where, I ask, does the turning point in the action come? We've defined "turning point" as whatever moment makes the end of a story inevitable.

"When he chains Fortunato."

"No, no. Much earlier. When Fortunato enters the catacombs."

"Maybe even earlier than that. Maybe before the story begins, at the moment when Montresor 'vowed revenge.' Everything after could be called the denouement, the playing out of his vow."

"Maybe there are lots of turning points—one each time Montresor suggests that they turn back and Fortunato's own pride keeps him from doing so."

Each one of these possibilities, I say, *works*. My class has done a first-rate job looking at sympathy and suspense in this perfectly crafted tale.

.▎7 ▍.

Araby

JAMES JOYCE

*In which we discover how important setting can be
in revealing character and theme.*

GRADE 8

There are almost too many settings in "Araby"—North Richmond Street, which is a dead or "blind" end, the garden of the house in which the boy, his uncle, and his aunt live, the streets in which the boys play at dusk, the lit doorway in which Mangan's sister stands, the front parlor with its window blinds drawn to within an inch of the frame, the marketplace on Saturday nights, the back drawing room with the broken window in which the priest died, the "high cold empty gloomy" upstairs rooms, Buckingham Street, the bare railroad carriage, and Araby itself, the bazaar that comes to town and to which the boy goes to buy a gift for Mangan's sister. In large part, it is through setting that Joyce tells the story of an adolescent "crush" and of the beginning of painful self-knowledge—and it is through the artful transformation of what darkness and empty space connote that Joyce shows us the boy's searing epiphany.

Early in "Araby" the boy, who is not named and who narrates his story, describes the setting of sky and street where he and his companions play in "the short days of winter . . . before we had well eaten our dinners."

> The space of sky above us was the colour of ever-changing violet and towards it the lamps of the street lifted their feeble lan-

terns . . . Our shouts echoed in the silent street. The career of our play brought us through the dark muddy lanes behind the houses when we ran the gantlet of the rough tribes from the cottages, to the back doors of the dark dripping gardens where odours arose from the ashpits, to the dark odorous stables where a coachman smoothed and combed the horse or shook music from the buckled harness.

What, I ask, does the boy's description tell us about him?

My class looks at me with the puzzled but kindly indulgence that one reserves for a demented aunt and explains, "The passage isn't about him. It's about where he's playing."

Yes, but the words are his, I say.

Students are accustomed to thinking about character in moral terms—to asking themselves is this character kind? is that one selfish? greedy? proud? But this passage isn't one of moral description. Slowly we piece together what it does reveal.

"Well, he's very conscious of setting. And he pays a lot of attention to color and sound."

Good.

"Maybe we could say that he sees beauty where others might not."

Excellent. Can you give us an example?

"Where he speaks of the coachman who 'shook music' 'from the buckled harness.'"

Good.

Someone adds, "And when he talks about the 'muddy lanes' and the 'dripping gardens' and the 'odorous stables.' He makes them sound almost beautiful—'dark' in different ways."

"The same sort of thing happens when he describes what the boys do as they run past the gang of rough kids. He says, 'we ran the gantlet.' It's like he's imagining himself part of a chivalric world. Maybe that's a way of turning what's ordinary or common into something better."

Very good—and what about the sentence, "The space of sky above us was the colour of ever-changing violet and towards it the lamps of the street lifted their feeble lanterns"? What do you notice?

Hands go up. "Everyone is intent on 'the career of our play,' but the boy is also focused on the sky. He keeps looking at it."

How do we know?

"Because he says its color is 'ever-changing'."

Good. Anything else?

"He personifies the street lamps."

And what does that personification reveal? What does he say the lamps are doing?

"'Lifting their feeble lanterns' toward the sky of 'ever-changing violet'—toward something beautiful—so maybe they're yearning for that beauty."

Great. So what does that perhaps tell us about him?

"That he, too, yearns for the beautiful?"

Very good. The next setting the boy speaks of is the marketplace on Saturday nights. Why is he there?

"He's there because each Saturday, after his uncle receives the week's wages, the boy and his aunt go out to buy groceries and the boy helps carry the parcels."

What's the marketplace like?

"The opposite of the streets the boys play in at dusk, even though both are nighttime settings."

How so?

"It's so crowded that he's 'jostled by drunken men and bargaining women.'"

Yes.

Someone else says, "It's noisy—but rather than echoes, he hears 'curses,' 'shrill litanies,' and 'nasal chanting.'"

Good.

"It's brightly lit—he calls the streets 'flaring' because of the gas lamps. I think that shows that he much prefers darkness to light."

Excellent. And how does he deal with this setting?

The student who talked about 'gantlet' takes the floor. "He wants to escape it, not be dirtied by it, and so he imagines that he 'bore [his] chalice through a throng of foes.' A chalice is a holy cup—the Holy Grail that King Arthur's knights search for—and chalices are used in church services. The boy thinks of himself as a knight, imagines Mangan's sister, with whom he is in love, as a sacred chalice, and regards the everyday world as a foe that sullies what is holy and perfect."

Great.

Someone else responds, "The everyday world does sully holy things—it makes church 'litanies' 'shrill' and associates them with 'pigs' cheeks.'"

Very good.
Now let's look at a different setting—the one he always connects with Mangan's sister.

> [I]f Mangan's sister came out on the doorstep to call her brother in to his tea we watched her from our shadow . . . if she remained, we left our shadow and walked up to Mangan's steps resignedly. She was waiting for us, her figure defined by the light from the half-opened door. Her brother always teased her before he obeyed and I stood by the railings looking at her. Her dress swung as she moved her body and the soft rope of her hair tossed from side to side.

"Later," someone says, "when he's waiting for his uncle to come home and give him money to go to the bazaar, he sees the same picture in his mind." We read that, too:

> I sat staring at the clock for some time and, when its ticking began to irritate me, I left the room. I mounted the staircase and gained the upper part of the house. The high cold empty gloomy rooms liberated me and I went from room to room singing. From the front window . . . I looked over at the dark house where she lived. I may have stood there for an hour, seeing nothing but the brown-clad figure cast by my imagination, touched discreetly by the lamplight at the curved neck, at the hand upon the railings, and at the border below the dress.

And I ask, *What elements are common to both descriptions?*
"Darkness, from which the boy views Mangan's sister. She's also in darkness, but surrounded by light—either from the doorway or the lamppost."
And how does darkness alter focus?
"It erases everything around the boy—erases reality, really—and lets him focus just on her."
Excellent.
"It lets him pretend that he lives in a world other than the one that he actually occupies."
Great.
Another hand goes up. "The light around her is like a halo. That makes her a kind of icon, a holy image."
And because she's backlit, what do we never see or hear of?

"Her face. We see only the 'soft rope' of her hair."

"Maybe Joyce is suggesting that the boy doesn't really know her."

Let's go further. What does the boy say the lamplight does?

"He says she is 'touched discreetly' by it 'at the curved neck, at the hand upon the railings, and at the border below the dress.'"

Why "touched" and why "discreetly"?

"A 'touch' is the lightest of actions and 'discreetly' here means something like 'without intruding or going any further than is proper'. So 'touched discreetly' expresses the boy's own preference for keeping a reverent distance."

Excellent.

Others begin to look as closely at the language. "Maybe the fact that he uses 'the' where it would be more natural to use 'her' is part of the same thing. He says, 'the figure,' 'the neck,' 'the hand,' and 'the dress,' rather than 'her figure,' 'her neck,' 'her hand,' and 'her dress,'—another way of keeping a respectful distance."

Great reading.

Encouraged, someone else adds, "Maybe, rather than just 'the neck,' he says 'the curved neck' to emphasize it as a curved form rather than as flesh. To come closer would be to trespass. Maybe he's in love but not ready for love."

Very good.

Before we leave these two passages, let's look at the architectural feature that Joyce includes in both.

At first my class is puzzled, and then someone says, "The railing! That's something that also creates distance and separation."

I add, *There's another dark setting associated with love, even though Mangan's sister is not mentioned in it.*

One evening I went into the back drawing-room in which the priest had died. It was a dark rainy evening and there was no sound in the house. Through one of the broken panes I heard the rain impinge upon the earth, the fine incessant needles of water playing in the sodden beds. Some distant lamp or lighted window gleamed below me. I was thankful that I could see so little. All my senses seemed to desire to veil themselves and, feeling that I was about to slip from them, I pressed the palms of my hands together until they trembled, murmuring; "O love! O love!" many times.

Someone raises her hand. "I have a question. Is 'love' in 'O love! O love!' Mangan's sister or love itself?"

We bandy this about for a minute or two, and decide that he calls to love itself.

"His hands, when he murmurs, 'O love! O love!'" someone else adds, "are held like hands in prayer."

"Maybe he's reached a kind of pinnacle of feeling in which even she can be replaced by pure longing, a kind of romantic ecstasy for which he no longer needs an actual image or trigger."

"That makes Mangan's sister essentially a path to feelings which make him feel fully alive, feelings of pain and joy at the same time."

"Maybe," someone else volunteers, "even his reference to the 'fine incessant needles of water' that 'impinge upon the earth' is a way of suggesting that pain and beauty are linked."

"If he can exist in a realm of pure abstraction, then he doesn't have to take any action at all. The passage in which he describes his ritual of following Mangan's sister every morning and then walking past her without speaking shows that he really is afraid to approach her."

I compliment the class and then return to the passage we were looking at a moment earlier, beginning, "I sat staring at the clock for some time." *As the boy contemplates the image in his mind of Mangan's sister, he says, "I may have stood there for an hour." What's odd about that?*

"It indicates that he's lost all track of time. But time is his whole concern. He's afraid he'll be too late for the bazaar if his uncle doesn't come home soon and give him the money. That's why he is 'staring at the clock' in the first place."

"Losing track of time is almost an acknowledgment that he finds love in his imagination more beautiful than love in reality could ever be."

Someone else takes up the thread. "It's as if he knows that buying some present for her at the bazaar won't express what he feels and won't make her love him. And then the worst thing will happen— his fantasy will end."

In talking about fantasy versus reality, we need to look at what immediately follows the sentence in which the boy says he lost track of time. What happens, and why is it ironic?

"The next sentence is,

When I came downstairs again I found Mrs. Mercer sitting at the fire. She was an old garrulous woman, a pawnbroker's widow, who collected used stamps for some pious purpose.

The gap between the vision of Mangan's sister and the reality of Mrs. Mercer couldn't be wider."

"Joyce is showing us someone who is the polar opposite of the boy's romantic fantasy—and is suggesting that that is the reality."

"Maybe Joyce is also suggesting that what the boy intends doing is not unlike what Mrs. Mercer, who's so unappealing, does. After all, he's going to Araby to buy something, and she's associated with pawnbrokers and buying and selling goods."

If these earlier settings reveal the boy's nature and illusions, I say, the settings of the final part of the story reflect the collapse of those illusions and the painful learning that follows.

When his uncle arrives home in a drunken state and gives the boy money to go to Araby, it's already past nine o'clock as he heads toward the station. Joyce writes,

I held a florin tightly in my hands as I strode down Buckingham Street towards the station. The sight of the streets thronged with buyers and glaring with gas recalled to me the purpose of my journey.

What shocks or surprises us here?
"He's forgotten where he's going and why."
Good.
"He's probably not really forgotten, but his mind is blocking it."
"And look what 'recalls' his purpose to him—'buyers.' He knows, on some level, that his mission belongs to the realm of the marketplace, the very thing he finds coarse."
Excellent.
We look next at Joyce's description of the railway carriage:

I took my seat in a third-class carriage of a deserted train. After an intolerable delay the train moved out of the station slowly. It crept onward among ruinous houses and over the twinkling river . . . I remained alone in the bare carriage. In a few minutes the train drew up beside an improvised wooden platform. I . . . saw by the lighted dial of a clock that it was ten minutes to ten.

How does this description make you feel?

"Uneasy."

"Every detail makes me uncomfortable—that it's a 'third-class carriage,' that the train is 'deserted,' that there's an 'intolerable delay,' and so on. It's as though the setting is telling him 'There's no point in going. You're already too late. What lies ahead will be as joyless as this train ride.'"

"The very word, 'improvised,' describing the landing platform, suggests that all of this is temporary—it's been thrown up in a minute and will be taken down soon. I know this is going too far, but I think it's the opposite of the love he dreams of, which is supposed to last forever."

Excellent.

"I think it may be important that one of the things he's always spoken of positively is described negatively. The upstairs room he sang in was 'empty,' but he calls the empty train 'deserted' and the third-class carriage 'bare.'"

Excellent.

Someone adds, "It's the same with the bazaar. He has always liked being in darkness, but now when he says 'the lights are going out' we get an awful feeling."

"He also says that "the stalls are being dismantled. What's still available for sale are 'porcelain vases and flowered tea sets'—not romantic offerings but unexciting domestic items for middle-aged couples and middle-class households."

We reread the conversation he overhears between two Englishmen and the shop girl in which the men are trying to pick her up, and, once we recognize it as a suggestive exchange, we see the moment as one in which the non-idealized face of love reveals itself to him. The weight of his folly and naiveté, what he calls his "vanity," in imagining himself mature and able to inspire and sustain love, and in which he has equated love with adoration, is borne in upon him.

Then we turn to the story's final description of setting:

I found myself in a big hall girdled at half its height by a gallery. Nearly all the stalls were closed and the greater part of the hall was in darkness. I recognised a silence like that which pervades a church after a service . . . two men were counting money on a salver. I listened to the fall of the coins.

"The things that he has sought," someone says, "—solitude, darkness, and silence—come back to mock him. The hall is nearly empty."

"And dark."

"And silent."

"But silence now is 'like that which pervades a church after a service'—a silence that says 'you're too late,' 'you've missed everything.' It's when, in a church, holy vessels no longer have any sacramental purpose."

There's an allusion to the Gospels in this passage as well.

"Do you mean 'two men were counting money on a salver. I listened to the fall of the coins'?"

"It puts everything into a commercial context."

Good. Can anyone summarize for us what we've noticed?

"An ironic shift in which the aspects of setting associated with his adoration of Mangan's sister are present, but have become things without beauty or meaning."

And so the boy releases the coins he has held in his hand.

I allowed the two pennies to fall against the sixpence in my pocket. I heard a voice call from one end of the gallery that the light was out. The upper part of the hall was now completely dark.

Gazing up into the darkness I saw myself as a creature driven and derided by vanity; and my eyes burned with anguish and anger.

What doesn't he see as he looks into the darkness?

"The image of Mangan's sister."

What does he see instead?

"Himself. 'Gazing up into the darkness I saw myself as a creature driven and derided by vanity; and my eyes burned with anguish and anger.' And he is overwhelmed by shame and embarrassment at all he has thought and done."

"He's so hard on himself, which shows how deeply he has felt things before and how deeply he feels them now."

"In a sense, his reaction now is as extreme as his feeling of adoration once was."

Should we say he grows up here?

"We could say that he begins to."

Excellent. Such moments of recognition, I remind the class, *are called "epiphanies," moments of a truth's "showing forth." Does anyone remember,* I add, *the description of the garden at the beginning of the story?*

"It's attached to their house and had in it a 'rusted bicycle pump.'"

"If it's rusted, that must mean that it cannot inflate a tire to let someone ride away from that place."

Excellent. What else does the garden contain?

"'A central apple-tree.'"

And in what story is there a central tree?

The class tries to think back to other things we've read this year, and then recalls something else. "There's a central apple tree in the Garden of Eden!" someone says. "It's the Tree of Knowledge and is linked to the loss of innocence."

"So," someone else says, excitedly, "the pump and the tree in the garden setting foreshadow in a way what the boy learns and what happens to him."

We talk a little about the fact that loss of innocence in stories of romance sometimes means loss of virginity. But here it is not loss of innocence in any sexual sense that the boy experiences, but the greater loss of the sense of an innocent world and of himself as an innocent within it. Where he thought there was beauty, and where he thought his own motives were refined and pure, he has discovered folly and vanity. The end of innocence and the beginning of self-knowledge are what Joyce has presented in "Araby" through brilliant manipulation of setting.

■ 8 ■

This Lime-Tree Bower My Prison

SAMUEL TAYLOR COLERIDGE

Pied Beauty

GERARD MANLEY HOPKINS

*In which we discover the lyrical
possibilities of grammar.*

GRADE 8

Pope's dictum in "An Essay on Criticism" that "The *Sound* must
seem an *Eccho* to the *Sense*" is the basic principle behind our study
of poetry. To that we add, after studying these two exquisite poems,
the more mundane point that grammar can be as important as figures of speech and sound in revealing a poem's essence. Samuel
Taylor Coleridge's "This Lime-Tree Bower My Prison" and Gerard
Manley Hopkins's "Pied Beauty" are, with a few glosses, accessible
to eighth grade students and exciting in their celebrations of the natural world. We study them side by side.

This Lime-Tree Bower My Prison

Because "This Lime-Tree Bower My Prison" is longer than any poem
my students have yet read, 20 lines longer than "My Last Duchess"
and more complex, I do what I would otherwise never do—I summarize the poem for them before we begin reading it together. My
summary usually goes something like this:

  *The poet Samuel Taylor Coleridge owned a cottage in the Lake
District of England—an area of hills, lakes, and green meadows with*

sweeping prospects. He wrote this poem, as he explains in an introductory note, when friends visited and he, having injured his foot, could not join them in their walk through the countryside. Confined to the tree-shaded bower beside his cottage, he felt disappointment and envy.

In stanza one, Coleridge imagines, as he sits home-bound in his bower, the path his friends may be taking—scaling down a shaded path beside a waterfall he's told them about, seeing the ash tree that arches over the path and the dripping weeds at the bottom of the waterfall.

In stanza two, he imagines his friends ascending from the dell to meadows and distant hills stretched out in the sunlight before them and, beyond that, blue water, a far-off ship, and islands that look purple in the distance. He imagines the particular pleasure that one of his friends, Charles Lamb, who has been confined to London by his work and the need to care for his sister, must feel at such a sight. By mid-stanza it is sunset, and Coleridge asks the sun to sink slowly, so that flowers, clouds, groves, and ocean may be suffused with reddish-gold for Charles to gaze upon as long as he wishes.

Stanza three returns to the lime-tree bower of the poem's beginning, but now Coleridge finds it beautiful. He notes the play of sunlight on the leaves, the darkening colors of the walnut trees and elms at twilight, the silence broken only by the sound of a bee, and he concludes that there is beauty in all of nature. He further concludes that deprivation can be a good thing if it teaches you to be joyful for the joy of others. Now feeling neither isolated nor deprived, Coleridge imagines that the same darkening sky and the same blackbird he sees are at that exact moment also seen by Charles.

Then we read the poem.

THIS LIME-TREE BOWER MY PRISON

Addressed to Charles Lamb, of the India House, London

In the June of 1797, some long-expected friends paid a visit to the author's cottage;* and on the morning of their arrival, he met with an accident, which disabled him from walking during the whole time of their stay. One evening, when they

---

* The friends were the poet William Wordsworth, his sister Dorothy, and the essayist Charles Lamb.

had left him for a few hours, he composed the following lines
in the garden-bower. —Coleridge

Well, they are gone, and here must I remain,
This lime-tree bower my prison! I have lost
Beauties and feelings, such as would have been
Most sweet to my remembrance even when age
5   Had dimm'd mine eyes to blindness! They, meanwhile,
Friends, whom I never more may meet again
On springy heath, along the hill-top edge,
Wander in gladness, and wind down, perchance,
To that still roaring dell, of which I told;
10   The roaring dell, o'erwooded, narrow, deep,
And only speckled by the mid-day sun;
Where its slim trunk the ash from rock to rock
Flings arching like a bridge;—that branchless ash,
Unsunn'd and damp, whose few poor yellow leaves
15   Ne'er tremble in the gale, yet tremble still,
Fann'd by the water-fall! and there my friends
Behold the dark green file of long lank weeds,
That all at once (a most fantastic sight!)
Still nod and drip beneath the dripping edge
20   Of the blue clay-stone.
                     Now, my friends emerge
Beneath the wide wide Heaven—and view again
The many-steepled tract magnificent
Of hilly fields and meadows, and the sea,
With some fair bark, perhaps, whose sails light up
25   The slip of smooth clear blue betwixt two Isles
Of purple shadow! Yes! they wander on
In gladness all; but thou, methinks, most glad,
My gentle-hearted Charles! For thou hast pined
And hunger'd after Nature, many a year,
30   In the great City pent, winning thy way
With sad yet patient soul, through evil and pain
And strange calamity! Ah! slowly sink
Behind the western ridge, thou glorious Sun!
Shine in the slant beams of the sinking orb,
35   Ye purple heath-flowers! Richlier burn, ye clouds!

Live in the yellow light, ye distant groves!
And kindle, thou blue Ocean! So my friend
Struck with deep joy may stand, as I have stood,
Silent with swimming sense; yea, gazing round
40 On the wide landscape, gaze till all doth seem
Less gross than bodily, and of such hues
As veil the Almighty Spirit, when yet he makes
Spirits perceive his presence.
                    A delight
Comes sudden on my heart, and I am glad
45 As I myself were there! Nor in this bower,
This little lime-tree bower, have I not mark'd
Much that has sooth'd me. Pale beneath the blaze
Hung the transparent foliage; and I watch'd
Some broad and sunny leaf, and lov'd to see
50 The shadow of the leaf and stem above
Dappling its sunshine! And that walnut-tree
Was richly ting'd, and a deep radiance lay
Full on the ancient ivy, which usurps
Those fronting elms, and now, with blackest mass
55 Makes their dark branches gleam a lighter hue
Through the late twilight: and though now the bat
Wheels silent by, and not a swallow twitters,
Yet still the solitary humble-bee
Sings in the bean-flower! Henceforth I shall know
60 That Nature ne'er deserts the wise and pure;
No plot so narrow, be but Nature there,
No waste so vacant, but may well employ
Each faculty of sense, and keep the heart
Awake to Love and Beauty! And sometimes
65 'Tis well to be bereft of promis'd good,
That we may lift the soul, and contemplate
With lively joy the joys we cannot share.
My gentle-hearted Charles! When the last rook
Beat its straight path along the dusky air
70 Homewards, I blest it! deeming its black wing
(Now a dim speck, now vanishing in light)
Had cross'd the mighty Orb's dilated glory,
While thou stood'st gazing; or, when all was still,

Flew creeking o'er thy head, and had a charm
75 For thee, my gentle-hearted Charles, to whom
No sound is dissonant which tells of Life.

Grammar

In order to read "This Lime-Tree Bower My Prison," students need
to know that direct objects ("its slim trunk") can precede subjects
("the ash") and main verbs ("flings"); that nouns ("the many-steepled
tract") can be followed by their adjectives ("magnificent"); that the
use of the same word in various grammatical forms can impart a particular beauty to phrases like "long lank weeds that . . . nod and *drip*
beneath the *dripping* edge of the blue clay-stone"; that imperatives
("kindle, thou blue Ocean!") can sound lyrical; that ordinary adjectives ("rich") can be made into exotic comparative adverbs ("richlier")
to exquisite effect; that ellipsis, the omission of understood words
or phrases, can produce moments of beauty when, instead of "This
lime-tree bower *feels like* my prison," a poet writes, "This lime-tree
bower my prison." Once students are trained to read with grammatical precision, they are ready to read with pleasure and understanding. Poems no longer seem vague conglomerations of words.

As we talk about grammar, a hand goes up. "I think there's a
grammatical error at the beginning of stanza three. But I kind of
like it. Where Coleridge writes, 'A delight/Comes sudden on my
heart,' shouldn't 'sudden' be 'suddenly'?"

*Absolutely. Instead of an adverb, he's used an adjective, and done it
on purpose. Can you tell why?*

"Maybe because he's describing something that happens 'suddenly' and 'sudden' feels more 'sudden' than 'suddenly.' Does that
make sense? We expect a third syllable and don't get it, and so we
notice the word, wait for its ending, and then are struck by the
abruptness or 'suddenness' of the phrase."

*Excellent. There's a name for the sort of deliberate grammatical
error you've noticed. It's called "enallage"—the substitution of one part
of speech for another.*

Someone else adds, "I have another example of enallage. When
Coleridge says, 'the bat/Wheels silent by,' 'silent' replaces 'silently.'
Because 'silent' is shorter word, it's more like silence."

Excellent.

Sound

We begin a discussion of sound by looking closely at stanza one. Its alliterative and assonantal effects are particularly gorgeous. Taking, almost at random, lines 5–16, and marking just the "*w*'s" and long "*a*'s" of "*a*sh," we follow sounds that seem to "wind down" through the passage just as the travelers are doing in the dell:

> They, meanwhile, . . .
> Wander in gladness, and wind down, perchance,
> To that still roaring dell, of which I told;
> 10 The roaring dell, o'erwooded, narrow, deep,
> And only speckled by the mid-day sun;
> Where its slim trunk the ash from rock to rock
> Flings arching like a bridge;—that branchless ash,
> Unsunn'd and damp, whose few poor yellow leaves
> 15 Ne'er tremble in the gale, yet tremble still,
> Fann'd by the water-fall!

Someone adds, "I noticed the long 'e.' It's everywhere in stanza one, and really nice. And it seems to appear in important words, like 'sweet' and 'heath.'" She takes us through the beginning of stanza one:

> Well, they are gone, and here must I remain,
> This lime-tree bower my prison! I have lost
> Beauties and feelings, such as would have been
> Most sweet to my remembrance even when age
> 5 Had dimm'd mine eyes to blindness! They, meanwhile,
> Friends, whom I never more may meet again
> On springy heath,

and adds that "the long 'e' then disappears from the stanza and returns with more force three lines later in 'The roaring dell, o'erwooded, narrow, deep' and then seven lines after that twice in 'the dark green file of long lank weeds.'"

Someone adds, "I have a comment about onomatopoeia. Single-syllable, heavy-stressed words one after another—'dark green file'; 'long lank weeds'—make me see the grasses standing separately."

Great.

"Did Coleridge do these things on purpose?" one of our skeptics asks.

I am prepared: *Some of writing is, of course, instinctive or becomes so,* I say, *but sometimes an earlier version of a poem can show us the conscious craft of a poet.* I have brought to class an earlier draft of this passage, and we set the two versions side by side.

> They, meantime, . . .
> Wander delighted, and look down, perchance,
> On that same rifted Dell, where many an Ash
> Twists its wild limbs beside the ferny rock,
> Whose plumy ferns forever nod and drip
> Spray'd by the waterfall.

Then we reread Coleridge's final version.

> They, meanwhile, . . .
> Wander in gladness, and wind down, perchance,
> To that still roaring dell, of which I told;
> 10   The roaring dell, o'erwooded, narrow, deep,
> And only speckled by the mid-day sun;
> Where its slim trunk the ash from rock to rock
> Flings arching like a bridge;—that branchless ash,
> Unsunn'd and damp, whose few poor yellow leaves
> 15   Ne'er tremble in the gale, yet tremble still,
> Fann'd by the water-fall!

"'Wander delighted' sounds choppy," someone says, "but 'Wander in gladness' has a full sound. And replacing 'look down' with 'wind down' adds physical action in which we see the travelers actually descend the path, and the sound of 'wind down' is so much better: the 'w's' alliterate, and the double vowel sound of 'ai' in 'wind' is like a winding turn."

Great.

"Emphasizing that 'w,' Coleridge has changed 'meantime' to 'meanwhile.'"

Nice.

"'Spray'd' isn't half as good as 'Fann'd.'"

Can you tell us why?

"For one thing, the 'f' connects 'Fann'd' with 'waterfall.' For another, 'Spray'd' tells us that the waterfall wets the ferns, but 'Fann'd' tells us that it moves them. Again, Coleridge introduces motion. 'Spray'd' makes me see droplets, but 'Fann'd' makes me see what Coleridge is actually talking about, the movement of the dark green weeds."

Excellent.

Someone adds, "I'll bet Coleridge must have worked on this poem a long time."

I'll bet he did, I say. How good, I think, that they are learning in this way about the effort a good writer takes. *A great poet who lived about a hundred years before Coleridge once said, "True Ease in Writing comes from Art, not Chance, / As those move easiest who have learn'd to dance."*

Someone makes me repeat the lines, I do, and then we go on.

"'Rifted' is just a synonym for a 'dell' or 'ravine.' 'Roaring' makes me feel like I'm actually hearing the sound of rushing water, like I'm there. It's the first of many natural sounds in the poem—the sound of bees and swallows and rooks' wings. Even the sound of no sound, of silence. Sound is even the very last thing Coleridge mentions. His last line is 'No sound is dissonant which tells of life.'"

"Is that statement—'No sound is dissonant which tells of life'— the same as 'No plot so narrow, be but Nature there'? Are both lines ways of saying that everything in Nature is beautiful?"

An excellent thought. Yes.

There's another aspect of sound—the repetition of words—that is a distinctive feature of this poem, I say. *We don't usually think of repetition as a poetic tool, just as we don't think of grammar in that way, but both are.*

Someone muses, "I've always thought of poetry as something with metaphors, but I don't think there are any in this poem."

I don't think so, either. A poem doesn't have to have metaphor to be beautiful.

Someone offers as our first example of repetition the phrase, "wide wide Heaven" at the beginning of stanza two. "I know this is obvious," she says, "but the repetition of 'wide,' with the 'ai' diphthong, really makes me understand how big the sky is."

Someone else says, "Coleridge also repeats nouns but with different adjectives. He does that with 'dell' and 'ash.' Listen." She reads lines 9–14, giving added emphasis to the appositive phrases, here italicized, that repeat key nouns:

> . . . that still roaring dell, of which I told;
> 10 *The roaring dell, o'erwooded, narrow, deep,*
>   *And only speckled by the mid-day sun;*
>   Where its slim trunk the ash from rock to rock
>   Flings arching like a bridge;—*that branchless ash,*
>   *Unsunn'd and damp* . . .

"And Coleridge makes adjectives follow rather than precede their nouns. If they appeared in normal adjective-noun order, they would just sound like talking. Now they sound like poetry."

Excellent.

Someone else has a different point to make about repetition. "The same words are sometimes repeated, but in slightly different form—like 'sun' and 'Unsunn'd,' 'gladness' and 'most glad,' 'joy' and 'joys,' 'gazing' and 'gaze,' and my personal favorite," she adds, smiling, "'nod and drip beneath the dripping edge of the blue clay-stone.'"

And there's a name for that—polyptoton, *the repetition of grammatically varied forms of the same word within the same sentence. The verb "drip," for example, becomes the participle "dripping." I love that line, too.*

Another student raises her hand. "You know where Joyce repeats 'dark' to describe the 'muddy lanes,' the 'dripping gardens,' and the 'odorous stables' in 'Araby'? He did what Coleridge is doing—repeating simple words to make things beautiful and vivid."

Nice. And since you've mentioned darkness, let's consider Coleridge's use of light, darkness, and color in this poem.

Light, Darkness, and Color

How much attention does Coleridge pay to light and darkness in stanzas one and two?

"Well, in both the bower and the dell of stanza one, there's a mix of light and darkness, with more dark than light. In stanza two, there is pure light instead of a mix of light and darkness."

What about color?

"In the dell, there are only dark green weeds, brown or black tree trunks and branches, and clay-blue stones. In stanza two, the colors become 'clear blue' and 'purple'—'purple shadow' actually, which is even more delicate than purple—and lighter green in the 'hilly fields and meadows.' And then mid-stanza there is a burst of color.

Coleridge tells the sun to sink slowly and the landscape to take on the fiery colors of sunset. At the end of the stanza, Coleridge compares the hues of sunset to God. So there's a lot of color in stanza two, and it gets more beautiful as it goes on."

Excellent. What about stanza three?

Someone else raises her hand. "There's really no color in stanza three. It's set in the lime-tree bower, and it begins with Coleridge's remembering the way sunlight on the leaves makes them 'transparent' and makes one leaf shade another. But the actual time is twilight, a time of darkness."

Good.

Someone else's hand goes up. "Coleridge now finds the bower beautiful. Light and shadow make the trees and leaves beautiful during the day, and the darkness and silence of the evening, in which he hears only the buzzing of bees, make the bower beautiful at night."

Very good.

Someone adds that she never before noticed how leaves in sunlight cast their shadows on other leaves, or, rather, she did, but never thought something as insignificant as that was worthy of mention in a poem. And then, describing stanza three, she says, "There's no color, just darkness, but what's really strange is that the darkness seems almost to become light."

Can you explain?

"Well, Coleridge says the ivy is covered with 'a deep *radiance*' and that the elm branches '*gleam.*' He watches a rook's 'black wing' through the 'dusky air' and sees it 'vanishing in *light.*' It seems like, in each case, what's dark is described as being light, even as merging into light."

Excellent.

She continues, "And we already know that Coleridge finds light magnificent from the passage of imperatives in stanza two, where he tells the clouds to 'richlier burn' and the blue Ocean to 'kindle' in the light of the setting sun."

Just to clarify, why does he issue these orders?

"For Charles's sake, so that Charles has something beautiful to look at and remember."

And what does that show about Coleridge?

"That now he feels connected to his friend, rather than alone and envious."

Good. Let's go back to stanza three. Is there anything we should add to our list of words Coleridge uses for the late light of the sun?

"Do you mean where instead of saying the sun's 'last light' he says its 'glory'?

Yes.

"'Glory' is, like 'radiance' and 'gleam,' a substitution for 'light,' somehow even more abstract, a step further from the physical phenomena and more closely linked to something almost divine."

Very good. And what is Coleridge's mood when he uses these words?

"He's no longer envious or unhappy, but full of quiet joy and calm. Maybe it follows from his mood at the end of stanza two where he associates the hues of sunset with the hues of God."

Let's look at that passage.

> So my friend
> Struck with deep joy may stand, as I have stood,
> Silent with swimming sense; yea, gazing round
> 40 On the wide landscape, gaze till all doth seem
> Less gross than bodily, and of such hues
> As veil the Almighty Spirit, when yet he makes
> Spirits perceive his presence.

I explain that *"gross" in line 41 doesn't mean "disgusting," but "composed of physical matter."* I ask, *Have any of you ever stared at something and then deliberately looked cross-eyed at it, letting the contours dissolve and just seeing colors and vague shapes?* Practically everyone has—and to prove it to me half the class, I find, is suddenly staring at me cross-eyed.

We have, then, some idea of what "Less gross than bodily" means. Coleridge says that those colors of sunset, spread over sky and land, seamlessly joining them, are the same colors through which God signals his presence to his angels. Coleridge suggests that those "hues" are like a "veil" "the Almighty Spirit" dons. His essence is not material and thus is not visible, but these hues bring his angels and us as close as possible to perceiving the presence of God.

Time

How conscious does Coleridge make us of time, and especially of present time?

"Very. The poem begins at mid-day, then becomes sunset, then dusk."

"And Coleridge keeps emphasizing the present moment through the use of 'now.'"

Where does "now" appear?

"As the first word of stanza two, in 'Now, my friends emerge,' and then in line 54, at 'and now, [the ivy on the elm trees] . . . Makes their dark branches gleam.' And most intensely in line 71 '(Now a dim speck, now vanishing in light).'"

Why all these "now's"?

"They emphasize the present moment. Coleridge is no longer thinking about what he will or won't remember at some future time, or about what he may have missed. He's just thinking of the beauty of the present moment."

"That's mostly because he's imagining Charles, at the same moment, seeing the same sky and rook and hearing the same 'creeking,' even though they're physically apart. He imagines that they are experiencing time and sunset simultaneously, and that that unites them."

Does anyone remember what Coleridge once thought the benefit of joining his friends on their walk would be?

"Yes—memories. Pictures in his mind."

What's different now?

"Now he doesn't think that at all. Its benefit, he thinks, is in *not* having gone, rather than in having gone. Remaining in the lime-tree bower has taught him that nature's beauty is everywhere, that he does indeed have memories stored up, and that hardship can be a good thing. Most of all, it's somehow taught him to think of others—to take pleasure vicariously in the pleasure of those he loves. And that sense of connection is expressed in the way space and time work and finally come together in the poem."

Pied Beauty

PIED BEAUTY

Glory be to God for dappled things—
    For skies of couple-colour as a brinded cow;
        For rose-moles all in stipple upon trout that swim;

Fresh-firecoal chestnut-falls; finches' wings;
5   Landscape plotted and pieced—fold, fallow, and plough,
      And all trades, their gear and tackle and trim.

All things counter, original, spare, strange;
      Whatever is fickle, freckled (who knows how?)
      With swift, slow; sweet, sour; adazzle, dim;
10 He fathers-forth whose beauty is past change.
      Praise him.

Gerard Manley Hopkins's "Pied Beauty" is also about nature and God, but shorter, quirkier, and syntactically more difficult than "This Lime-Tree Bower My Prison."

What, I ask, *is the grammatical relationship of the last three lines of stanza one to the first three?* I'm hoping my class will see that "chestnut-falls," "wings," "landscape," "trades," "gear," "tackle," and "trim" are additional objects of the preposition even in the lines where "for" is absent, rather than just interesting words thrown down. If my question is too hard, I rephrase it, trying not to give too much away, and ask, *What words are objects of the preposition "for" in this stanza?* or even, *What are the ten objects of the preposition "for" in this stanza—or 13, if we count "fold, fallow, and plough"?*

Once the class sees the syntax, we are free to talk about Hopkins's images and words. We picture to ourselves the brown and white or black and white hides of cows, the tones of the sky, the rose-colored spots on trout, the black and white "pied" feathers of magpies, the mahogany and lighter brown of chestnuts, the red and black of fireplace sparks, the greens and browns and gold of fields.

A hand goes up. "I expected 'plough' to be a verb, but Hopkins makes it an adjective—or noun, really. The oddness made me really focus on the line."

Someone else adds, "I have another example of Hopkins's replacing one part of speech with another. Instead of 'stippled,' he writes 'all in stipple.' I guess he really likes nouns. His writing makes me look at words closely, and when I have to do that, I see what they describe."

Excellent.

"I think it's interesting that the last two lines of stanza one are different from the three before it. They focus on man-made things—even farmed fields are man-made."

Yes. And what can we conclude from that?

"Maybe that there is beauty everywhere, in the natural world and in the activities and implements of men as they shape that world— in all things 'pied.'"

"I think the category of 'pied beauty' is strange. The things that Coleridge describes as beautiful in "This Lime-Tree Bower My Prison" are things that, once he speaks of them, we know we've always known to be beautiful. But Hopkins is different—he's challenging us, saying, 'Look. This is beautiful, too, even though you've never regarded 'pied' things as a category by itself."

Excellent. Let's move on to stanza two.

> All things counter, original, spare, strange;
>   Whatever is fickle, freckled (who knows how?)
>   With swift, slow; sweet, sour; adazzle, dim;
> 10 He fathers-forth whose beauty is past change.
>   Praise him.

My class naturally assumes that all these nouns and modifiers are also objects of the preposition "for." *They are not*, I say.

Our clue is in the next-to-last line of the poem, "He fathers-forth whose beauty is past change." Who can explain what "fathers-forth" means? I ask.

"Brings into being?"

Good. And what's the grammatical subject of "fathers-forth"?

"He."

And what does "whose beauty is past change" modify?

"'He'? God?"

Good. So what would the natural word order of line 10 be?

"He whose beauty is past change fathers-forth."

Yes. And what's wrong with that as a sentence?

"It's not a complete thought."

"'Fathers-forth' needs a direct object."

Exactly. Let's find one in this stanza.

There is general silence and mild consternation. Then someone calls out, "I think I've found it. Is the direct object of 'fathers-forth' 'All things'? And maybe 'Whatever'?"

Exactly. Bravo! So, instead of more objects of the preposition "for," of what do the first three lines of stanza two consist?

"Two direct objects and their modifiers."

Do you remember "Coleridge's line, 'its slim trunk the ash from rock to rock / Flings'? I ask the class. It's constructed just like this stanza is— with the direct object placed before the subject and the verb.

"Yes," someone says. "I forgot."

"That was easier, though," someone else adds, "because things were closer together. I wish I'd remembered that!"

We are learning that poems are not just collections of pretty words and images. They make grammatical sense if we look hard enough. But we haven't yet approached the heart of "Pied Beauty."

Why does Hopkins define God as He "whose beauty is past change"? I ask. What contrast is he creating?

"He has accustomed us to think of beauty as variation. And then, he does this stunning turn-around, saying that God's beauty is without variation, unchanging in time or space, singular, and that that makes it more beautiful than anything else."

"Maybe that's why both the first and last lines of 'Pied Beauty' refer to God and tell us to praise Him. He is the frame upon which the world and the poem hang. Beginning and ending the poem with God is Hopkins's way to demonstrate, even in the look of the poem, that God is beyond all that He creates and supports."

Tremendous work, all of you.

▪9▪

On My First Sonne

BEN JONSON

Ode to Stephen Dowling Bots, Dec'd.

MARK TWAIN

*In which we think about tone, and compare
a great poem to an awful one.*

GRADE 8

To this exquisite Ben Jonson poem about grief, loss, and sources of comfort, I append, by way of clarification, the comically lugubrious "Ode to Stephen Dowling Bots, Dec'd." from Mark Twain's *The Adventures of Huckleberry Finn*. Placed side by side, these two poems illustrate, better than any of my words can, the beauty of the Ben Jonson elegy and the value of understatement in shaping reader response.

On My First Sonne

ON MY FIRST SONNE

Farewell, thou child of my right hand and joy!
My sinne was too much hope of thee, lov'd boy.
Seven yeeres tho' wert lent to me, and I thee pay,
Exacted by thy fate, on the just day.
5 O, could I loose all father now! For why
Will man lament the state he should envie?

To have so soone 'scap'd worlds and fleshs rage,
And, if no other miserie, yet age?
Rest in soft peace, and, ask'd, say here doth lye
10   BEN. JONSON his best piece of *poetrie*,
For whose sake, henceforth, all his vowes be such
As what he loves may never like too much.

Ben Jonson's spellings delight, rather than confuse, my students. In fact, my class finds "incorrect spelling" particularly heartening—the double "n's" and final "e's" of "sonne" and "sinne," the "ie" endings of "envie," "miserie," and "poetrie"; the missing apostrophes in "worlds" and "fleshs."

I explain that *"Benjamin" is a Hebrew name that combines* ben, *"child or son of," and* yamin, *"right hand," and that first sons were very often given their father's names.*

"Then the first line is like a pun, with Ben Jonson privately speaking his son's name and publicly saying how treasured his son was to him."

Exactly. Does everyone know what being someone's "right hand man" means?

"That that person is the one you rely on most, the one you want always by your side."

And does that apply here?

"Oh, yes. Because what the father wants more than anything is to have his son by his side again."

Good. What we will look most closely at, I tell the class, *is what this poem shows about the speaker's effort to deal with his grief and to find comfort.*

I continue, *Who can guess what "lent to me" in line three might mean?*

My students begin gamely. "When you loan something, the person you loan it to knows that it's only temporary and that it has to be returned. So when Jonson writes, 'Seven yeeres tho' wert lent to me,' maybe he's saying that God is the lender and his son, for however long he has him, is a loan from God."

Excellent. Then Jonson says, "and I thee pay." Who is the "thee"? God or his son?

"Would God be capitalized?"

That's often, but not always, the case.

Someone else ventures, "Jonson has just said, 'Seven yeeres tho' wert lent to me.' If 'thee' were God, Jonson would have stopped talking to his son, and he's not ready to do that yet. So 'thee' must be his son."

Good point.

Someone counters, "But his son can't hear him."

You're right, of course. So why does Jonson address his son?

"Maybe he can't bear the thought that his son is gone, and talking to his son lets Jonson feel as though his son is still there. Even though he knows in his heart that his son can't hear him, he pretends his son can to comfort himself and control his tears."

Good.

If the first four lines form a unit, in which Jonson speaks directly to his son, what in line 5 suggests that Jonson's grief suddenly overwhelms him?

"In line 5, he cries out, to no one in particular, 'O, could I loose all father now!' That 'O' and the exclamation point at the end tell us how sad he is."

And for what does Jonson wish in "O, could I loose all father now!"?

"That he had never been a father?"

Almost. Look at the adverb, "now," and at the verb, "if only I could."

She corrects herself and says, "He wishes that he could somehow stop feeling like a father now."

Yes.

Someone asks, "Is 'loose' just an old spelling for 'lose'?"

It might be, or it might actually be "loose"—or both. If it's "loose," what is Jonson saying?

No hands go up.

What does one loosen?

"Ropes?"

Good.

"Knots. And ties and bonds."

So . . . ?

"If it's 'loose,' it's a metaphor in which he's saying how physically bound he is to his son, and that he feels tied to him by love."

Good.

"Instead of saying 'all my feelings as a father' Jonson just says 'all father.' I think that compression is really good. It conveys the full weight of the word 'father.'"

Nice. And what happens next? We read again:

5 O, could I loose all father now! For why
   Will man lament the state he should envie?
   To have so soone 'scap'd worlds and fleshs rage,
   And, if no other miserie, yet age?

"What happens next is that Jonson asks a question. Two, actually. He asks why people in general grieve when death is a state they should 'envie.'"
And the second question?
"It's the same question, but, rather than saying what death brings you, it says what death lets you avoid."
Very good. By the way, can anyone explain what "fleshs rage" might be?
"If it's when your body gets angry at you, or assaults you, then, I guess, sickness."
Perfect. Let's go on. How are these lines different from the first four?
"He's no longer talking to his son."
"He's talking about people generally rather than about himself."
"I think the purpose of these two questions is to try to convince himself that death is a blessing, so maybe we could say that he's found a new way to control his pain—not by imagining his son alive, but by imagining his son dead."
"I agree," someone adds, "but the fact that these lines are questions rather than statements also indicates how hard it is for him and how great his sorrow is."
Excellent, all around. Let's go on now to the poem's conclusion.

    Rest in soft peace, and, ask'd, say here doth lye
10 BEN. JONSON his best piece of *poetrie*,
    For whose sake, henceforth, all his vowes be such
    As what he loves may never like too much.

What do you notice?
"He's talking to his son again, as he did before."
"But now he's referring to himself in third person as 'BEN. JONSON' and 'his' and 'he.' That's new. I think that shows that he's able now to create a little distance between his grief and himself."
Very good.

A hand goes up. "Is Jonson calling his son 'his best piece of *poetrie*'?"

Yes. What about "ask'd, say"?

"I think that means, if or when you are 'ask'd' who you are, answer, 'I'm "Ben Jonson's best piece of *poetrie.*"' So Jonson is now assuming that his son is in heaven among the dead, who 'ask' him who he is. In other words, Jonson has accepted his son's death."

Excellent. And what about "here doth lye"?

The class pauses for a moment and then someone suddenly raises her hand. "Does 'here' actually mean 'here'? In this very spot? I mean, is this the moment of burial, and is he 'lying' his son in the grave at this moment?"

"Oh! So that's why the poem begins, 'Farewell,' right?"

Right.

Another hand goes up. "It makes this moment even harder for him if it's the actual moment of burial. I didn't realize that."

What about calling his son "his best piece of poetrie"?

"That's such a loving thing to say. Especially since this poem is itself so good."

"Jonson is describing all the work of his life, all his writing, as not worth as much to him as his little son."

Exactly. What about the final two lines?

> For whose sake, henceforth, all his vowes be such
> As what he loves may never like too much.

"Aren't 'love' and 'like' the same?" someone asks.

"And how can you 'like' your child 'too much'?" a mildly alarmed student asks.

A "paradox," I say, is a statement that seems to contradict itself, as this line seems to do. Paradoxes seem illogical but really are logical, so Jonson must be making some sort of distinction between "love" and "like." Let's suppose that, by "like," Jonson means "become accustomed to" or "expect to have forever."

Someone else, pleased at having understood something that has been puzzling her, says, "That's his 'sinne'!—to have forgotten that his son is just 'lent' to him and that all things are impermanent."

Excellent.

Another hand goes up. "There's something else. These final four lines have lots of pauses in them. There's 'Rest in soft peace, and,

ask'd, say,' and there's 'For whose sake, henceforth,' and then no
pause at all, just a flowing last line and a half which reads, 'all his
vowes be such/As what he loves may never like too much.' When
you're crying, you sometimes can't catch your breath. Maybe these
pauses are like that—a kind of weeping rhythm. And as he grows
calmer, he can get a full line out. So even in how he writes these
lines we see Jonson as beginning to accept his loss."

Very nice.

Ode to Stephen Dowling Bots, Dec'd.

Now, I say, we'll read a very different sort of poem, also marking some-
one's death. I explain that it comes from *The Adventures of Huckle-*
berry Finn by Mark Twain, in which a young girl named Emmeline
Grangerford makes it her practice to read obituaries and write
poems about dead people she doesn't know. This one, Huck tells
us, is "about a boy by the name of Stephen Dowling Bots that fell
down a well and was drownded." The "Dec'd." in the title, I explain,
is a newspaper's abbreviation for "deceased," which Emmeline has
included because she thinks it's elegant. I ask someone to read her
poem to us.

ODE TO STEPHEN DOWLING BOTS, DEC'D.

And did young Stephen sicken,
　　And did young Stephen die?
And did the sad hearts thicken,
　　And did the mourners cry?

No; such was not the fate of
　　Young Stephen Dowling Bots;
Though sad hearts round him thickened,
　　'Twas not from sickness' shots.

No whooping-cough did rack his frame,
　　Nor measles drear, with spots;
Not these impaired the sacred name
　　Of Stephen Dowling Bots.

Despised love struck not with woe
　　That head of curly knots,

Nor stomach troubles laid him low,
Young Stephen Dowling Bots.

O no. Then list with tearful eye,
Whilst I his fate do tell.
His soul did from this cold world fly,
By falling down a well.

They got him out and emptied him;
Alas it was too late;
His spirit was gone for to sport aloft
In the realms of the good and great.

By the time she's finished, we're all laughing.
What makes this so funny? I ask.
"Well, it's supposed to be sad, right?"
*Right. That's Emmeline's purpose—to make her readers feel sad.
What was Jonson's purpose?*
"To find comfort and master his grief."
"And to pay tribute to his son."
*Yes. The aims of these two poems couldn't be further apart. What
makes this poem incapable of making us feel sad?*
"For one thing, the author doesn't feel sad. And she doesn't seem
to know anything about Stephen Dowling Bots, except that he had
curly hair and fell down a well. The rest is filler. It's all he didn't die
of this, and he didn't die of that."
Excellent.
"Even his name sounds kind of silly. It ends abruptly in 'Bots.'"
"Her rhymes are as abrupt as his last name, and lots of the lines
feel like they were composed solely to rhyme. For example, what
does it mean to say that 'sad hearts . . . thickened'? Nothing at all."
"'Ode to Stephen Dowling Bots, Dec'd.' is the opposite of 'On
My First Sonne,' where we are hardly conscious of the rhyme. Our
whole focus there is on the meaning of the lines and the feelings in
the poem."
Excellent.
"The rhymes in 'Ode to Stephen Dowling Bots' are so repetitive that we can't help but focus on them. There's 'Bots' a couple of
times, and 'shots,' 'spots,' and 'knots.' And there's 'die,' 'cry,' 'eye,' and
'fly.' It's really awful."

Deliberately awful, I say. *It takes a kind of genius to write such a terrible poem for one of your characters, as Twain does. What about line length here?*

The class looks more closely at the poem and then someone says, "The Stephen Dowling Bots lines are shorter, usually four "feet," followed by three "feet," but the lines in "On My First Sonne" are longer—ten syllables each, even an eleventh."

And?

"I think that maybe the short lines make us even more conscious of the rhymes. We hear them sooner."

Good.

Another hand goes up. "I noticed something else—in 'On My First Sonne,' sometimes the thought doesn't end where the line ends, but goes on. Some lines are enjambed—for example, 'For why/Will man lament the state he should envie?' That's like 'My Last Duchess,' which we read last year. When lines are enjambed, the rhyme becomes less obvious."

Exactly. We stop for a minute to review formal terms—pentameter, tetrameter, trimeter, dimeter, enjambment, and end-stopping.

Someone explains, "If you want to write something that makes your audience weep, you can't include the phrase, 'stomach troubles.' Or combine 'stomach troubles' with the fancy poetic word 'list' for 'listen.' And then you can't begin a stanza with 'They got him out and emptied him' as though he were a bucket and end it with 'the realms of the good and great.' Emmeline keeps bouncing around from one kind of language to another, and it's just silly."

Excellent. We call these sorts of alternations "shifts in diction or tone."

"And the poem is not sensible. A person can fall down a well, but how can a 'soul'?"

We've had a wonderful time demolishing Emmeline's poem. Before we go I ask, *Can someone summarize what placing these two poems side by side has shown us?*

"Maybe that trying to force an emotion doesn't work, but trying to control an emotion does. It's the difference between understatement and hyperbole."

Excellent.

"And it's okay to laugh at poetry that's really bad. And important to know the difference."

.. 10 ..

Twelfth Night

WILLIAM SHAKESPEARE

*In which we discover the importance of image
categories and juxtapositions.*

GRADE 8

The lady Olivia, who is courted by the noble Orsino, Duke of Illyria,
and by silly Sir Andrew Aguecheek, has fallen desperately in love
with a young manservant of the Duke's who is really a woman in
disguise. That woman, Viola, has washed ashore in a shipwreck in
which her twin brother Sebastian appears to have been lost. She
has made her way to the Duke's palace looking just like Sebastian.
There, she has introduced herself as "Cesario," been taken into
the Duke's service, and promptly fallen in love with the Duke. He,
thinking her a lad, albeit a lovely one, dispatches her to woo the lady
Olivia for him.

A seemingly intractable romantic situation is thus created for all
three figures: Olivia, Orsino, and Viola. But it is not quite intractable because Sebastian has survived the shipwreck and has washed
ashore on Illyria also. As Act IV begins, he is walking about the
town and is met, in succession, by three sets of persons who mistake
him for "Cesario."

Sebastian first encounters Olivia's jester, Feste, who insists that
Olivia has sent him to fetch "Cesario." Then Sir Andrew Aguecheek,
fresh from an aborted duel with "Cesario," rushes onstage. In the
mistaken belief that he is again confronting "Cesario," and with a

swift, "Now, sir, have I met you again. There's for you," Sir Andrew smacks Sebastian. We see now how beautifully Shakespeare has constructed this portion of the plot. Sebastian does exactly what a bold and manly youth, so approached, would do: "Why, there's for thee, and there, and there," and he strikes Sir Andrew three times in rapid succession.

We laugh at this wonderfully unexpected further confusion of identity, at Sebastian's swift reprisal in which Sir Andrew, ready to bully "Cesario," gets his own back, and at the question Sebastian asks no one in particular, "Are all the people mad?"

Sir Toby Belch, Olivia's uncle and Sir Andrew's handler, doing exactly what he did a moment before when Sir Andrew and Viola were dueling, wades into the fight and finds himself facing a young man who is surprisingly "well-fleshed."

Why is this so funny? I ask.

"For the second time in less than a minute, a bully gets his own back," someone says, pleased. "It's so quick!"

"Part of what's funny is the shock Sir Andrew and Sir Toby both experience, since both of them approach Sebastian so smugly."

"It gets even funnier," someone adds. "We don't expect a third interruption, but we get one just when we think the limit of confusion has been reached."

Someone contradicts her. "We might be expecting a third interruption, but we fully expect that it will be as hostile as these others. What happens next, however, is brilliant! Olivia, fetched by Feste, arrives in a frenzy of fear for 'Cesario.' So what we get is not a third hostile encounter but one in which 'Cesario' is showered with affection."

"And Sebastian is as baffled by her as he was by Sir Toby and Sir Andrew and Feste. We get to laugh at his confusion and her error at the same time."

When Olivia tells Toby he is a ruffian fit only for mountains and caves, and then, in most gentle and loving terms, urges "Cesario" home with her, what is Shakespeare doing?

"Using this scene to solve the love triangle?"

Exactly.

Another hand goes up. "We've seen the encounters between Viola and Olivia drag on and on—Olivia pleading for Viola's love and Viola evading her, so we expect slow-paced encounters between the two.

Now everything happens in a flash. Olivia begs 'Cesario' to return home with her, and he immediately says yes."
Very good.
"I think it's also funny that she's basically shocked when he says he will be 'ruled' by her. She wants him to agree to her love, but totally doesn't expect it."
Good.
As puzzling to Sebastian as his encounter with a Fool and a fighter are the blandishments of this lovely woman. If he is dreaming or mad, so be it—he will follow her. Suddenly Shakespeare deepens this moment by giving Sebastian lines of lyrical response linked to images of the sea—of drowning in "Lethe," of being carried along by a running "stream."
From the play's inception, characters have learned that there are things one cannot control or solve, that once struck by love, for example, one is swept along, or "turned into a hart," or driven to do "I know not what." In four rhyming lines of great beauty, Shakespeare reminds us of all those things. *What about these lines?* I ask:

> What relish is in this? How runs the stream?
> Or I am mad, or else this is a dream.
> Let fancy still my sense in Lethe steep
> If it be thus to dream, still let me sleep.

Why these particular images?
"Sebastian bound himself 'to a strong mast' to ride the flood and, by the report of Antonio, who 'took him from the breach of the sea,' Sebastian was barely alive when rescued. Water meant danger. Now," the student continues, "Sebastian's imagery indicates that immersion in water is no longer associated with danger and death, but with love and with exquisite and blissful dreaming."
Great.
"And," someone else adds, "the 'salt water' of the sea and of Olivia's and Sebastian's tears has been replaced with the fresh water of a running stream."
Excellent. So what do Sebastian's water images emphasize about the direction in which the plot is going?
"Maybe that we're moving beyond the play's romantic sorrows and difficulties to its solution."

At this point, I continue, *Shakespeare does something remarkable—he places before us a new problem and possibly the harshest scene of the play. What comes right after this moment?*

"It's the scene with Malvolio imprisoned by the other servants and Sir Toby."

Malvolio, as my students already know, is the exceedingly sour steward in the lady Olivia's household, "sick," as she herself tells him, "of self-love." By the beginning of Act IV, Malvolio has been fooled into believing that Olivia pines for him. His yellow stockings, cross-gartering, and bizarrely suggestive behavior in her presence have so alarmed her that she instructs that he "be looked to" and unwittingly assigns that task to the very members of her household who have tricked him in the first place. They place him, at Sir Toby's instruction, "in a dark room and bound."

"They are getting their own back," my student continues, "by pretending that he is possessed by the fiend and that, to be cured, his devils must be exorcised. They're repaying him for his high-handedness."

And where is Malvolio during this scene? Remember, I warn the class, *that Shakespeare's stage had no curtain, and so everyone who came onstage also had to exit.*

"Malvolio would have to be shouting from offstage. He can't be onstage because he's begging to be released from the room he's in, and if he were onstage he could just walk off whenever he wanted to."

Good. And how does he describe the room he is in?

"He says he has been 'laid . . . here in hideous darkness' and that it is 'as dark as ignorance.'"

That Shakespeare dramatizes the imprisonment of Malvolio in a scene placed between the two Sebastian-Olivia scenes is no accident, I say. *What's Shakespeare up to?*

My students pause, and then someone ventures, "Maybe we are meant to see Malvolio, prompted by self-love, as Sebastian's opposite—in every way."

Ideas begin to tumble out. "Sebastian is amazed and grateful at Olivia's love, and regards himself as undeserving. Malvolio believes himself the undisputable object of her desire and is led to that conclusion by personal vanity and gross logical errors."

Great. What, by the way, are some of those logical errors? We list examples of Malvolio's folly and blindness in the letter scene.

"He convinces himself that Olivia, who has urged him to behave more pleasantly to Feste, is now advising him to 'be opposite with a kinsman, surly with servants' and that Olivia, dressed in black mourning and affecting a mood of gravity, 'commended' yellow stockings, cross-garters, and smiles."

"He knows that Olivia has rejected Sir Andrew Aguecheek with his 'three thousand ducats a year' and Orsino, whom even she says is noble,

> Of great estate, of fresh and stainless youth,
> In voices well divulged, free, learn'd and valiant,
> And in dimension and the shape of nature
> A gracious person,

and yet he convinces himself that she lusts after a steward."

"He persuades himself that Maria, whom he's treated with arrogance and who probably has a grudge against him, is a reliable source of news."

"We've seen how direct Olivia is, both in rejecting romantic advances and in expressing her own feelings of love. Yet Malvolio thinks she'd communicate her adoration through a cryptic note. To serve and know one's mistress so ill is also a sign of Malvolio's absolute self-absorption."

Great points. And what about Sebastian? How is he Malvolio's opposite? In what sort of setting does Sebastian appear a moment after Malvolio's imprisonment scene?

It's a space flooded with sunlight, we decide. Sebastian's first words are "This is the air; that is the glorious sun." Instead of references to "hell" and "darkness" we hear of "heaven" and of service that is "golden." We are no longer in the presence of a character who thinks he deserves Olivia's love but of someone whose modesty tells himself he does not—no longer in the presence of someone who seeks "some rich jewel" but of someone who has received such an object unsought and who values it only as evidence that he is not mad and that his encounter with Olivia is not imaginary.

Someone notices that "The pearl is the only jewel, in a play otherwise filled with gifts of jewels, which is given not to win love but to reflect it."

Nice.

Encouraged, someone adds, "Like the sunlight, the pearl is also kind of a symbol for Sebastian, just as the opal was for Orsino. I mean, pearls come from the sea, as Sebastian has, and, just the way Sebastian sees and knows himself and Malvolio does not, the pearl shows you your own image when you look at it."

Great.

The sunlit and out-of-doors setting of IV.iii is, we agree, an analogue for Sebastian's state of mind, just as the previous setting was for Malvolio's. Like the water imagery in IV.i, the images of light in IV.iii mark the play's movement towards happiness. I remind the class that when Sebastian is first washed ashore on Illyria he said, not out of self-pity but to warn his friend Antonio from his side, "My stars shine darkly over me."

Hands shoot up. "Now over him is 'the glorious sun' and 'heavens' that will 'shine.'"

In contrast to the confined space of IV.ii, space in IV.iii extends outward and upward. At the scene's end, Sebastian and Olivia go off to plight their troth, I point out, *underneath the chapel's "consecrated roof," and even that interior reference directs the eye upward.*

"And," my class adds, "there are lots of references to movement here, in contrast to the preceding scene."

For example?

"As the scene begins, Sebastian has just returned from traversing the town."

Good.

"And, while he doesn't find Antonio, he learns that Antonio, for his part, 'did range the town to seek me out.'"

Good.

"Maybe we could even say there is motion as Sebastian contemplates Olivia's competence, because he speaks of her ability to 'take and give back and 'sway' the affairs of her household."

Okay.

I explain that *Shakespeare's juxtaposition of Malvolio and Sebastian throws into relief not only the character traits but also the predisposition of thought of each man. Sebastian in Act IV and Malvolio in the letter scene of II.v face similar cognitive questions. With limited evidence, each must decide what is true and what action is appropriate. Malvolio's methods and conclusions are as false as Sebastian's are sound.*

"Both men have soliloquies, and both soliloquies turn on the same question—the love of Olivia."

Good.

"In his soliloquy, Sebastian explores every counterargument he can think of, while Malvolio ignores everything that does not prove his case."

Yes. Examples?

"From the letter Maria has composed and left on the ground for anyone to find, Malvolio jumps immediately to the conclusion that he is its intended recipient and the object of Olivia's passion."

"I love the part where, to make the letters M.O.A.I. mean "Malvolio,' he needs to move them around, to, in his phrase, 'crush this a little' so that it will 'bow to me.' When logical inference will not yield the desired result, Malvolio disregards whatever is unclear or ambiguous."

"He even wants to dominate an envelope."

We all laugh and then continue. "When he's read the whole letter he bursts out, 'Daylight and champaign'—open countryside—'discovers not more.' It's a conclusion that's really ironic, since it leads him to dress and behave in a manner that results in just the opposite setting, darkness and enclosed space."

Great.

While we've been talking about Malvolio, one student has continued to look at Sebastian's soliloquy. "In his soliloquy, and in contrast to Malvolio, Sebastian struggles to decide whether his perceptions are reliable or whether he, or perhaps she, is mad. 'Yet,' 'though' and 'but'—words that signal an objection to, or a qualification of, a prior statement—appear eight times in 14 lines of his 21-line soliloquy. I counted. And those words introduce or create sentences of significant length, a rhythm utterly different from that produced by Malvolio's staccato outbursts."

Excellent.

"Sebastian's thinking is shaped by his natural modesty. He seeks a conclusion that is not governed by personal desire and he proceeds step by logical step."

"He doesn't even reach a definite conclusion," someone adds, "about whether he or Olivia or both are mad. What he does do, just as he did when he tied himself to the mast at sea, is decide that in a world in which nothing is certain, one can nonetheless act."

So what does Shakespeare reward in this play?
"Modesty."
"Clear thinking."
"A ready heart."

▪▪ 11 ▪▪

No Second Troy

WILLIAM BUTLER YEATS

*In which we follow a series of interrogatives
in a verse argument.*

GRADE 9

No Second Troy

Why should I blame her that she filled my days
With misery, or that she would of late
Have taught to ignorant men most violent ways,
Or hurled the little streets against the great,
Had they but courage equal to desire?
What could have made her peaceful with a mind
That nobleness made simple as a fire,
With beauty like a tightened bow, a kind
That is not natural in an age like this,
10 Being high and solitary and most stern?
Why, what could she have done, being what she is?
Was there another Troy for her to burn?

If my class doesn't know the story of Helen, I explain that a prince
of Troy carried her off, a married queen of Sparta and the most
beautiful woman of the world; that the Greeks followed, laid siege
to the city of Troy, and, in the tenth year of the war, burned it to the
ground. I add that Yeats was all his life in love with Maude Gonne,
an upper-class Irish revolutionary.

Originally "No Second Troy" was part of a twelfth-grade poetry unit, taught in combination with Robert Burns's "Mary Morison." When the curriculum changed, I moved "No Second Troy" to the beginning of the ninth-grade sonnet unit. It is not a sonnet at all, having 12 lines instead of 14, but rather a kind of proto-sonnet that beautifully illustrates the basic sonnet form of argument and resolution. Here the argument is one that the speaker has with himself, as he struggles to justify his impulse to forgive the woman about whom he writes.

The subject matter in early sonnet tradition, I tell my class, *was love*. As we examine this poem we find that it, too, is about love. We read the poem through, despite the fact that much of it is initially unclear to us. What the class can see is the syntax, and so I ask, *How many sentences does the poem have?*

"Four."

What kind of sentences are they?

"Questions."

How long are the questions?

"The first two are five lines each, and the last two are each just a single line."

Good. And what makes the last two questions so much shorter than the first two?

"They have no details in them."

Good.

The first question, "Why should I blame her that she filled my days/With misery," seems straightforward. The speaker, my students sense from the "why should I" construction, appears to be fighting against the natural impulse we all have to blame someone who has caused us pain.

Someone notes, "The poem begins as an argument the speaker is having with himself or, more precisely, as a recognition that 'she' has hurt him but that he wants to forgive her."

Good.

What's not clear to my students, though, is what Yeats means by the next part of the first question:

> . . . or [why should I blame her] that she would of late
> Have taught to ignorant men most violent ways,
> Or hurled the little streets against the great.

We talk about the device of metonymy, the use of one thing in place of another with which it is closely associated, such as, someone suggests, "crown" or "throne" for "king." But "streets" does not immediately call up something else, so we talk about who might live on small and winding lanes and who might live on great avenues, and then decide that "little streets" and "great" might be metonymies for the powerless poor *versus* the powerful rich.

Going further and applying what a few students know of Irish-English political history, we decide that those "great" streets might be inhabited by wealthy British or by Irish who are pro-British. If we're right, the speaker might, we decide, be suggesting that "she" "of late" tried to foment a violent form of political rebellion, and might have succeeded, if "the little streets" had "courage equal to [their] desire."

How, then, might we categorize the two parts of the speaker's first question?

"Maybe as first personal and then political."

Good. And what is implied about her courage when Yeats says that the "little streets" lacked sufficient courage?

"That she was very courageous."

Good.

We go on to Yeats's second question:

What could have made her peaceful with a mind
That nobleness made simple as a fire,
With beauty like a tightened bow,

and I ask, *If the first question presents negative things about her, what does the second question do?*

Posed that way, the answer is easy. "It praises her mind and her beauty."

"It also criticizes the time into which she was born—it is not, according to the speaker, 'an age' in which 'nobleness' and sternness can find a proper object or direction."

Good. Let's look at Yeats's comparisons in that second question. To what is her beauty likened?

"To 'fire,' and fire itself is compared to something 'simple,' which is a very strange way of describing fire."

"And to a 'tightened bow,' another odd way of speaking of beauty."

"These images have something in common—they both suggest danger and destructive force."

Great! And how does the speaker sum up the essence of her beauty in line 10?

"He calls it 'high and solitary and most stern.'"

A hand goes up. "Why do all the adjectives in that line have 'ands' between them?"

What do you think the reason may be?

A grimace and silence. I rephrase the question. *What do those 'ands' do to the line, "Being high and solitary and most stern"?* which I read very slowly.

Someone answers, "I think—at least the way you've read it—they slow it down and make it more stately."

And can you hear the three stresses that Yeats gives the last three monosyllables, "and most stern"?

"Yes. And the vowel sounds of the line are themselves long and therefore slow—'ee' in 'Being,' 'ai' in 'high,' 'aw' in 'solitary,' 'o' in 'most,' and 'er' in 'stern.'"

Someone adds, "The sounds themselves suggest her loveliness. And I think the 'ands' make each quality not only stand out, but also seem sort of 'solitary.'"

Nice. Let's go on, I say, *to the last two questions of the poem.*

Why, what could she have done, being what she is?
Was there another Troy for her to burn?

Aside from being shorter, how do these two questions differ from the others?

A student fond of questions of logic raises her hand. "The first begs the question but still leaves open the possibility of disagreement, the possibility of the speaker's saying that she could have done otherwise than she did. But I think the second question, which is also the conclusion of the poem, closes down that possibility. Its answer is historical fact. There is, in Maude Gonne's day, 'no second Troy.' The title itself answers the last line with a simple 'no.'"

Great.

"It's interesting," a student who has been following the poem's interrogatives closely says, "that there are three interrogative pronouns in line 11, 'Why, what could she have done, being what she is?' but two of them no longer function as interrogatives. The 'Why' that opens the line is a kind of exclamation or interjection meaning something like 'hey!' and the second 'what' is an interrogative turned into a relative pronoun. So the speaker, even in line 11, is tamping down his questioning."

Great.

"I think he has made peace with himself, has argued on her behalf against himself, and his conclusion, implicit in the poem's title but not completely established until the end, asserts his continuing love for her, despite the misery that that love brings."

I can think of nothing to add or ask, and simply say, *That was great.*

⊪ 12 ⊪

When, in Disgrace with Fortune and Men's Eyes

My Love Is Strength'ned, Though More Weak in Seeming

AND

Full Many a Glorious Morning Have I Seen

WILLIAM SHAKESPEARE

In which we delight in the beauty of Shakespeare's imagery and think about how sonnets work.

GRADE 9

I introduce Shakespeare's sonnets to my students in as simple a way as I can, describing them as 14-line poems that rhyme in an interwoven, rather than in a couplet, pattern. I say that Shakespeare's sonnets are divided into three four-line units called "quatrains"— from the word for "four"—with a two-line rhyming conclusion called a "couplet," and that the thought units of a sonnet correspond, roughly, to those four divisions. And I add one more thing— that "sonnet" means "little song."

And having said all I want initially to say about the form of the sonnet, I add this: that sonnets are arguments in poetic form. There is a thesis, which may be a statement or a question, then an enlargement of that thesis, perhaps by illustration or perhaps by contradiction, and a resolution or explanation. I add that what I've just said is only minimally accurate, but is enough for us to begin with. I say that each sonnet of Shakespeare's is different and will prove, in all sorts of ways, the insufficiency of my definitions.

29. WHEN, IN DISGRACE WITH FORTUNE AND MEN'S EYES

When, in disgrace with Fortune and men's eyes,
I all alone beweep my outcast state,
And trouble deaf heaven with my bootless cries,
And look upon myself and curse my fate,

Wishing me like to one more rich in hope,
Featured like him, like him with friends possessed,
Desiring this man's art, and that man's scope,
With what I most enjoy contented least;

Yet in these thoughts myself almost despising,
Haply I think on thee, and then my state,
Like to the lark at break of day arising
From sullen earth sings hymns at heaven's gate;

For thy sweet love rememb'red such wealth brings
That then I scorn to change my state with kings.

I love teaching Sonnet 29 for two reasons, the first being that it so accurately describes the state of near despair—what students call "being depressed"—and thus shows them that these poems are about feelings they know. The second reason is the perfection of its third quatrain in answering the first quatrain and in fusing content with style.

We begin by reading the poem aloud twice. The second time we stop at each word whose meaning either has changed or is difficult to unlock, and we note that a number of these words have two meanings. For example, "Fortune" in line 1, from the Latin *Fortuna*, can mean the goddess of destiny or of wealth. "Rich in hope" in line 5 can mean "having the prospect of great wealth" or "full of hope." "Art" in line 7 can be "craft," perhaps poetic craft, or "craftiness," and "scope" in the same line can be intellectual or social power and range. "Enjoy" and "contented" in line 8 can each have the more common present-day meanings of "take pleasure in" and "be satisfied by" or the less-common meanings of "possess" and "filled with." "Yet" in line 9 is "still" or "even though," and "haply" in line 10 is "it sometimes happens" or "fortunately" or both. While the most usual Elizabethan meaning of "sullen" in line 12 is "dark" or "gloomy," "sullen" can also mean "sulky" or "ill-humored"—it can, that is, operate literally to describe the earthy ground or figuratively to describe a state of depression.

Such doublings are not simply a matter of verbal playfulness; if they were, they would hardly be worth mentioning. They embody the essential point of Sonnet 29: that the world, like these words, can be seen in many ways, and that feelings of despair or joy are not necessarily a reflection of how things are, but of how they are perceived—a truth to which Hamlet, speaking of his own depression, gives voice when he says, "There is nothing either good or bad but thinking makes it so."

The other piece of information we need is ornithological. The lark, I explain, nests on the ground. Its flight upward, at dawn, is perpendicular, and as it ascends and re-ascends, it sings beautifully. It is silent in its downward flight. I add that it rises so high as to seem to disappear from sight.

We look at the three quatrains in succession to consider the relationship of structure to argument. The first, we find, describes the speaker's despair. Nothing is going well, no one regards him well, he weeps, he cries out to heaven for succor, no succor comes, and he hates his situation.

Someone points out that the first line, "When, in disgrace with Fortune and men's eyes," ends with "eyes" and that the next line, "I all alone beweep my outcast state," begins with "I," and asks whether it is perhaps relevant to the solipsistic nature of despair that the first quatrain is full of "I" sounds?

An excellent possibility, I say.

We reread the quatrain, listening for that sound and for whatever seems to produce a constrained feeling. We find that there is little overall fluidity. Someone notices that there is a pause after the very first word of the poem, "When," and someone else notes that the lines are end-stopped. *Nor,* I suggest, *do the sounds of the first quatrain flow easily into each other. Saying "I all alone" requires the reformulation of the mouth with each initial vowel sound.* We repeat the phrase together, paying attention to how our mouths are moving, and then look again at quatrain two. *How does Shakespeare develop the argument of the sonnet in the second quatrain? I ask.* "Is the first 'him' in the line, 'Featured like him, like him with friends possessed,' the same as the second 'him,' or different?" *Which better expresses the speaker's sense that everybody else is in possession of something that produces happiness?* "A different 'him.'" *Good. I think that's your answer. A great poet will make the most powerful and dramatic choice.* I mention, too, that that line, "Featured like him, like him with friends possessed," is an example of chiasmus, the grammatical figure in which the order of words in one clause is inverted in the other, and, as a mnemonic, I write the Greek letter X, called "chi," on the board.

"There's a second example of chiasmus in the same quatrain," someone urges. "It's 'With what I most enjoy, contented least.' Could we say that the chiasmic pattern, in which something turns back upon itself, might also represent the inward-turning of depression?" *Excellent idea. And now let's define how the argument proceeds in quatrain two.*

New hands go up, and someone answers, "Quatrain two expands upon quatrain one through specific examples—the poet envies those who have hope, beauty, friends, talent or cunning, intellect or access."

"Quatrain two reveals to us what it is to be depressed—one feels envious of everyone for everything, and thinks oneself worthless and lacking in all things."

Then someone asks, "Could we say that the sentence begun in the first quatrain spills over into the second quatrain because the speaker's despair is so strong as to be uncontainable?" *Certainly. What about quatrain three? Where does it take the sonnet's argument?*

"The speaker suddenly thinks of a dear friend or lover, and is filled with joy. His despair evaporates. To borrow a phrase from the final couplet, the third quatrain argues that 'sweet love rememb'red' cures despair. So the second part of the poem offers a solution to the problem set out in the first part."

Excellent. And how, in poetic terms, does Shakespeare show that shift in feeling?

"Lines are no longer end-stopped. They flow into one another, an analogue, perhaps, to the sense of connectedness the speaker suddenly feels. Lines 10 to 12 are enjambed, so that what we get is 'And then my state like to the lark at break of day arising from sullen earth sings hymns at heaven's gate.'"

We all try to say this without stopping for a breath. Hardly anyone can, but that's not because of caesurae—pauses—in the lines. Nor do we have to reposition our mouths for each sound. Words flow into each other.

Someone says, "The sounds in these lines are really nice, and the assonance and alliteration link words to each other."

Tell us what you hear.

"There's the 'l-k' of 'like' and 'lark,' with the same 'k' in 'think' in the preceding line and in 'break' in this line."

Great.

"The 'a' in 'break' is the same as in 'day,' and the 'ar' of 'lark' and 'arising' are the same. And then once more we hear the beautiful, full 'a' in 'gate.'"

"Running through the last line of the third quatrain," someone adds, "are lots of soft 's's' and 'h's in 'sullen,' 'sings,' 'hymns,' and 'heaven's.' Everything flows together."

"'Yet in these thoughts myself almost despising' and 'Like to the lark at break of day arising' each have an extra syllable, the unstressed '-ing' of 'despising' and 'arising.' The consequent lengthening of quatrain three perhaps increases our sense of expansion after the constriction of the preceding quatrains."

Excellent.

I add that the literal meaning of "despising" is "looking down," from the Latin *de-specere*. The hint is quickly picked up, and our endings expert says how witty it is that the two "-ing" words in quatrain three suggest diametrically opposite motion.

We talk about the deliberate contrasts Shakespeare creates between the imagery of the first quatrain and the imagery of the third quatrain, in which "hymns" and "sings" replace "cries," and in which "heaven" is no longer distant or "deaf," for now the poet and the lark sing at its very "gate."

"To go back to the question about the poem's argument, quatrain three asserts that what saves one from despair is a sense of oneness and connection—of the self to the beloved, to nature, and to God." *Great.*

We look at the couplet and someone points out that now the whole sonnet is to be understood as one sentence and one single forward movement, celebrating "love rememb'red."

Another student notices that the couplet, like the third quatrain, returns to things addressed earlier. "The phrase, 'such wealth brings,' fulfills the speaker's earlier wish to be 'like to one more rich in hope' and the reference to 'kings' in the final line is especially telling because the poet has envied ordinary men their gifts, but now does not envy even the most extraordinary of men, kings and monarchs."

We conclude that while the couplet does not move the argument forward, it does restate, emphatically and handsomely, the sonnet's claim about the transformative power of love.

102. My Love Is Strength'ned, Though More Weak in Seeming

My love is strength'ned, though more weak in seeming;
I love not less, though less the show appear:
That love is merchandized whose rich esteeming
The owner's tongue doth publish everywhere.

Our love was new, and then but in the spring,
When I was wont to greet it with my lays,
As Philomel in summer's front doth sing
And stops her pipe in growth of riper days;

Not that the summer is less pleasant now
Than when her mournful hymns did hush the night,
But that wild music burdens every bough,
And sweets grown common lose their dear delight.

Therefore, like her, I sometime hold my tongue,
Because I would not dull you with my song.

Sonnet 102 is less well known, but no less beautiful, than Sonnet 29—perhaps more so. It is a sonnet of apology and explanation to the beloved who thinks the poet's love is diminished. Sonnet

102 is, in a sense, a sonnet for older folk or for those who equate restraint with grace. Like Sonnet 29, it is about song, and it, too, makes exquisite use of nature.

We begin by looking at its argument and at where and how that argument is positioned in the poem. My students tell me that the first quatrain sets the parameters of the argument: the opening lines assert that the poet's love not only is undiminished, although "the show" of that love—its expression in verse—is less frequent, but that his love has actually increased. The next two lines assert a general principle of conduct: that "publishing" one's love, through either what one says or what one has printed, cheapens that love, "merchandizes" it.

Someone suggests that the poetic device of synecdoche, which here attributes action not to the "owner" but to "the owner's tongue," is a way of suggesting the idea of idle gossip and the dissociation of feeling from speaking on the part of those who "publish" their love.

The second quatrain recites the history of the poet's adoration, analogizing it to the seasons in which the nightingale ("Philomel") sings ("spring" or "summer's front") or is silent ("riper days"). Like the songbird who "stops her pipe in growth of riper days," so he, in the "spring" of their love, sang constantly of that love in his verse. The analogy to the nightingale continues, beautifully, through the first three lines of the third quatrain.

I ask my class, *Are there perhaps two different arguments in these middle stanzas?*

They suggest that, in likening his silence to the nightingale's, the poet is saying that his silence now is as natural a response as his vocal expressions of love were before.

And what, I continue, *is the non-metaphoric equivalent of the "wild music [that] burdens every bough"? And whose might it be?*

Someone who remembers the reference to "music from the spheres" in *Twelfth Night* says that, since Elizabethans regard harmony in music as an echo of the divine ordering of the universe, then "wild," and thus disordered, "music" is the verse of lesser poets and would-be lovers, who clamor like birds of mid-summer. Here we discover that the second excuse the poet proffers for his poetic silence is not natural but aristocratic—he will not scramble with rivals to praise her, and what he feels for her is felt too deeply to be made "common."

Then we direct our attention to the concluding couplet. In the best of sonnets, the couplet does not represent a dropping off of energy, or even, as in Sonnet 29, a strong summation, but a turn, a further movement. The end of Sonnet 18 ("Shall I compare thee to a summer's day?") does that: after explaining why the beloved exceeds in every way the beauty of summer, and promising that the beloved's "summer" will be "eternal," the poet uses the couplet of Sonnet 18 ("So long as men can breathe or eyes can see, / So long lives this, and this gives life to thee.") to say that "this," the sonnet he is writing at this very moment, "gives life to thee." In the same way, the couplet of Sonnet 102 turns the poem back on itself. We look again at the lines,

> Therefore, like her, I sometime hold my tongue,
> Because I would not dull you with my song,

and I ask whether we can detect a third explanation here for the poet's silence? The class sees that whatever we find will turn on the phrase, "I would not dull you," and the first reading suggested is "I would not want to bore you."

That's fine, I answer, *but perhaps not as grammatically precise as it might be. What if we read "dull" as the opposite of "burnish"?*

"Then," a student says, "the poet is making a third argument, this time from modesty: 'My verse is not good enough to capture your loveliness or to express the depth of my love.'" Someone else sees quiet wit and paradox in the couplet: "The poet has written a gorgeous, sensuous sonnet that offers the beloved the ultimate praise— that he, a poet capable of creating such loveliness, has not the skill to praise her adequately, and thus 'sometime' falls silent."

Another hand goes up. "I just noticed the two caesurae in line 13 ('Therefore, like her, I sometime hold my tongue')—after 'therefore' and again after 'like her.' He's doing what he says he sometimes does generally—holding his tongue."

Great.

We come up for air, and then make a few comparisons to Sonnet 29. The most obvious is that in Sonnet 29 the simile of the lark comes very late and occupies just two lines of text. Its delay is quite deliberate. The absence of metaphoric beauty throughout most of Sonnet 29 has exactly replicated the dry and desiccated state of the speaker; when the image appears it refreshes and revives the spirit and invests the poem with vitality. What happens in Sonnet 102 is very different. Here we have a glorious extended metaphor that dominates two quatrains. It is not only one of the most lovely comparisons in all of Shakespeare's sonnets, an absolute proof that the poet of this "lay" is capable of anything, but also a device of indirection—as metaphor always is—and therefore wholly suited to the sonnet's argument against overt expression.

33. Full Many a Glorious Morning Have I Seen

Full many a glorious morning have I seen
Flatter the mountain tops with sovereign eye,
Kissing with golden face the meadows green,
Gilding pale streams with heav'nly alchemy,

Anon permit the basest clouds to ride
With ugly rack on his celestial face,
And from the forlorn world his visage hide,
Stealing unseen to west with this disgrace.

Ev'n so my sun one early morn did shine
With all triumphant splendor on my brow;
But out alack, he was but one hour mine,
The region cloud hath masked him from me now.

Yet him for this my love no whit disdaineth;
Suns of the world may stain when heav'n's sun staineth.

Sonnet 33, like Wordsworth's "Composed Upon Westminster Bridge, September 3, 1802," immerses the reader immediately in the beauty of the morning. The sun "gilds" the "mountain tops," "meadows," and "streams," and the very first phrase of the sonnet, "Full many," itself suggests joyful abundance. A line is devoted to each setting—mountains, meadows, and streams—which sunlight, called "glorious morning," shines upon and transforms, until the whole world is made beautiful and transmuted to gold by "heav'nly alchemy."

"The very phrase that brings that quatrain to a close," someone says, "'heav'nly alchemy,' is nice, with its rhyming 'ly' syllables, its repeated 'eh' vowels, and its chiastic 'l's.'"

We speak of what the first quatrain shows us—that love, expressed in the sun's action of "kissing with golden face the meadows green," works a kind of magic, transforming the world and making what is beloved appear beautiful. And it is essential to the purposes of the sonnet that so much beauty be asserted in the first quatrain, in order that the sharpest and most startling contrast can be made in the second quatrain. If we seek a principle to describe this alteration, it is something like the unreliability of all things.

We should include, I urge, *in "all things," the unreliability of grammar itself.* Quatrain one seems like it's a complete thought* even though it ends with a comma.

> Full many a glorious morning have I seen
> Flatter the mountain tops with sovereign eye,
> Kissing with golden face the meadows green,
> Gilding pale streams with heav'nly alchemy,
>
> Anon permit the basest clouds to ride . . .

But immediately in quatrain two we find a second verb, "permit," that replaces "flatter" as central to the direction of the argument.

"Could we say," a student asks, "that the grammar of the sentence does what the clouds do, which is to erase the effect of the sunlight?"

Bravo!

"And could we say that we have been fooled grammatically, just as the speaker has perhaps been fooled into thinking that the sunlight would last?"

Bravo again.

As we begin to talk about the third quatrain, I find that not every student realizes that the "sun" in the phrase, "Ev'n so my sun one early morn did shine," is not the actual sun but a person, the speaker's friend or beloved.

The poetic pattern to which we are accustomed, the pattern that is easiest for us all, is the presentation of a human situation followed by a metaphoric analogy. That is how Sonnet 29 operates ("and then my state, like to the lark") and how Sonnet 102 operates ("When I was wont to greet it with my lays, / As Philomel in summer's front doth sing") but Sonnet 33 inverts that order. It begins with a meta-

---

*This insight, I tell my class, comes from *Shakespeare's Sonnets,* ed. with analytic commentary by Stephen Booth, Yale University Press, 1980.

phor that runs for two whole quatrains, and the only indication we have that quatrain three is not a continuation of the metaphor but is rather its application to a human situation is the introduction of personal pronouns in phrases such as "my sun," "my brow," "he was but one hour mine," and "masked . . . from me now." This shift is elegant in its compression, and elegant again in that the personified sun becomes an actual person. In any event, once everyone realizes that this sonnet is not simply a complaint about bad weather, we are "good to go."

One student says, grimly, "The friend or lover whose love has seemed to transform the speaker's world, just the way sunlight has transformed nature, is treacherous or, if we want to be kinder, weak enough to 'permit' base, dark clouds to obscure it from view."

Every student has had the experience of being best friends with someone who suddenly is best friends with someone else. No student needs more than this to understand the emotional pain that the speaker feels.

Yet instead of concluding in resentment the poem ends in generosity and forgiveness. Like Sonnet 102, Sonnet 33 is an apology. Here the speaker is not excusing himself to the beloved, but, as in "No Second Troy," excusing the beloved to himself. The speaker knows, of course, that cloud formations and the movement of the sun across the sky are natural phenomena, not acts of will, yet in the couplet he pretends that the relationship of sun to cloud is indeed a matter of the sun's permitting the clouds to obscure its face, and takes that false model as a moral guide. We talk about this conclusion as a kind of ironic joke the speaker makes at his own expense, as if saying, "I will pretend that my rationale is valid, that reasoning, in which one argues from the cosmic, and therefore greater, case to the lesser, holds here, and so I will find my beloved's desertion acceptable."

The sun/cloud metaphor has until this point in the sonnet done what metaphors like the lark and Philomel are supposed to do: it has mirrored what is happening in the human sphere. But suddenly, in the last line of Sonnet 33, "Suns of the world may stain when heav'n's sun staineth," the metaphors become very dense. When we read "Suns of the world" we hear the pun, "sons of the world," mortal and sinful men, of whom the speaker is, necessarily, one. And in the closing phrase we hear "heaven's son," Christ, the son of God.

We are, the speaker is saying, sinners all, and therefore we all are in need of grace and forgiveness, such as that which he offers to his inconstant friend or lover.

Together, we arrive at the conclusion that, as a final sign of the act of forgiveness that the speaker imposes upon himself, the speaker says the "sun [that] staineth" is "heav'n's," thereby asserting that it is no less beautiful, no less adored, and no less capable of bestowing beauty than it would be if it did not "permit the basest clouds to ride with ugly rack on his celestial face."

.ı 13 ı.

Goodfriday, 1613, Riding Westward

JOHN DONNE

*In which we look at the structure of Donne's
argument and the power of paradox.*

GRADE 9

Great religious verse, I tell my students, *does not convince us of the validity of the poet's faith; rather, it shows us what it feels like to believe.*

John Donne wrote "Goodfriday, 1613, Riding Westward" as one continuous poem, with no stanza divisions. What I have done below, for ease in reading, is to break the poem into units of thought corresponding to what my students felt was the way the poem's argument divided. Line numbers appear at each of our divisions.

GOODFRIDAY, 1613, RIDING WESTWARD

Let mans Soule be a Spheare, and then, in this,
The intelligence that moves, devotion is,
And as the other Spheares, by being growne
Subject to forraigne motions, lose their owne,
And being by others hurried every day,
Scarce in a yeare their naturall forme obey:
Pleasure or businesse, so, our Soules admit
8 For *their* first mover, and are whirld by it.

Hence is't, that I am carryed towards the West
10 This day, when my Soules forme bends towards the East.

There I should see a Sunne, by rising set,
And by that setting endless day beget;
But that Christ on this Crosse, did rise and fall,
14 Sinne had eternally benighted all.

Yet dare I'almost be glad, I do not see
That spectacle of too much weight for mee.
Who sees Gods face, that is selfe life, must dye;
What a death were it then to see God dye?
It made his owne Lieutenant Nature shrinke,
It made his footstoole crack, and the Sunne winke.
Could I behold those hands which span the Poles,
And tune the spheares at once, peirc'd with those holes?
Could I behold that endless height which is
Zenith to us, and our Antipodes,
Humbled below us? Or that blood which is
The seat of all our Soules, if not of his,
Make durt of dust, or that flesh which was worne
28 By God, for his apparell, rag'd and torne?

If on these things I durst not looke, durst I
Upon his miserable mother cast mine eye,
Who was Gods partner here, and furnish'd thus
32 Halfe of that Sacrifice, which ransom'd us?

Though these things, as I ride, be from mine eye,
They'are present yet unto my memory,
35 For that looks towards them;

and thou look'st towards mee,
36 O Saviour, as thou hang'st upon the tree;

I turne my backe to thee, but to receive
Corrections, till thy mercies bid thee leave.
O thinke mee worth thine anger, punish mee,
Burne off my rusts, and my deformity,
Restore thine Image, so much, by thy grace,
42 That thou may'st know mee,
and I'll turne my face.

   Students associate poetry with imagery. Donne's devotional verse
contains extraordinary images—tender, physical, sometimes even

sexual, in which everyday things become illustrations of the spiritual and profound. His poems are also, and just as much, intellectual banquets, structures built upon an ascending series of logical turns, leading to dramatic and stunning conclusions.

Trusting to the power and appeal of Donne's logic, we approach "Goodfriday, 1613, Riding Westward" in a different way. Usually, we first comb through a poem to clarify its language, its allusions, and its images. In this case, we leapfrog over those things and begin with the question, *Where do shifts in thought come?*

"The first eight lines form, I think, a unit."

Why?

"I'm not sure what a 'Spheare' means here, but I do see that Donne compares 'mans Soule' to 'a Spheare' in the first line and that the next seven develop aspects of that comparison."

Good. "Spheare" refers to those same Ptolemaic crystalline spheres that Olivia alludes to in Twelfth Night *when she says to Viola, "I had rather hear you to solicit that / Than music from the spheres." Do you remember? So, what's our next logical unit?*

"I think maybe just the next two lines, just a single couplet, because they describe what the speaker is doing. And because now he's talking about himself rather than about people in general."

Good. Do you want to find the next unit of the argument also?

"Maybe the next four lines,

> There I should see a Sunne, by rising set,
> And by that setting endless day beget;
> But that Christ on this Crosse, did rise and fall,
> Sinne had eternally benighted all."

Why are these lines a unit?

"Well, they end in a period, which is sort of a clue. But they might be two separate units because in the first two lines Donne uses metaphor, and in the second he speaks non-metaphorically. But on the other hand," she continues, "they're both about the same thing, and the word 'benighted' does continue the metaphor of the preceding couplet. Okay. I'm sure. It's a four-line unit."

A hand goes up. "The imagery here reminds me of Sonnet 33 where Shakespeare plays upon 'sun' and 'son.' But what's different is that Donne uses paradox. The 'setting' sun, or dying Christ, creates 'endless day'—light, not darkness."

Excellent. So are we agreed that these four lines form a second unit of argument? Heads nod and I continue, *Where might we say the next shift in argument comes?*

"I think the next unit of thought is a very long one—from line 15 through line 28, or maybe even through line 32."

Let's assume, just for the moment, that it runs through 28. What does it contain?

"Does 'Yet dare I almost be glad' mean something like, 'I know I shouldn't be, but I'm almost glad that I'm not facing Jerusalem'?"

Yes.

"I just wanted to be sure. So these lines consist of a list of what he, because he loves God, would find it unbearable to witness."

Very good. And what form does that list take?

Someone else answers, "It's a series of rhetorical questions. But I have a question. Two, really. The direction you're facing has nothing to do with what goes on in your mind, does it?"

Of course not.

"So what's Donne doing?"

Maybe making an abstract idea so literal that we almost laugh and then don't, because it's also serious. We sort of just catch our breaths and wait to see where he's taking us. It's a form of wit and part of what makes Donne's verse so unusual. How about your second question?

"In saying that if he were looking east the 'spectacle' would overwhelm him, isn't he also saying that the Crucifixion is always unfolding in the present?"

Yes. Excellent point.

Another hand is raised. "In these lines, the argument moves from the lesser case to the greater. For example, he says that if seeing 'Gods face' is death then seeing God's agony and death is something more than death."

Good. We call arguments from the lesser case to the greater a mi-nori, "from the lesser."

Someone else has a question. "What would we call an argument from the greater to the lesser? Donne is also arguing, in this passage, that if Nature itself reacts cataclysmically to Christ's death, with earthquake and eclipse, how can he, a mere mortal, sustain such a vision?"

That's called a fortiori, "from the stronger." Thank you both for pointing these things out. Let's continue dividing the poem into its logical units. Shall we say this unit stops at 28 or at 32? Anyone?

"It's a hard choice. Lines 29 to 32 are the fourth question in the series of questions that begins at line 15."

"And Donne begins this question about Mary with 'If on these things I durst not looke,' as if he's saying, 'then how can I look on Mary?' That makes the rhetorical question about Mary the climax of the series, so maybe we should call it part of the same logical unit."

"But maybe not, because the other questions focus on the physical aspects of the body of Christ—his hands, his height, his blood, and his flesh. Lines 29 to 32 are different."

We decide not to decide. *It's more than enough, I say, to have seen as much as you have. What's the next logical division?*

"Can I divide a unit mid-line?

Why not?

"Then 33 to the middle of 35. I think this is an important turn or change in the poem. Until this moment, Donne has spoken of not seeing, or not wanting to see, the aspects of the Crucifixion. Now he says he *does* see them—in his memory."

Good.

"And then, in the rest of line 35, which becomes chiasmic, he says Christ sees him, just as he sees Christ in his 'memory.'"

"There's something else that he does in line 36 that's new—he, for the first time in the poem, speaks directly to Christ. He says, 'O Saviour.'"

Yes.

The student who has mentioned chiasmus goes on. "Her comment emphasizes, as the chiasmus does, the tightness of the connection between the speaker and Christ."

Good. And what does the next logical division of the poem seem to be?

Someone else replies, "The last six lines, 37 to 42, are a single unit. Donne changes course and now says that his turning his back on the east is purposeful, and that the purpose is not 'pleasure or businesse,' as he said it was in the poem's opening. Instead, it is 'to receive / Corrections.'"

By which he means . . . ?

"I think it's very literal. When you're whipped or scourged, it's your back that's struck. He is asking Christ to 'correct' him in this way, until Christ, in his 'mercies,' leaves off."

"And then," someone adds, "he says something remarkable—at least remarkable to us. 'O thinke mee worth thine anger.' He's saying that he hopes he's worth God's scourging. And that in that scourging his 'rusts'—his corruptions—will be burnt away."

"After that," someone goes on, "he pleads that God 'Restore thine image,' which must mean something like, 'Let your goodness become part of me.' And adds, 'by thy grace,' which, I think, means that even the process of burning away his 'sinnes' cannot make him pure enough to see God—only God's grace can do that."

"And then, in the beautiful, concise turn at the very end, he says that when that happens, 'I'll turne my face.'"

"The poem's final turn," someone adds, "is on the word 'turne.'"

"And perhaps reflects the turning 'Spheares' we hear about at the beginning."

Great job, everyone, I say as the class ends.

◾ 14 ◾

Pride and Prejudice

JANE AUSTEN

In which we distinguish between direct and indirect discourse, and talk about Austen's wit.

GRADE 9

Pride and Prejudice, "light and bright and sparkling," can seem to students flat and full of big words, any one of which might be substituted for any other. It once seemed so to me.

To counter that impression, I do several things: I suggest synonyms and grammatical rearrangements that are less felicitous than Austen's, I point out passages where what seems to be simple narrative is actually indirect discourse, and I encourage my students to read lines aloud, dramatically. We look at what exclamatory speech can reveal and at how Austen makes battles of wit between Elizabeth and Darcy into intimate exchanges. Much of the novel's greatness, we find, turns on Austen's absolute control of language and tone.

The Narrative Voice

My class has read the novel quickly in preparation for a slow second reading and close discussion. *Today let's begin*, I say, *with the moment after Mrs. Bennet expresses concern that Mr. Bingley, who has just gone off to London, may be forever "flying about."*

> Lady Lucas quieted her fears a little by starting the idea of his being gone to London only to get a large party for the ball; and a report soon followed that Mr. Bingley was to bring twelve ladies

and seven gentlemen with him to the assembly. The girls grieved over such a number of ladies; but were comforted the day before the ball by hearing, that instead of twelve, he had brought only six with him from London, his five sisters and a cousin. And when the party entered the assembly room, it consisted of only five altogether; Mr. Bingley, his two sisters, the husband of the eldest, and another young man.

What's Austen making fun of here?

"The community and its tendency to gossip—and to regard gossip as reliable. First, there are supposed to be twelve ladies coming, then six, and then, when the Bingley party actually appears, there are only two."

"And the phrase, 'a report soon followed,' emphasizes how quickly rumors get started."

Suppose Austen had written "the girls fretted" rather than "the girls grieved"?

"'Fretted' isn't funny. 'Grieved' is funny, as is its opposite, 'were comforted,' because they're much too extreme for the occasion. We 'grieve' when someone dies or when there's some great and irreparable loss. The girls are worried that there will be too many ladies at the dance. It's an example of satiric overstatement."

What if, instead of "Lady Lucas quieted her fears a little by starting the idea," Austen had written, "Lady Lucas quieted her fears a little by suggesting the idea"?

They pause for a moment and then someone says, "'Starting' makes us think about how rumor travels; 'suggesting' doesn't necessarily even imply the spread of gossip."

Very good.

Someone adds, "The rumors and misinformation here not only are presented as silly, but also are corrected by the end of the paragraph. Later in the story these very things—gossip and rumor and misinformation—become serious. Jane's feelings are misread, Wickham's lies about Darcy prejudice Elizabeth, and Lydia's elopement and the gossip it engenders nearly ruin the Bennet family. It's interesting how Austen introduces a major theme in such a casual way."

Excellent point.

We look next at a couple of other gently satiric passages. The first is the description of the Bingley sisters:

They were of a respectable family in the north of England; a circumstance more deeply impressed on their memories than that
their brother's fortune and their own had been acquired by trade.

*Why does Austen include the phrase, "a circumstance more deeply
impressed on their memories than that" when she could simply write,
"They were of a respectable family in the north of England; their brother's fortune and their own had been acquired by trade"?*—which is
how I, as a young reader, would have absorbed the passage. *What's
Austen doing?*

"If that phrase were omitted, we would simply have background
information about the Bingleys—where they were from and what the
source of their wealth was. The sentence would tell us that although
they are rich, they are not landed gentry. But 'a circumstance more
deeply impressed on their memories than that' reveals that they con-
veniently forget their origins and pretend to higher social rank than
they actually have, and further suggests that such airs are hardly
their fault, since who can control what makes or doesn't make an impression on one's memory? What Austen's really doing is exposing
their pretensions while seeming to be non-critical."

Excellent.

Enthusiasm for finding examples of Austen's subtle exposure of
the Bingley sisters' pretensions grows. Someone else offers the following:

His sisters were very anxious for his having an estate of his own,
but though he was now established only as a tenant, Miss Bingley was by no means unwilling to preside at his table.

"If, instead of the *litotes*, the double negative, of 'was by no means
unwilling,' Austen had written 'was willing,' it wouldn't be funny.
If she'd written 'was eager' it would be closer to the truth, but still
would fail to characterize Caroline Bingley negatively. 'By no means
unwilling' suggests not only that Caroline's eagerness is unseemly
but also that someone of the rank to which she professes would not
'preside' at a rented table. The *litotes* tells us how quick Caroline is
to drop her airs when her own interests are involved."

Excellent.

Someone who has been busily rummaging through the text since
this part of the discussion began raises her hand, having found what

she was looking for. "Austen makes the same point much later when she writes that Caroline, thinking it 'advisable to retain the right of visiting at Pemberley,' 'paid off every arrear of civility to Elizabeth.' 'Advisable' is a great word here. 'Proper' or 'polite' or even 'civil' would suggest a reserve of genuine courtesy in Caroline. 'Advisable' suggests self-interest."

Great. Thank you.

Let's look now at what Austen does, not so much with word choice as with word placement. We read the lines that follow Mr. Bingley's return of Mr. Bennet's visit,

> An invitation to dinner was soon afterwards dispatched; and already had Mrs. Bennet planned the courses that were to do credit to her housekeeping . . .

and I ask, *How does Austen emphasize Mrs. Bennet's precipitousness?*

"'Soon afterwards' is a neutral term about time, but 'already' suggests excessive and preemptive haste, so the sequence of terms is one method of emphasis."

"Another way Austen emphasizes Mrs. Bennet's precipitousness is by changing the natural word order. We'd say 'Mrs. Bennet had already planned . . . ,' but beginning the clause with 'already had,' putting half the verb before its subject, carries with it comic urgency."

Excellent. Character, then, can even be reflected in grammatical order.

Indirect Discourse

Indirect discourse, I tell my students, *consists of words that belong to a particular character but are not placed inside quotation marks.* Then we look at the first sentence of *Pride and Prejudice*:

> It is a truth universally acknowledged, that a single man in possession of a good fortune, must be in want of a wife.

Is that true? I ask. The class looks blank. *Does every rich man who is single want a wife?*

"If by 'want' you mean 'desire,' then no. If by 'want' you mean 'lack,' then yes because it's a tautology."

Excellent. What verb do we use to assert that something is shown to be true?

"Proved?"

And what verb does Austen use here?

"Acknowledged."

And . . . ?

"They're not the same things—an 'acknowledged' truth is simply something that a bunch of people agree about."

Good. What about "must be in want of a wife"? When do we use "must be"?

"When we hope something is true but are only guessing."

"When we're saying how much we want something to be true— as in 'it *has* to be.'"

So whose voices are we hearing?

"I'm not sure, but I don't think it's the young man's. Maybe the community's."

Excellent. Then why does Austen write, "universally"?

"To be satiric because the community regards itself as the whole universe."

Great. So what's Austen done in the very first sentence of the novel?

"She's playing one meaning against the other. If we don't read carefully, we don't realize that the young man may not share the community's eagerness. She's actually suggesting, at the very beginning of her story, that there may be a difference between what's true and what people take or want to be true."

Excellent.

"That's sort of what the novel's about."

We turn to a passage of narrative interspersed with moments of indirect discourse. Mr. Bennet, after teasing Mrs. Bennet for refusing to call on Bingley, makes a visit himself, and Bingley returns the courtesy. *Is there anything funny here?* I ask:

> In a few days Mr. Bingley returned Mr. Bennet's visit, and sat about ten minutes with him in his library. He had entertained hopes of being admitted to a sight of the young ladies, of whose beauty he had heard much; but he saw only the father. The ladies were somewhat more fortunate, for they had the advantage of ascertaining from an upper window, that he wore a blue coat and rode a black horse.

"Austen pretends an anticlimax is a climax. Nothing happens, but the Bennet girls think something has happened. Bingley doesn't get to see them and they don't get to see him—although they crowd around an upper window in their eagerness."

Good. And what have they, in fact, seen?

"'A blue coat' and 'a black horse.'"

Is that phrase Austen's or the girls'? Is it the same voice as the rest of the paragraph?

They think for a moment, and then someone answers, "Its rhythms are different, and its vocabulary is so simple that it sounds like part of a nursery rhyme: 'He wore a blue coat and rode a black horse.' Maybe what we're hearing is the girls saying this to each other. Maybe Austen is using indirect discourse to suggest how excited and naive the girls are."

"I agree. I think she's gently satirizing them."

Now let's look at the rest of that passage we began a moment ago.

An invitation to dinner was soon afterwards dispatched; and already had Mrs. Bennet planned the courses that were to do credit to her housekeeping, when an answer arrived which deferred it all. Mr. Bingley was obliged to be in town the following day, and consequently unable to accept the honour of their invitation, &c. Mrs. Bennet was quite disconcerted.

Whose voices might we be hearing within the narrative?

"'To do credit to her housekeeping,' reflects Mrs. Bennet's own expectation and sense of her own expertise. And maybe the formal language of the apology is Mr. Bingley's voice. Austen could have just written, 'Bingley planned to be in town the following day, and declined their invitation.'"

"I agree," someone adds. "'Was obliged' and 'the honour of,' are formulae that people use in polite society so as not to give offense, especially when they are declining an invitation, and Bingley is very polite."

"The '&c.' is either what Bingley actually writes in his note to Mrs. Bennet, or Austen's way of indicating that he's just saying what well-bred people always say."

Very good. Let's see if there's indirect discourse in the next sentence also.

She could not imagine what business he could have in town so soon after his arrival in Hertfordshire; and she began to fear that he might be always flying about from one place to another, and never settled at Netherfield as he ought to be.

"I definitely hear Mrs. Bennet's voice. 'As he ought to be' is not Austen's judgment but Mrs. Bennet's. It reflects the comic fact that although she hasn't even met him, she views him as her son-in-law and has an opinion about where he should or should not be going, and when."

Great.

Someone adds, "I think 'always flying about' is her voice also. She always speaks in absolutes, and reaches conclusions with no evidence to support them."

Good.

The Exclamatory Mode

Let's see if we can hear Mrs. Bennet's voice in the actual lines Austen assigns her. We choose the moment when she returns from the Meryton Assembly, and I ask someone to read Mrs. Bennet's lines as though she's almost out of breath:

> "Oh! my dear Mr. Bennet," as she entered the room, "we have
> had a most delightful evening, a most excellent ball . . . Jane was
> so admired, nothing could be like it. Everybody said how well
> she looked; and Mr. Bingley thought her quite beautiful, and
> danced with her twice. Only think of *that* my dear; he actually
> danced with her twice."

We find that Mrs. Bennet's sentences are full of superlatives and are chopped into short exclamatory phrases. We hear the same speech patterns as Mrs. Bennet describes Darcy:

> "So high and so conceited that there was no enduring him!
> He walked here, and he walked there, fancying himself so
> very great!"

"Her compliments to Bingley at Netherfield," someone says, "demonstrate the same excitement and excess, and are also constructed of short phrases and superlatives. And she's very funny because she thinks she's being subtle in promoting Jane's virtues to Mr. Bingley, but is completely obvious."

"[If] it was not for such good friends I do not know what would become of her, for she is very ill, indeed, and suffers a vast deal, though with the greatest patience in the world, which is always the way with her, for she has, without exception, the sweetest temper I ever met with. I often tell my other girls they are nothing to *her*. You have a sweet room here, Mr. Bingley."

Someone adds, "Her shift of topic with no transition is also pretty funny."

"Later, her sudden turnaround concerning Darcy is hilarious. And it shows all the characteristics of her speech. Austen writes like a playwright would." And the student reads the lines to us with wonderful breathlessness:

"Good gracious! Lord bless me! only think! dear me! Mr. Darcy! Who would have thought it! And is it really true? Oh! my sweetest Lizzy! how rich and how great you will be! What pin-money, what jewels, what carriages you will have! Jane's is nothing to it—nothing at all. I am so pleased—so happy. Such a charming man!—so handsome! so tall!—Oh, my dear Lizzy! pray apologise for my having disliked him so much before. I hope he will overlook it."

Someone, who has been listening quietly adds, "Mrs. Bennet isn't the only character who uses exclamations. Caroline Bingley does too, and that's really ironic because Caroline Bingley regards Mrs. Bennet as ill bred, which of course is true, but she's more like Mrs. Bennet than she realizes."

That's great, I say. *Find an example for us.*

She picks a passage that combines indirect discourse and the exclamatory mode. "It's where Caroline and Mrs. Hurst express their supposed concern for Jane after Elizabeth reports that 'Jane was by no means better.'"

The sisters, on hearing this, repeated three or four times how much they were grieved, how shocking it was to have a bad cold, and how excessively they disliked being ill themselves; and then thought no more of the matter.

"It's brilliant," someone says. "Austen knows exactly what trying to sound sincere sounds like—the exclamatory 'how's,' the misuse of 'grieved' and 'shocking,' the sudden shift of focus from Jane's health to their own, and the dismissive anticlimax."

"In her direct discourse, Caroline does the same things. The passage in which Caroline compliments Darcy on his library at Pemberley is full of the same sort of exclamations meant to demonstrate deep feeling and superlatives designed to flatter Darcy." We read,

"What a delightful library you have at Pemberley, Mr. Darcy! . . . And then you have added so much to it yourself, you are always buying books . . . Charles, when you build *your* house, I wish it may be half as delightful as Pemberley."

Let's talk for a minute about "delightful."

"Austen emphasizes it, since she begins and ends this passage with it."

Good.

"It's clearly not the right word to describe a library or a great estate, so it establishes Caroline's falseness."

Good. And what does it imply?

"An act of judgment, I think."

Great. Go on.

"To say something is 'delightful,' or, as Caroline has a moment before, that something is 'shocking,' is to indicate that you have judged what you've seen and that you regard yourself as qualified to judge. It's mildly condescending. At least it is when dealing with those of lower rank. When dealing with Darcy, whom Caroline hopes to impress, it's calculated to indicate to him that she belongs to the class that has the right to condescend to others—Darcy's own—and that she is, therefore, a suitable mate."

How ever did you figure that out?

"I don't know. I just did."

Great. We've talked about similarities between the exclamatory speech of Caroline Bingley and Mrs. Bennet. Are there also differences?

"Caroline Bingley uses exclamations to express feelings she doesn't have or thinks will be to her advantage to convey."

Very good. And Mrs. Bennet?

"Her exclamations are always sincere."

Excellent. We all agree, and we also agree that it is a mark of great writing to use the same rhetorical method for such different purposes.

Since we are talking about the exclamatory mode, I ask, *Is there anyone else in the novel who uses it?—perhaps not with regularity, but at critical junctures?*

Someone remembers what Elizabeth says at the moment of her epiphany, after she reads and rereads Darcy's letter and tests its assertions against her memory of events, and so we read that passage aloud:

"How despicably have I acted!" she cried.—"I, who have prided myself on my discernment!—I, who have valued myself on my abilities! who have often disdained the generous candour [tendency to put the best interpretation on things] of my sister and gratified my vanity, in useless or blameable distrust.—How humiliating is this discovery!—Yet, how just a humiliation!—Had I been in love, I could not have been more wretchedly blind. But vanity, not love, has been my folly.—Pleased with the preference of one, and offended by the neglect of the other, on the very beginning of our acquaintance, I have courted prepossession and ignorance, and driven reason away, where either were concerned. Till this moment, I never knew myself."

A hand goes up immediately. "If Caroline Bingley's 'how this' and 'how that' is a mark of her insincerity, and Mrs. Bennet's 'what jewels, what carriages' a mark of her lack of restraint and her 'mean understanding,' Elizabeth's 'how's' are a sign of how deeply she feels things and how completely she understands them. It is language put to its right use."
Excellent.

Elizabeth Bennet and Aristotle

Since we are looking at Elizabeth's moment of recognition and self-knowledge, I decide to talk briefly about tragic form and *The Poetics*. I say that what makes *Pride and Prejudice* so remarkable is in part owing to Austen's superimposition of tragic structure upon a comic base.

According to Aristotle, a perfect tragedy, as *Oedipus Rex* is perfect, is one in which the protagonist experiences a moment of *anagnorisis*, "recognition," and, if possible at the same time, a turn or reversal of fortune, a *peripeteia*. Austen gives Elizabeth Bennet such a moment of *anagnorisis* when she reads and rereads Darcy's letter and suddenly understands that she has allowed herself to be flattered by Wickham and that she has been wrong in virtually all her judgments of Darcy. The moment seems to Elizabeth also to be one of *peripeteia* in that, at the moment that she realizes she might indeed find Darcy the very man she could love, she recognizes that her refusal of his proposal has been cast in a manner unlikely to produce any renewal of it.

The *anagnorisis* is real; the *peripeteia* is false. Darcy still loves her and will propose again, and everything he does between his first and second proposal conspires to that effect and proves his love and worth. There is a second and happier *anagnorisis* in the story, not one in which Elizabeth learns of her own flaws, but in which Elizabeth learns of Darcy's secret assistance to the entire family in arranging for Wickham to marry Lydia. Without the first *anagnorisis* this would not, I tell the class, be a great novel; without a false *peripeteia* it would not be a romantic comedy.

The Conversations of Elizabeth and Darcy

My tiny lesson in Aristotle finished, I ask, *Who besides Elizabeth learns and changes?*

Hands go up quickly. "Darcy. He softens, as his behavior at Pemberley demonstrates, and later we find it's because he has taken all her criticism to heart."

"Unlike all the other characters in the novel, Darcy and Elizabeth are able to change. They both have the ability to stand outside themselves and reassess what they've done and how they've thought."

"Mr. Bennet reassesses his behavior as a father—but, to be fair, only a little and only temporarily."

Dialogues between Elizabeth and Darcy, I say, *reflect in playful terms the same moral ability that both have to stand back and see themselves.*

We start with the conversation between Elizabeth and Darcy at Netherfield when she is nursing Jane. Bingley and Caroline are discussing qualities of character and Darcy says,

"My feelings are not puffed about with every attempt to move them. My temper would perhaps be called resentful.—My good opinion once lost is lost forever . . .

"There is, I believe, in every disposition a tendency to some particular evil, a natural defect, which not even the best education can overcome."

"And *your* defect is a propensity to hate every body."

"And yours," he replied with a smile, "is willfully to misunderstand them."

What's happening between them here?

"Rather than taking offense at her exaggeration, he finds it charming, and steps back from it to respond not to her criticism of him but to describe her mode of thinking."

Excellent.

"His reply shows how tenderly indulgent of her he really is, and how much he enjoys this exchange."

Yes.

"I don't know why, but there's something intimate about this."

"Maybe part of intimacy is being so interested in someone that you sense and can articulate precisely what that person is like."

Excellent.

We look next at how they speak to each other at the Netherfield ball. They are dancing a half-hour set with each other, and Elizabeth says,

> "It is *your* turn to say something now, Mr. Darcy.—I talked about the dance, and *you* ought to make some kind of remark on the size of the room, or the number of couples."
>
> He smiled, and assured her that whatever she wished him to say should be said.
>
> "Very well.—That reply will do for the present.—Perhaps by and bye I may observe that private balls are much pleasanter than public ones.—But *now* we may be silent."
>
> "Do you talk by rule then, while you are dancing?"

A hand goes up. "Although Elizabeth claims that they are not talking about anything, they really are. In fact, this is also a kind of intimate conversation. You can't tease someone about something without intimacy of some sort."

"They are also joking about the etiquette of dancing that says couples should converse, and by that joking are placing themselves outside the social circle and into a small circle of their own. There's something intimate about that."

Excellent.

"I love the part where she says the very thing that she says she will perhaps speak of 'by and bye.' It's not exactly *praetoritio*, telling your listeners you will not speak of something that you fully identify and therefore speak of, but it's like that. In saying what she may speak of later, she's already spoken it and it's not saved for the future. She's being funny, and they are laughing, or at least smiling, together. It's kind of sexy. They're flirting without admitting it."

There's another part of this same conversation, I point out, *where Elizabeth says,*

"We have tried two or three subjects already without success, and what we are to talk of next I cannot imagine."

"What think you of books?" said he, smiling.

"Books—Oh! no.—I am sure we never read the same, or not with the same feelings."

"I am sorry you think so; but if that be the case, there can at least be no want of subject."

"He refuses to be insulted or put off. And it's really funny that they create a conversation about needing a topic for a conversation."

"All these exchanges suggest that both of them can move outside themselves and see themselves from a different angle. I think that's the same as the ability of Elizabeth and Darcy to rethink their own behavior. And that shared ability—they are both so intelligent—is one of the things that makes us feel how much they belong together."

Great. Let's end with the dialogue between Elizabeth and Darcy that precipitates his proposal. They are at Rosings, and Elizabeth is seated at the "instrument." To Darcy's cousin, Colonel Fitzwilliam, in mock dismay, and pretending Darcy can't hear what she's saying although he is standing beside her at the piano, Elizabeth says,

"Your cousin will give you a very pretty notion of me, and teach you not to believe a word I say. I am particularly unlucky in meeting with a person so well able to expose my real character, in a part of the world where I had hoped to pass myself off with some degree of credit. Indeed, Mr. Darcy, it is very ungenerous in you to mention all that you knew to my disadvantage in Hertfordshire—and, give me leave to say, very impolitic too—for it is provoking me to retaliate, and such things may come out, as will shock your relations to hear."

"I am not afraid of you," said he, smilingly.

Elizabeth goes on to describe to Colonel Fitzwilliam Darcy's "dreadful" behavior in Hertfordshire where,

"He danced only four dances, though gentlemen were scarce; and, to my certain knowledge, more than one young lady was sitting down in want of a partner."

Darcy excuses himself, lamely, as not having the talent "of conversing easily with those I have never seen before."

"My fingers," said Elizabeth, "do not move over this instrument in the masterly manner which I see so many women's do. They have not the same force or rapidity, and do not produce the same expression. But then I have always supposed it to be my own fault—because I would not take the trouble of practicing. It is not that I do not believe *my* fingers as capable as any other woman's of superior execution."

Darcy smiled and said, "You are perfectly right. You have employed your time much better. No one admitted to the privilege of hearing you, can think any thing wanting. We neither of us perform to strangers."

Who, I ask, has the last word in these exchanges?
"Darcy."
And what sort of last word is it?
"It is always kind, always indulgent of Elizabeth, always an attempt to link them."

"In saying, 'We neither of us perform to strangers,' he's saying the most intimate thing of all—that they are not strangers—and I think he's talking not just about the past but, as he and she often do, about this immediate 'performance' and perhaps about the future as well."

Very good. We often think of wit as a rhetorical method to keep someone at bay. Austen uses it to bring these characters together.

"In these exchanges," someone else adds, "Elizabeth and Darcy are light and nimble. So when later, at Pemberley, neither lover can speak easily to the other, we know that they are both really in love."

Excellent. Tomorrow we will look at Elizabeth's first conversation with Wickham, and at Austen's description of the grounds of Pemberley, the changing prospect along its roads and from its different windows, its comparison to Rosings, and the significance of such settings. For now it's lunchtime, and my class leaves this refined world to return to our more raucous one.

.∎ 15 .∎.

The House Slave

RITA DOVE

*In which we find that good poems can address
issues of social justice without stridency.*

GRADE 10

THE HOUSE SLAVE

The first horn lifts its arm over the dew-lit grass
and in the slave quarters there is a rustling—
children are bundled into aprons, cornbread

and water gourds grabbed, a salt pork breakfast taken.
5   I watch them driven into the vague before-dawn
while their mistress sleeps like an ivory toothpick

and Massa dreams of asses, rum and slave-funk.
I cannot fall asleep again. At the second horn,
the whip curls across the backs of the laggards—

10 sometimes my sister's voice, unmistaken, among them.
"Oh! pray," she cries. "Oh! pray!" Those days
I lie on my cot, shivering in the early heat,

and as the fields unfold to whiteness,
and they spill like bees among the fat flowers,
15 I weep. It is not daylight yet.

Let's start, I say, with your reaction to this poem.
    "What struck me was that while it describes something awful,
there's so much in it that is beautiful."

Such as?

"Such as saying that the cotton fields at dawn 'unfold to white-ness,' or that the slaves sent out to pick cotton 'spill' 'like bees among the fat flowers.'"

Another student adds, "I think phrases like 'dew-lit' and 'the . . . before-dawn' are beautiful ways to describe the time just before sunrise."

Ivory can be beautiful, too. What about "like an ivory toothpick"? Is this simile beautiful? Is it different from the images you've just mentioned?

"It's different in, I think, two ways at least. The images we've mentioned are things that are moving or result from movement, and they're natural things. An 'ivory toothpick' is man-made and as stiff and lacking in motion and life as anything can be."

There is strong agreement. "A toothpick is hard, unbending, and even able to inflict pain. And ivory is costly. Ivory toothpicks are luxury items, frivolities. So the simile is saying that the plantation mistress is hard and self-indulgent. I'm not sure how I would de-fine 'beauty,' but I don't find the phrase 'like an ivory toothpick' beautiful. It emphasizes her whiteness and her lack of human feeling."

Good. Would someone compare the description of the "mistress" with the description of the "Massa"?

"There's no simile or metaphor for him like there is for his wife. The speaker just says 'and Massa dreams of asses, rum and slave-funk.' The line stands out because it's the only crude thing in the poem, and the crudeness is emphasized by the repetition of the 'ass' sound in 'Massa.'"

Someone adds, "It's the only time the speaker describes some-thing other than what she sees or hears. In the rest of the poem a limited third-person point of view is strictly maintained and every-thing is understated. There's even a kind of understatement when the speaker says that 'sometimes' she hears her sister's voice and that on 'those days' she weeps."

What about the last line, "It is not daylight yet"? Is that an example of understatement, too?

"The speaker 'weep[s],' and the day hasn't even begun. I think Dove is suggesting, in an understated way, that there will be much worse pain to follow."

"I agree. Dove selects a relatively benign moment, shows how painful it is, both to participants and witness, and leaves us to infer how unbearable slavery's worst abuses and horrors are."

"Could the last line, 'It is not yet daylight,' be figurative as well as literal?—could it mean that there is no deliverance—no 'daylight'?"

Perhaps.

"I was thinking," someone quietly says, "that both 'The House Slave' and Richard Wilbur's 'Love Calls Us to the Things of This World' are poems of early morning, poems of dawn. Can we call this poem an aubade?"

"That's great," a friend says. "*This* dawn music is not the music of the lark or lover's lute, but a brass horn that doesn't call lovers from their beds, but slaves to whippings and work."

Great, both of you.

"If Dove is modeling this poem on the medieval and Renaissance aubade," someone adds, "then she's criticizing the western European tradition through the poem's form as well as through its content."

Since you mention sound, let's look a little more closely at sound in this poem. What follows the braying "first horn"?

"'A rustling,'" someone says, "as the half-awake slaves rush to gather their belongings and go to the fields."

And then?

"The 'second horn,' when 'the whip curls across the backs of the laggards' and then the screams, among which the speaker sometimes hears her sister's voice."

"And the cries seem to get louder as the exclamation mark after the second 'pray' tells us."

"I was wondering why the house slave's sister cries 'O! pray!' rather than, for example, 'O! God!' I think perhaps 'O! pray!' is the most innocuous of possible cries, one that she can't hold in and yet the one least likely, for itself, to elicit further blows."

"Maybe she's telling herself to pray she lives through this moment, but, in any event, I agree that she is perhaps trying to muffle any suggestion of accusation."

Is there any other sound in the poem?

"Maybe the snores of the 'Massa,' although they are only implied."

"The poem's last line begins, 'I weep,' so the last sound of which we are conscious is the muted weeping of the house slave, audible only to the house slave herself."

Excellent. And are there contrasts in the poem, other than those we've noted?

"Actually, a lot. I hadn't thought before of contrast as a way the poem is shaped. There is contrast between the sisters—one is a field slave and the other a house slave, one cries out loud and the other weeps quietly."

"There's the dreamless sleep of the mistress and the night fantasies of the Massa."

"And contrast between the slave owners who sleep through the morning and the slaves who must rise before dawn."

"I think paradox might also be called a contrast. The speaker is 'shivering,' not in the cold but in the early 'heat.'"

"Another contrast is between images of beauty and the reality of slavery."

What about point of view? Are there contrasting points of view in the poem?

"Ah!" someone blurts. "From a distance the movement of dark-skinned slaves among the cotton boles appears pastoral and idyllic, 'like bees among . . . flowers.' Up close, in the heat and exhaustion, with whips at their backs, it is a horror."

Good. One last question: Can we call this a narrative poem?

The class is evenly divided between "descriptive" and "narrative." The "narrative" faction argues that the poem tells what happens in the early morning. The "descriptive" camp counters that action in the poem is less important than its imagery. We decide that Dove seamlessly fuses narration and description in this short and excellent piece.

▪ 16 ▪

A Good Man Is Hard to Find

AND

The River

FLANNERY O'CONNOR

*In which we set aside religious preconceptions
in order to consider the beliefs of others.*

GRADE 10

A Good Man Is Hard to Find

"But what's the point? There's this irritating grandmother in the story and then, when I feel a little sympathy for her, 'The Misfit' shoots her, and then nothing happens to him. She's dead, and the story just ends."

"And in 'The River' a little boy walks into a river and drowns. He thinks he's finding God. He hasn't hurt anybody—okay, he's taken his babysitter's handkerchief and book, which is then stolen from him by a creepy adult at his parents' party, but he doesn't deserve to die. What kind of stories are these?"

My students don't like Flannery O'Connor. They're not of Miss Prism's mind, that "The good ended happily and the bad unhappily. That is what Fiction means," but they do expect some moral correspondence in what they read. In *The Adventures of Huckleberry Finn*, they point out, Huck gets to "light out for the territories," and in *The Scarlet Letter*, Dimmesdale admits his guilt and finds final absolution. But "The River" and "A Good Man Is Hard to Find" seem to belong to an amoral universe. So I begin slowly. *You said the grandmother was "irritating." Irritating how?*

A cascade of complaints follows. "She's a know-it-all, a busy-body."

"Everything is really her fault: the family is taking a vacation to Florida, and she secretly brings the cat in a basket under her valise, and the cat leaps onto Bailey's neck and causes the car accident."

"She wants Bailey to make a detour to see an old plantation house and totally misdirects him. Not only has she mistaken Georgia for Tennessee, but also she's lied about there being a 'secret panel' in the house with 'a treasure in silver' buried behind it to get the children, John Wesley and June Star, to join in her nagging of their parents. Her detour takes them down a dirt road where her son Bailey loses control of the car, the car overturns, and the killers reach them."

"When she recognizes The Misfit, that oddly-named killer, she stupidly calls out, 'You're The Misfit!' and that cry dooms them."

What else is irritating about her? How does she regard herself?

"Her pride is so irritating—she's proud of how she dresses for the trip, proud of being the first in the car, proud of her 'naturally sunny disposition.'"

"Insofar as she thinks about life and death, her thoughts go no further than deciding to wear white gloves, a straw hat with white violets on the brim, and a sachet with matching violets at her collar, so that, should anything happen, whoever finds her body will know that she was 'a lady.' That's her idea of 'being ready to meet her Maker.'"

"And she regards being a 'lady' as the only true virtue, yet she thinks of herself as a Christian."

"When she gets into a spat with that bratty child, June Star, she says, 'All right, Miss . . . Just remember that the next time you want me to curl your hair.' Her moral rule is tit for tat."

"In fact, her religious understanding is so superficial and she's so vain that she even thinks she can reform and redeem The Misfit."

"I hate that she talks in clichés."

"And in grandiose phrases. After the accident, although there's nothing wrong with her, she says, 'I believe I have injured an organ.'"

"That sort of language is part of what she thinks is ladylike."

"On top of which, she's a racist. As they're driving, she says, 'Oh look at the cute little pickaninny!' and then she tells the watermelon story in which 'a nigger boy' is the butt of the joke. Yet she thinks of herself as completely without bias."

O'Connor's genius has made these characters so real that my students have almost forgotten that they're not. I ask, *Can we agree that O'Connor has created a brilliant portrait of a vain, silly, morally blind woman?*

We agree, and then someone makes an important point. "The rest of the family is stupid and coarse and unkind—so there's no one in the story to like and no one to feel sympathy for."

Is part of your problem with the story not feeling sympathy for anyone? "Yes."

Is that also the problem the characters themselves have—feeling no sympathy for anyone but themselves?

"Maybe. That's interesting to think about."

Let's talk about how our sympathies progress as we read the story. You, I say, turning to the student who began the discussion, *said that at a certain point you dislike her less. Did anyone else have that reaction?*

Several hands go up.

Can you pinpoint where the change comes?

"For me it was just after Bailey and John Wesley are led off to the woods by The Misfit's assistants, Hiram and Bobby Lee. O'Connor writes, 'There was a pistol shot from the woods, followed closely by another,' and continues,

> Then silence. The old lady's head jerked around. She could hear the wind move through the tree tops like a long satisfied insuck of breath. 'Bailey Boy!' she called.

I suddenly see her as an 'old lady,' weak and helpless. The detail that her 'head jerked around' suggests that she's not in control of her body. And then she hears the wind. I think that's the first time she pays attention to anything outside herself without commenting on it. There's something more internal happening now."

Good.

Another hand goes up. "This passage made me feel more sympathetic, too. But for me it's that her cry is not just 'Bailey' but 'Bailey Boy.' She's crying out to her son, who has just been killed. It's a cry of grief."

Someone else adds, "My sympathy began a little earlier, when Bailey is being marched off to the woods and calls out, 'I'll be back in a minute, Mama, wait on me!' and she cries, 'Come back this instant!' Suddenly he becomes fully real to me. And both of them, in a kind of terror that makes them unable to think, speak irrationally. The very illogic of his promising to come back and of her insisting that he do so is moving. Maybe I become sympathetic to her when she gets past all the posing and all the clichés and begins to feel something—partly because I'm surprised that she can."

Someone else selects the climax itself. "For me, she becomes sympathetic later, after Bailey's wife and the baby and June Star are taken off to the woods and she hears a scream and three more gunshots. The Misfit is now wearing Bailey's Hawaiian shirt, which Hiram and Bobby Lee have brought back from the woods, and she and the Misfit are talking about Jesus. Suddenly, The Misfit's

> voice seemed about to crack and the grandmother's head cleared for an instant. She saw the man's face twisted close to her own as if he were going to cry and she murmured, 'Why you're one of my babies. You're one of my own children!'

At this moment of maximum stress, shirt and wearer merge as her panic deepens, but she's also feeling something new—love and empathy. It's the first time that what she says to The Misfit is truly about him and not prompted by her desire to save herself."

Excellent.

"I agree. She's no longer speaking in clichés, not even clichés of redemption. The last thing she does is to reach out to someone who has hurt her, and that's what kills her. O'Connor writes that The Misfit 'sprang back . . . and shot her three times through the chest.'"

"Is she supposed to be like Jesus here, just before she dies?"

If she is . . . ?

"If she is, then she's not what she was before, because this one moment has redeemed her."

And if it has, how must we regard The Misfit?

"As an agent of redemption?—but he's a killer!"

What does The Misfit say just after he shoots her?

"He says, 'She would of been a good woman . . . if it had been somebody there to shoot her every minute of her life.'"

Does that make sense? Any ideas?

"Maybe that she's 'good' in this final moment because she's forced to think of real things, of life and death, her own and others', and not of lace collars and white gloves."

Good.

"Maybe O'Connor is suggesting that no matter what follows, the grandmother's moment of selfless love is of value."

And if we're right, what is O'Connor saying about redemption?

"That it can come through anyone, even through someone who is himself evil, himself a sinner. And that it may be joined to pain and loss—that there's nothing easy about it."

Very good. What about The Misfit's punishment?

"There isn't one."

"Maybe O'Connor is saying that if God wants The Misfit to be punished he will be, and if God doesn't want him to be punished, he won't be, and it must be left in God's hands."

Good. Let's talk about The Misfit a little more. What's odd about him?

"His politeness."

"His interest in Christ. Maybe 'interest' isn't the right word— he's a non-believer whose whole life is shaped by his non-belief. So in a sense, he is religious. He talks about Christ's raising the dead and says,

> 'If He did what He said, then it's nothing for you to do but thow away everything and follow Him, and if He didn't, then it's noth- ing for you to do but enjoy the few minutes you got left the best way you can—by killing somebody or burning down his house or doing some other meanness to him. No pleasure but meanness.'

The Misfit is crazy, but he's also more serious about religion than anyone in the story. I'm really confused."

"I don't know how to regard him either," a friend offers. "Maybe with mixed feelings, because he's crazy but his behavior has been shaped by what he believes, and we tend to think consistency is a virtue. But he's certainly no hero."

The River

Maybe you'll get to like "The River," too, I say. Let's begin with a summary.

"A little boy, 'four or five,' is picked up in the early morning by Mrs. Connin, his baby-sitter, who takes him along with her own children to the river to hear The Reverend Bevel Summers preach and heal. The boy lives with irresponsible parents who party and have hangovers, farm him out to sitters, and make a joke of everything. On a whim, when Mrs. Connin mentions the name of the preacher, Harry says his name is Bevel, too. What we see eventually in Harry—or maybe we should call him Bevel—is a hunger for meaning, for something that's not a joke."

"And a desire for connection. He pockets the handkerchief Mrs. Connin gives him to wipe his nose, along with the book entitled 'The Life of Jesus Christ for Readers Under Twelve' that once belonged to Mrs. Connin's 'great grandmamma'."

And then?

"They get to the river where people are assembled, and The Reverend preaches that 'There ain't but one river and that's the River of Life, made out of Jesus' Blood . . . All the rivers come from that one River and go back to it like it was the ocean sea.'"

What happens next?

"The preacher takes the boy and baptizes him in the river." We read,

"If I Baptize you, . . . you'll be able to go to the Kingdom of
Christ. You'll be washed in the river of suffering, son, and you'll
go by the deep river of life. Do you want that?"

"Yes," the child said, and thought, I won't go back to the apartment then, I'll go under the river.

"You won't be the same again," the preacher said. "You'll
count."

And what happens that night?

"Bevel returns home that night to his parents' general indifference. A man at the party walks off with the children's Bible that Bevel has hidden in his jacket, saying that, since it's dated 1832, it's a 'collector's item.' And when his mother asks, 'What did that dolt of a preacher say about me? . . . What lies have you been telling today, honey? . . . tell me what he said . . . Tell me,' all the sleepy child can answer is, 'He said I'm not the same now . . . I count.' The next morning, when he wakes and both parents are still sleeping off their hangovers at noon, Bevel makes a breakfast of party left-overs, soggy crackers with anchovy paste, ginger ale that has been standing around all night, some raisin bread heels and half a jar of peanut butter, takes 'a car-token' and 'half a package of Life Savers' from his mother's purse, and finds his way to the river."

A hand goes up. "I think O'Connor has a sense of humor, a subtle one. For example, when Bevel sets out from his apartment and takes 'half a package of Life Savers,' he is, in a sense, being saved."

Very nice, and we all smile.

Another hand is raised. "I thought at first O'Connor might be making fun of fundamentalist preaching and fundamentalist adherents, but I don't think so. The alternative to the faith healers are the dissolute and indifferent sophisticates. That's no better. For every person who believes in an absolutely literal reading of the Bible there's someone else who thinks Bible stories are a joke or Bibles are just profitable items to sell to antique book dealers. That's more to be mocked. And the preacher's words bring joy to Bevel."

Excellent. Before we continue with our summary, let's talk a bit about Mrs. Connin.

"She's poor, and ignorant, and opinionated, but basically kind to Bevel. And when she brings him home to his indifferent, partying parents, she is sufficiently disgusted with them not to take the money. I think that's a really important comment about *them.* And the only reason that Bevel can leave the next day and make his own way to the river is that his parents are asleep, with no thought of him."

And how does the story end?

"Bevel remembers the bus route and the highway and dirt path Mrs. Connin took, and reaches the river, followed by a concerned Mr. Paradise who has seen Bevel walk past the gas station. Bevel wades into the river and drowns."

How does O'Connor handle that moment?

"She presents Bevel's drowning from a double perspective—Bevel's and Mr. Paradise's, and those perspectives are completely different. Bevel is so young that he confuses the literal with the figurative and keeps putting his head underwater, trying to enter the actual river and follow it to the Kingdom of Christ, but 'it,' he thinks, keeps pushing him back—which is simply his body's automatic response to seek air. Mr. Paradise, the religious skeptic of the story, sees from a distance the boy drowning and rushes towards the water, holding a peppermint stick he has brought for the child. Bevel, in turn, sees Mr. Paradise but, given Mr. Paradise's bulk, takes him to be 'something like a giant pig' bounding after him, 'shaking a red and white club,' a repetition of the horror of the day before when Mrs. Connin's sons got Bevel to set the shoat loose and the pig charged the terrified child. Bevel's world consists of indifferent parents and bullies who trick him. So he keeps trying to enter the stream and finally, after several attempts, in which he wades deeper and deeper out, he is caught by a current. The description of his drowning is almost beautiful." She reads,

> He plunged under once and this time, the waiting current caught him like a long gentle hand and pulled him swiftly forward and down. For an instant he was overcome with surprise; then since he was moving quickly and knew that he was getting somewhere, all his fury and fear left him.

And then?

"Mr. Paradise tries to rescue Bevel several times. Failing, he 'rose like some ancient water monster and stood empty-handed, staring with his dull eyes as far down the river line as he could see.'"

Should we, I ask the class, feel sorry for Bevel?

"Perhaps we should not feel sorry for him, although certainly the rational—and ironically named—Mr. Paradise does. Maybe the ending says that Bevel is far from 'paradise.' I don't know. But Bevel believes he has found Christ and peace. I think O'Connor might say that if you die seeking the 'kingdom of heaven,' as Bevel does, or feeling a rush of love for 'the least of them,' as the grandmother does, then your death is blessed—even if you misunderstand things, as both Bevel and the grandmother do."

Lovely point. Are there other ways in which the two stories are alike? Can we, for instance, compare the Reverend Bevel Summer's function in the story with The Misfit's?

"Maybe it's like The Misfit's, in that each brings someone else to God."

Good. According to Mr. Paradise, The Reverend is a fraud. What about that?

"Well, whether the agent of redemption is a criminal or a fraud perhaps doesn't matter."

What about the placement of the redemptive moment in each story—when does it occur and what permanent value has it?

"It occurs in each case at the conclusion of the story or, to be more exact, it concludes the story—I guess because it's what each story is really about."

"And it's followed, in each case, by the death of the person who finds God. With that person's death, the revelation also disappears. Revelation, both stories therefore suggest, is personal and internal. It's not something others even know about. So, maybe O'Connor is also saying that whoever would find God must seek Him anew. Faith isn't just a matter of what your family believes or what an institution tells you."

Very good. Anything else? The class is quiet. We've gone "about as far as we can go," and that has been far indeed, especially in a secular classroom. Our ability to go this far is a testament to O'Connor's art.

.▪ 17 ▪.

Devotions of a Painter

ANTHONY HECHT

Poem

ELIZABETH BISHOP

In which we compare two superb ecphrastic poems.

GRADE 11

Eleventh-grade English includes ten weeks of close study of two or three poets. I have sometimes taught the verse of Anthony Hecht and Elizabeth Bishop and, in those years, have often assigned, for comparison, these two ecphrastic poems—poems which, like "Musee des Beaux Arts" by W. H. Auden and "Ode on a Grecian Urn" by John Keats, respond to real or imagined visual art.

Hecht's "Devotions of a Painter" describes, if not a specific Monet painting, a recognizable composite. Bishop's poem, simply called "Poem," is about an unprepossessing Nova Scotia landscape, painted by an uncle and made, through her writing, luminously real.

Devotions of a Painter

DEVOTIONS OF A PAINTER

Cool sinuosities, waved banners of light,
Unfurl, remesh, and round upon themselves

In a continuing turmoil of benign
Cross-purposes, effortlessly as fish,
5 On the dark underside of the foot-bridge,
Cast upward against pewter-weathered planks.
Weeds flatten with the current. Dragonflies
Poise like blue needles, steady in mid-air,
For some decisive, swift inoculation.
10 The world repeats itself in ragged swatches
Among the lily-pads, but understated,
When observed from this selected vantage point,
A human height above the water-level,
As the shore shelves heavily over its reflection,
15 Its timid, leaf-strewn comment on itself.
It's midday in midsummer. Pitiless heat.
Not so much air in motion as to flutter
The frail, bright onion tissue of a poppy.
I am an elderly man in a straw hat
20 Who has set himself the task of praising God
For all this welter by setting out my paints
And getting as much truth as can be managed
Onto a small flat canvas. Constable
Claimed he had never seen anything ugly,
25 And would have known each crushed jewel in the pigments
Of these oily golds and greens, enamelled browns
That recall the glittering eyes and backs of frogs.
The sun dispenses its immense loose change,
Squandered on blossoms, ripples, mud, wet stones.
30 I am enamored of the pale chalk dust
Of the moth's wing, and the dark moldering gold
Of rust, the corrupted treasures of this world.
Against the Gospel let my brush declare:
"These are the anaglyphs and gleams of love."

In "Devotions of a Painter" Anthony Hecht focuses on the creative impulse of the artist. We begin as with a riddle. *Who is the "painter" of the title?* Eventually we piece together clues—a "foot-bridge," "water," "lily-pads," "poppy" flowers, "an elderly man in a straw hat"—and, with or without the help of pictures, identify the speaker as Monet and the setting as the garden at Giverny, with its

footbridge spanning the lily pond. But it is not with these things
that the poem begins. Instead, we hear,

> Cool sinuosities, waved banners of light,
> Unfurl, remesh, and round upon themselves
> In a continuing turmoil of benign
> Cross-purposes, effortlessly as fish,
> 5 On the dark underside of the foot-bridge,
> Cast upward against pewter-weathered planks.

Hecht is a master of language, and these words and combinations
exactly reflect what light on moving water does. A student says that
"sinuosities" is itself sinuous—its five syllables move in soft curves,
as light does on water. The next line, "Unfurl, remesh, and round
upon themselves," is likewise a miracle of sound replicating sense.
The mouth recircles with each word as it reforms, again and again,
the "r" sound—I make my students say this phrase aloud with me—
and yet the movement of the mouth is comfortable, easy—as free
and easy as "waved banners of light" in water. "These lines," someone declares, "are delicately, perfectly onomatopoetic."

And we begin to understand "cool" as literally cool to the touch—
in other words, "cool" in the way water is. "Waved" is a further clue,
a pun of sorts. We appear to be on the foot-bridge, looking with
Monet down at the water. In a wonderful simile, the play of sunlight
on water is likened to fish in water—not to fish exactly, but to something better, to the "effortlessness" of their movement.

Someone comments on the sounds of "effortlessly as fish." "It's
all 'essy,'" she says, "even the 'f's' are soft, and the word slips from
the tongue." We're pleased with ourselves: we've pictured the exact
motion Hecht describes, we've had that picture reinforced by sound,
and we've located the subject of the sentence ("sinuosities") and its
predicate ("unfurl, remesh, and round upon"). We see exactly how
light on water moves.

Except that suddenly we discover we are not looking at water at
all, but at the reflection of water on "the dark underside of the foot-
bridge." How fascinating it is ("How awesome an introduction to the
poem," someone says) that, just the way paintings capture the three-
dimensional world on two-dimensional canvas, the two-dimensional "underside" of the bridge captures a world reflected onto it.

Through Hecht's brilliant and subtle syntax, the canvas has become the wooden bridge.

We look next at that syntax. The six-line sentence has teased us with many possible endings—after "round upon themselves," after "cross-purposes," after "fish," and after "foot-bridge"—until we finally come to a stop at "pewter-weathered planks." The sentence's turn or pivot comes not at the verbs in line 2, but much later, in the prepositional phrase of line 5 ("On the dark underside of the foot-bridge") and in the participial phrase of line 6 ("Cast upward against pewter-weathered planks"), both modifying the noun "sinuosities," six lines distant. Hecht's sentence is a marvel of interweaving, of grammar that "unfurl[s], remesh[es], and rounds upon [itself]." The looseness of its arrangement and the tiny caesurae, the pauses, that each additive phrase demands replicate the movement and pauses of "waved banners of light."

Next we notice the exactitude with which Hecht captures what we all have seen but perhaps never have articulated—the tiny details of life that the artist registers: the way "weeds flatten with the current," the way dragonflies hover:

> Weeds flatten with the current. Dragonflies
> Poise like blue needles, steady in mid-air,
> For some decisive, swift inoculation.

Someone says, "We hear that flattening in the long vowels of 'weeds' and 'flatten,'" and someone else notes that the commas that surround and separate "steady in mid-air" imitate the dragonflies' stasis. The simile, "like blue needles" is, we agree, just right, and rendered even better by the wit of the next line, "For some decisive, swift inoculation."

We discover, in the next lines, that our focus shifts again, now from the air to the water:

> 10   The world repeats itself in ragged swatches
> Among the lily-pads, but understated,
> When observed from this selected vantage point,
> A human height above the water-level,
> As the shore shelves heavily over its reflection,
> 15   Its timid, leaf-strewn comment on itself.

"Among the lily-pads" seems like a good moment to have another look at two other Monet images. I show the class a photograph from a 1922 *New York Times* article, in which Monet and a gentleman stand on the bridge, beneath which we see the pond full of lily pads. I also show them a color reproduction of Monet's "Wisteria," now in The Hague museum. It was painted very close to the end of Monet's life, is beautiful in its rich colors, is typical of Monet's work in that the horizon is above the picture's frame, but is most interesting in that we see wisteria blossoms—Monet planted them along the shore—not as they would appear were we on land, but as reflected in the water. This means that we see not the drooping bells of the flowers, but the cups that those bells create, which are directly visible on land only if one crouches down below a spray of wisteria and looks upward. The image is extremely helpful in demonstrating the play of perspective Monet dealt in, and which Hecht deals in here. And we talk about the miracle of an artist's rendering water not simply as blue, but as blue, green, pink, purple, and gold, all the colors of the land, and yet making us know, with absolute certainty, that we are seeing water.

We look at line 14, "As the shore shelves heavily over its reflection," to see how sound and rhythm together create onomatopoeia. The sound of "shelves" is echoed in "heavily," but the two extra end syllables of the dactyl "heavily" throw "shelves heavily" off balance, imitating the shore's almost precarious overhang. Someone locates Hecht's wit again in "Its timid, leaf-strewn comment on itself," as if, like the dragonfly, "the shore" is invested with will and purpose.

Although there is no stanza break, we sense a transition at line 16, created by the anaphora of "Its" in line 15, referring to the reflection of the overhang, and "It's" in line 16:

15   Its timid, leaf-strewn comment on itself.
　　　It's midday in midsummer. Pitiless heat.
　　　Not so much air in motion as to flutter
　　　The frail, bright onion tissue of a poppy.

Where sentences a moment before ran six lines, now they contain four, even two, words. The compression itself suggests how hot it is, for in such heat, no one has the strength to speak a word more than necessary. The next sentence also lacks subject and verb: "Not so much air in motion as to flutter/The frail, bright onion tissue of a poppy." And after this "bridge" of heat coming exactly in the middle of the poem, in which now our tactile sense rather than our visual sense is temporarily engaged, we hear the artist's voice. "Devotions of a Painter" is carefully balanced, carefully structured:

> I am an elderly man in a straw hat
> 20 Who has set himself the task of praising God
> For all this welter by setting out my paints
> And getting as much truth as can be managed
> Onto a small flat canvas. Constable
> Claimed he had never seen anything ugly,
> 25 And would have known each crushed jewel in the pigments
> Of these oily golds and greens, enamelled browns
> That recall the glittering eyes and backs of frogs.

Monet's language immediately characterizes him, someone says, as modest, humble—"an elderly man in a straw hat"—described by his age and what he wears, not by what he has done. Now begins a string of unexpected words. According to his own report, he is serving God, praising him for—and we expect the word "beauty," but get "welter." *What's "welter"?* I ask, and, if no one knows, we look it up together and find that it is more commonly used as a verb than as a noun, and that that verb means "to roll or twist, to turn or tumble or writhe or wriggle about"—all this motion and moving life, all this mess. It is almost a joke. "A serious joke," someone says.

And what, I ask, does he say he is "getting . . . onto a small flat canvas"?

"Not the scene," someone answers, "but, again unexpectedly, 'truth' or, to be more accurate, as much of it as 'can be managed.'"

Hecht attributes to Monet admiration for the English landscape painter John Constable, who himself spoke of painting as aiming at "truth," and who, like Monet, constantly found something new in settings he painted and repainted. Hecht's Monet is pleased to think that Constable would have "known each crushed jewel in the pigments/Of these oily golds and greens, enamelled browns." Monet's craft consists not only of seeing and painting, but also, as with all great artists of the past, of grinding his own pigments—of the careful work that precedes or underlies what the public calls "art." Someone hears in all of this the modesty of great artists, including Hecht, and their devotion to truth. We muse for a moment about what perhaps has drawn Hecht to write this poem and decide that in some way he speaks not just for Monet but also for himself.

The poem continues, in lines 28–29, with,

> The sun dispenses its immense loose change,
> Squandered on blossoms, ripples, mud, wet stones,

and we seem to hear both voices, Hecht's in the wit of line 28, Monet's in the subject matter of line 29. And then we hear Monet's voice and perhaps Hecht's, joined in the poem's conclusion:

> 30   I am enamored of the pale chalk dust
>   Of the moth's wing, and the dark moldering gold
>   Of rust, the corrupted treasures of this world.
>   Against the Gospel let my brush declare:
>   "These are the anaglyphs and gleams of love."

A hand goes up. "What are anaglyphs?"

The Oxford English Dictionary, I say, in an ongoing effort to get my students to use it, *defines "anaglyph" as "something carved in low-relief" or as "a kind of photographic image where red and green images overlay each other to produce a broader range of color," but neither of those definitions seems to make sense here. The low-relief and bas-relief carvings on ancient Egyptian tombs were also sometimes called "anaglyphs" and*, I continue, *I think it's in that sense that Hecht uses the term—as a synonym for "signs," just as some of the carved images in the tombs and pyramids were regarded as "signs" before Egyptologists learned to decipher them. So the line becomes, "These are the signs and gleams of love." Does that make sense?*

My very accommodating class says yes, and this time I ask the question about another word in the same line. *Why "gleams"?*

"Maybe because 'gleams' reminds us of light on the water and on the underside of the bridge—and because it also suggests something luminous and divine."

Another hand. "What is meant by 'Against the Gospel'?"

A student replies, "I think, maybe, Hecht uses 'against' because the Gospels counsel choosing spiritual things over things of 'this world,' and Monet is saying that things of this world are themselves to be treasured as signs of God and avenues to devotion."

There is more discussion: "Maybe, but maybe not. The whole line is 'Against the Gospel let my brush declare,' so maybe it means 'my brush' is 'placed alongside,' or 'agrees with.'"

Both are excellent possibilities, I say, and add, *I don't know the answer either.*

Our discussion of words moves in yet another direction. Someone proposes, tentatively, that Hecht's use of "enamored" in,

30   I am enamored of the pale chalk dust
       Of the moth's wing, and the dark moldering gold
       Of rust, the corrupted treasures of this world,

is perhaps deliberate; it seems to echo "enamelled" a little earlier at line 26 where Monet speaks of Constable's never seeing anything ugly and then speaks of colors that we might regard as ugly, "oily golds and greens, enamelled browns/That recall the glittering eyes and backs of frogs."

"Perhaps by the similarity in sound Hecht is emphasizing that even those 'enamelled' browns deserve 'enamored' love," someone suggests.

"It's amazing," someone else says, "to speak of loving 'the corrupted treasures of this world.' To see the world as 'corrupted,' as fallen from grace and perfection, is, I suppose, a very religious attitude, as it is to love it."

We end our discussion by going back to the title of the poem, "Devotions of a Painter."

"'Devotions,'" a student suggests, "usually refers to the act of prayer. Monet defines painting as a devotional act, as 'praising God' by 'getting as much truth as can be managed/Onto a small flat canvas.'"

"So," someone else concludes, "in a sense, this poem is both ecphrastic and religious. It acknowledges and asserts that all that God creates is beautiful and that the artist, in paint or words, perhaps brings us closer to devotion."

Poem

POEM

About the size of an old-style dollar bill,
American or Canadian,
mostly the same whites, gray greens, and steel grays
—this little painting (a sketch for a larger one?)
has never earned any money in its life.

Useless and free, it has spent seventy years
as a minor family relic
handed along collaterally to owners
who looked at it sometimes, or didn't bother to.

10 It must be Nova Scotia; only there
does one see gabled wooden houses
painted that awful shade of brown.
The other houses, the bits that show, are white.
Elm trees, low hills, a thin church steeple
—that gray-blue wisp—or is it? In the foreground
a water meadow with some tiny cows,
two brushstrokes each, but confidently cows;
two minuscule white geese in the blue water,
back-to-back, feeding, and a slanting stick.
20 Up closer, a wild iris, white and yellow,
fresh-squiggled from the tube.
The air is fresh and cold; cold early spring
clear as gray glass; a half inch of blue sky
below the steel-gray storm clouds.
(They were the artist's specialty.)
A specklike bird is flying to the left.
Or is it a flyspeck looking like a bird?

Heavens, I recognize the place, I know it!
It's behind—I can almost remember the farmer's name.
30 His barn backed on that meadow. There it is,
titanium white, one dab. The hint of steeple,
filaments of brush-hairs, barely there,
must be the Presbyterian church.
Would that be Miss Gillespie's house?
Those particular geese and cows
are naturally before my time.

A sketch done in an hour, "in one breath,'
once taken from a trunk and handed over.
Would you like this? I'll probably never
40 *have room to hang these things again.*
Your Uncle George, no, mine, my Uncle George,
he'd be your great-uncle, left them all with Mother

when he went back to England.
You know, he was quite famous, an R.A. . . .

I never knew him. We both knew this place,
apparently, this literal small backwater,
looked at it long enough to memorize it,
our years apart. How strange. And it's still loved,
or its memory is (it must have changed a lot).
50 Our visions coincided—"visions" is
too serious a word—our looks, two looks:
art "copying from life" and life itself,
life and the memory of it so compressed
they've turned into each other. Which is which?
Life and the memory of it cramped,
dim, on a piece of Bristol board,
dim, but how live, how touching in detail
—the little that we get for free,
the little of our earthly trust. Not much.
60 About the size of our abidance
along with theirs: the munching cows,
the iris, crisp and shivering, the water
still standing from spring freshets,
the yet-to-be-dismantled elms, the geese.

Reading these two poems back-to-back, we are struck by how different they are. "If," my students say, "we had to speak of the movement
of 'Devotions of a Painter,' we might call it a movement outward.
With 'Poem,' the movement is not outward to encompass ever more
of the world, but inward, inward to the most inward point of all, the
place of private memory."

Lovely, I reply.

Hecht's verse, my students say, draws attention not only to his
felicities of language—to "sinuosities" and "welter," for instance—
but also to his range of reference: Monet and Constable, the Gospels
and anaglyphs. He clearly loves language—puns, onomatopoeia,
coinages of words, grammatical rearrangements that tease and en-
lighten, assonance and alliteration, witty personifications—and it is
part of the elegance and intellectual richness of his voice that we
are made so conscious of language when we read "Devotions of a
Painter." In "Poem," on the other hand, such devices, insofar as they

are present, are muted or, inversely, made obvious, as if to call attention away from language and to something else. Bishop's puns, for example, directly register with us even before, or just as, they are spoken, not afterwards: she points them out to us in the manner in which a friend, talking to us, might nudge us to say here's a joke. "Collaterally" in stanza one is a little pun that follows a homey metaphor about dollar bills, and "backwater" in stanza five, meaning both an out-of-the-way place and water in the back meadow, is prefaced by "literal" to indicate that a pun is in the offing.

Hecht's voice in much of his verse is stately and erudite; Bishop's here is personal and colloquial, and her vocabulary is relatively simple. We find some examples: she says, "Heavens, I recognize the place, I know it!"; she talks of someone's "speciality," of "the bits that show," of things "about the size of," of the painting's being "handed along," and so on. And there are lots of "its"—"its" that refer back to particular nouns ("it has spent seventy years as a minor family relic") and "its" that don't, that are broader in their reference.

There is nothing anywhere in the poem in the category of what students call "big words," nothing to look up in the O.E.D. Rather, there are words we know that, somehow, mean more than we usually attribute to them, that strike deeper. The little painting is "useless and free" and we think, when we read that phrase in stanza one, that "free" is just a playful extension of the monetary comparisons of the painting to "an old-style dollar bill," slightly larger than ones in current use. But when the word reappears later in "the little that we get for free," we realize that "free" is something far more. We recall that in Bishop's "At the Fishhouses," which we've read earlier, the same key words appear—"cold," "clear," "gray," "utterly free"—and with the same evocative power. But they remain sensory rather than intellectual terms. And the colloquial, non-intellectualized epiphanic "How strange" in "Poem" is very similar, we feel, to her epiphanic "how unlikely . . ." in "In the Waiting Room," coming just after the young Elizabeth says she knew that "nothing stranger / had ever happened, that nothing / stranger could ever happen," the ellipsis after "how unlikely . . ." itself suggesting insight receding into non-verbalized knowledge.

Someone suggests that Bishop's disinclination to cast experience in abstract terms is perhaps most easily seen if we compare the wit of the line in "Devotions of a Painter" where Hecht says Monet wants to get "as much *truth* as can be managed/Onto a small flat canvas," to Bishop's almost comically down-to-earth, aesthetic undercutting of what her uncle gets onto his small canvas—"titanium white, one dab" and "white and yellow, fresh squiggled from the tube."

"I think," someone adds, "that another way to look at differences between the two poems is to consider who the speaker is."

Good. Go on.

"In 'Devotions of a Painter,' it is Monet, who seems to be thinking rather than actually speaking, as he describes what he sees and what he tries to do. We, together with Hecht, are somehow present, hearing, observing, but not occupying physical space. It's a little like the way we and Hecht and Renoir watch the *tableau vivant* in 'The Deodand.' In 'Poem,' on the other hand, the painter's voice is not the one we hear; it's Bishop's, looking at the painting."

Someone adds, "Actually, there is no physical setting in 'Poem'— the only setting is the one in the painting itself. But in 'Devotions of a Painter' we are not looking at a painting at all. Rather, we're looking at the setting that inspires Monet's paintings."

Someone sees this as central, and adds, "That's the very point. That's it. The Nova Scotia landscape is not one that can be entered in reality—only in memory."

Bravo, all of you.

The student continues, "In Bishop's 'Crusoe in England,' we saw something similar, I think, where Crusoe recites the line about memory from 'Daffodils'—'They flash upon that inward eye.' Back in England, rescued, Crusoe longs for his island, which has, somehow, become dear to him. The island can exist now only in memory, and the objects which have been salvaged and which the local museum wants to display, 'the flute, the knife, the shriveled shoes, my shedding goatskin trousers . . . the parasol,' have no value for him. 'How can anyone want such things?' he asks. Crusoe's list sounds a little like the list that ends 'Poem,' but the list that ends 'Poem' is comprised of things that still have value because they exist in memory."

Our discussion of place and memory leads us to think about time. "In one poem—no, in both," my students correct themselves, "time is erased."

"In 'Devotions of a Painter,' we are transported to Giverny and to the years Monet lived there; he speaks to us and time collapses. We do not think of time. But in 'Poem,' we are terribly conscious of time—of the Nova Scotia of Bishop's childhood, the place of her growing up, and further back in time when her great-uncle painted the scene she looks at in present time. Time is associated with what she knew and loved."

Someone stops us briefly in our comparison. "Are 'knew' and 'loved' the same thing?"

An excellent question. I think, at least for "Poem," the answer is "yes."

Someone wants to correct our earlier conclusion: "Time is collapsed in the Bishop poem, too, not because it is ignored, but rather because it is so fully taken into account. Through a shared connection across time, a connection to the scene the painting depicts, time dissolves."

Someone else continues, "Then the function of ecphrasis here is different from its function in 'Devotions of a Painter.' In 'Devotions of a Painter' the aim of ecphrasis is to assert that all creation is beautiful and that art in the hands of certain artists is devotional because it captures the beauty of creation. Ecphrasis in 'Poem' has a different purpose: it stimulates 'memory,' and memory is the source of 'abidance'—of the 'little' that we get to hold onto and keep in life."

"I know we've said," someone begins, "that Bishop's poem takes us inward. I think this poem, or maybe I should say its effect, is a kind of paradox. The more personal the direction in which we, or Bishop, goes, the less share-able what we experience and can describe is. Yet, by the strangest of paradoxes, that unshare-ability becomes what ties us together because, deep in each of us, is something that is ours alone. As years pass and fewer people exist who have those same memories, or as years pass and the things we remember themselves vanish or are changed, that unshare-able place is one to which we go alone. I think it's that experience that the poem speaks to. So, ironically or paradoxically, what's most personal is also most universal. I think that's what gives this poem its great beauty and power."

Superb.

Let's look now at the painting Bishop describes. What's the first thing we're told about it?

"How small it is—'about the size of an old-style dollar bill.'"

What details emphasize its littleness?

"Just about everything. The church steeple is called 'thin,' a 'gray-blue wisp,' 'a hint of steeple,' and it's even likened to 'filaments of brush hairs, barely there.' The cows are called 'tiny,' the geese 'minuscule,' the blue sky covers 'a half inch' of the canvas below the steel-gray storm clouds, the bird flying to the left is called 'specklike.'"

Another hand goes up. "Right after calling the bird 'specklike,' Bishop says, 'Or is it a flyspeck looking like a bird?' I think that's really interesting, the way she can't tell whether the steeple is a thin painted line or just a hair from the paintbrush that got stuck on the canvas. The possibility that extraneous objects, a bit of brush hair or a tiny insect, have somehow gotten stuck to the canvas makes us conscious, through those realities, of the making of the painting and brings us back in time to the actual moment of its creation."

Excellent.

Another hand goes up. "Bishop says that 'up closer' a 'slanting stick' appears to be 'a wild iris, white and yellow.' She's ostensibly just correcting herself, something she does in her poetry that also makes it very personal, but at the same time she's saying something about how the closer you look, the more you see."

Good. Did anyone notice any other aspect of "littleness" in the poem?

A hand goes up. "Is it fair to include the small amount of time that presumably went into the painting's making? Bishop calls it "A sketch done in an hour, 'in one breath.'"

Very fair. And why all this littleness? What else is little?

"Littleness becomes the very heart of the poem," someone says, "when in the last stanza she speaks of 'the little that we get for free, / the little of our earthly trust. Not much. / About the size of our abidance.' Her very sentences here are little. And she's asking, what stays with us? what can we keep? what abides? And maybe hearing in the back of her mind the echo of hymns she used to sing, such as 'Abide with Me.'"

Someone adds, "And she's saying that not only is what abides 'little' but that 'life and the memory of it' are 'compressed,' and compression, too, makes things smaller than they are."

We talk next of the progression of the poem, as we did with "Devotions," which, we found divided into two 15-line parts with a mid-poem bridge:

It's midday in midsummer. Pitiless heat.
Not so much air in motion as to flutter
The frail, bright onion tissue of a poppy.

The structure of "Poem" is looser, but just before the first epiphany, there is something similar, a moment in which not just the subject matter of the painting but also the temperature of the air, something you can't quite paint, is felt and asserted with sureness:

> The air is fresh and cold; cold early spring
> clear as gray glass; a half inch of blue sky
> below the steel-gray storm clouds.

Another hand is raised. "The 'is' in the phrase, 'The air *is*,' is important. And the 'specklike bird,' two lines later, '*is* flying.' Up to this point, Bishop has simply pointed out the details of the painting; there have been no present tense verbs. Now we and she enter the picture's space. And the 'presence' of present tense readies us for the sudden explosion of recognition at the beginning of stanza three. Her excitement as stanza three begins is so great that she repeats herself ('I know it!') and breaks off after just two words ('It's behind—'), and when she finds the barn, 'titanium white, one dab,' she's looking for, she calls out, 'There it is.' Suddenly, the items in the painting become specific. The church is 'the Presbyterian church' and one of the houses becomes 'Miss Gillespie's house.' And then, laughing at herself, at her own excitement, she concludes the third stanza with,

> Those particular geese and cows
> are naturally before my time.

But they are 'particular' geese and cows, not just generic ones. They, too, she seems to be saying, were once alive, were once seen."

Excellent. And what happens at the end of "Poem" when we hear of those same items a third and final time?

"She has just spoken of 'the little of our earthly trust. Not much. / About the size of our abidance,' and goes on, at line 61, after 'our abidance':

> along with theirs: the munching cows,
> the iris, crisp and shivering, the water
> still standing from spring freshets,
> the yet-to-be-dismantled elms, the geese.

I think 'along with theirs' is beautiful. The cows, the iris, the water, the elms, the geese all are preceded by the definite article 'the,' which means that they are specific to a particular time, that they have had identity and being, like us."

Someone picks up from this point. "And now the adjectives describing them are different. Before, these things were described by size and color; now, by action that they themselves perform: the cows are 'munching,' the iris 'shivering,' the water 'standing.' And then, in the final line, I think something even more extraordinary happens. The elms, which will be 'dismantled,' are not 'yet' so; they still exist and partake of being. And then, somehow, because everything has been made so real, no adjective and no participle is needed. The weight of the word 'geese' itself is sufficient."

Lovely.

Another hand goes up. "I think it matters that 'the yet-to-be-dismantled elms' is not the final item. If it were, 'Poem' would end on a note of regret, emphasizing the loss that is inevitable. The poem has shown us that, but by ending with 'the geese,' Bishop is also showing us that something 'abides.'"

What of the title? I ask. Can we say anything about that before we end?

"It's an odd title, so unprepossessing."

"Does it refer to her poem, or to her great-uncle's painting? Or to both?"

How might it refer to both?

"Perhaps because one work of art creates another, and both, by reflecting a shared love of a particular place, and by a shared modesty and precision, express what poetry can do."

∎ 18 ∎

Rites and Ceremonies

ANTHONY HECHT

*In which we discover the searing power
of understatement.*

GRADE 11

With younger students, the best way to teach a poem is to read
it through with them, identify any problems, and then discuss it
in detail and depth. With older students and a poem as long and
richly allusive as "Rites and Ceremonies," I assign the reading of the
poem, with glosses, as homework, freeing us to use class time for
discussion.*

"Rites and Ceremonies" seems an unlikely title for a poem about
the Holocaust. We expect something more dramatic and searing.
But as we talk, we find the title aptly chosen. I begin by asking,
What are "rites and ceremonies"?

"Shared and prescribed communal expressions of feeling."

"Usually associated," someone adds, "with transitional events in life."

"It can be something as small as a military salute when a soldier's
coffin is brought home."

"Yes, and it's interesting that a rite or ceremony that small can
have tremendous power. Why should that be?

"Maybe because," a classmate ventures, "once we associate the
rite with an event, the rite becomes symbolic of all that that event
contains, a kind of shorthand of feelings."

---

*The extensive notes that I give to my students when we read "Rites and Ceremo-
nies" are available at www.pauldrybooks.com/products/teaching-particulars.

Excellent.

"We could therefore say that rites and ceremonies are ways of remembering things."

Yes. Good.

Another hand goes up. "I understand that rites and ceremonies can summon up pain and grief by the least gesture or word, but they also give us ways of containing our feelings. They have formal beginnings and endings and, when a ceremony or rite ends, that signals to us that we need to return to our lives, no matter what we feel. So they also provide consolation."

Good.

Another question is posed. "I understand all we've said, but I still don't understand the applicability of the title to this poem. Much of the poem is historical narrative rather than the description of a rite or ceremony."

Does this poem, I ask, *include any rites or ceremonies?*

My students pause and then someone says, "The opening and closing parts of the poem"—the poem is divided into four sections—"are, either in whole or in part, prayers."

Good.

Someone adds, "Not just personal prayers, but prayers that are part of the liturgy or composites of lines from different books of the Bible, such as Job and Psalms and Isaiah, and so on."

Yes.

There is a further objection: "But ceremonies and rites involve acts of some sort. I know we can kind of call 'prayer' action, but it's not really physical."

What would you say is the quintessential religious action? For example, what's the first devotional act we hear about in Genesis? My students think back to Genesis in sixth grade.

"Sacrifice. We hear of it even before we hear of prayer."

Good. Where and through what means?

"In the story of Cain and Abel, on an altar, with fire."

Precisely.

"And then with Isaac—Oh, my god. Are you saying that Hecht is likening the ovens of the Holocaust and the pogrom in Strasbourg to the ceremony of sacrifice? To burnt offerings?"

No. I think he's suggesting that reading in order to shoot it down, in order to show that to regard such things as sacrifice is obscene. Chris-

*tian clerics, for whom Christ's suffering is a sign of God's love, have
sometimes, in trying to offer comfort and ease guilt, "thanked the Jews"
for being killed in the Holocaust, for being "sacrificed." But at the beginning of Part III, in a matter-of-fact voice that Hecht uses only there
and at the beginning of Part IV, he says, "The contemplation of horror
is not edifying, /Neither does it strengthen the soul."*

We stay with the question of what constitutes "rites and ceremonies" a little longer. *Does anyone remember the word "ceremony"
appearing anywhere in the poem?* It is a very long poem, ten pages in
our text, and the word appears just once. But someone does recall it,
and finds it for us.

"My god," she blurts out a second time, apologizes, and goes on,
"I'm sorry, but this is horrible. The word appears in Part II, in which
Hecht describes the townspeople of Strasbourg in 1349, gathered to
watch the burning of the Jews, whom they have accused of poison-
ing the wells. Hecht writes:

> Everyone who was not too sick was down
> To watch the ceremony.

He calls that a 'ceremony.' He's being ironic, but he's also describing
exactly what it is. The community stops all work and gathers, as if
for a festive performance."

My class is appalled by what they have discovered. A second hand
goes up. "The Corso in Part III of the poem—that's a ceremony, too."

There is another collective gasp. She continues, "Hecht writes, 'It
is the first Saturday in Carnival,' the day of the heats. 'First down
the gantlet, twenty chosen asses,' and between them and 'the next
heat, the buffaloes,' are the Jews, chosen by 'Christ's Vicar' himself,
the Pope. They are stripped and made to race the Corso, along both
sides of which spectators 'have whips and sticks with bunting tied
around them' and the viewers and 'their dears' crowd the course,
drinking and laughing. It is a Church-devised annual event, this
ceremony, this shaming and torturing of Jews, a raucous ceremo-
nial beginning of the Lenten season, which is a time, supposedly, of
reflection and repentance."

"The running of the Jews entertains and pacifies the mob even
more, as the Church well knows, than the 'juggling,' 'acrobats,' and
'palm-reading.'"

So, I say, giving my class a moment to recover, *in how many ways does Hecht use the term "Rites and Ceremonies" in the poem?*

"As sincere ceremony in Parts I and IV, ironically in Parts II and III."

"That means," someone adds, "that the title is, in fact, all-inclusive—it covers everything in the poem."

"Could we argue," a third student asks, "that the poem, taken as a whole rather than viewed in its separate parts, is a ceremony and rite of remembrance?"

We well might, I say.

Someone adds, "Maybe that's what Hecht seeks to do here—to bear witness, so that these events he recounts are remembered the way that rites and ceremonies are."

Very good.

Another hand goes up. "Something we didn't mention before, but that I think is important, is that genuine rites and ceremonies are historical—they link present to past. That's what Hecht does in this poem—he places the Holocaust within the historical context of Jewish suffering and brings past moments into the present."

"I agree. The most graphic and extended moment in the poem is the Strasbourg pogrom."

"Perhaps Hecht does that so that our 'contemplation' is not just 'of horror' but also of the perpetrators and enablers of horror."

Very good.

"In other poems we have read, Hecht shows himself to be deeply interested in explaining evil—in 'The Feast of Stephen,' for example, or in 'Behold the Lilies of the Field,' or in 'The Deodand.' These poems are set in times and situations removed from, and unrelated to, the Holocaust—Jerusalem during the time of Jesus, ancient Rome during the reign of Valerian, Paris in the 1880s and Algiers in the 1950s—but they explore, perhaps even obsessively, the impulse to evil, the sadism of the bully, and, in every poem, the horror of witnessing evil. Perhaps these poems were prompted by the questions the Holocaust raised for Hecht, questions that he returns to, again and again, in many different forms."

Excellent.

"I agree, and I think the question that occupies him is not really the theological one of why God lets these things happen and does not intervene, but Lear's question—'Is there any cause in nature that make these hard hearts?' Where does such evil come from? These are questions about human behavior, questions about the psychology of cruelty, not questions about God."

"I think that's true, and the fact that stanza three of 'The Room' begins, 'It is twenty years now,' confirms the fact that Hecht never lets these questions go. And if that is obsessive, it is also the reaction of a supremely moral man."

Bravo, all of you.

Someone raises an additional point. "In addition to the sufferer and the perpetrator, Hecht also focuses on two other figures, the indifferent bystander and the true witness."

Whom in the poem do you place in the category of "indifferent bystander"?

"The docent at the cathedral of Strasbourg and Du Bellay in Rome, people with the same access to events that Hecht has—greater access, in fact—who refuse to see or acknowledge or feel."

And in the category of "true witness"?

"Hecht himself, and the voices he adopts. He is 'there' in the gas chambers, and he is there in Strasbourg in 1349. He hears 'the screaming' in the forest of Buchenwald, he hears the docent, he sees the heats in Rome and expresses false solicitude for Du Bellay. In other words, he fulfills the commandment to remember and feel what others feel."

Someone adds, "Implicit in his role as witness is the obligation for all of us to do the same. While the 'contemplation of horror is not edifying,' perhaps knowing what motivates evil is. And, while Hecht is never didactic, there is a line in Part IV, an imperative, that really affected me. It begins like a question, but is, in fact, an admonition. Hecht, talking about those of us who have survived, says,

> And to what purpose, as the darkness closes about
> And the child screams in the jellied fire,
> Had best be our present concern.

He enjoins us, the 'remnant,' to know and to act upon that knowledge."

Someone adds, "We have an obligation not just to the future but also to the past. This is a little corny, but when we participate in rites and ceremonies I think we participate not just for ourselves, but for those who have lived before us, even centuries before us, and died, and whose feelings and griefs we bear and carry with us, too."

"Is that," someone asks, "what the final prayer in Part IV means?" We read it together.

> Father, I also pray
> For those among us whom we know not, those
> Dearest to thy grace,
> The saved and saving remnant, the promised third,
> Who in a later day
> When we again are compassed about with foes,
> Shall be for us a nail in thy holy place
> There to abide according to thy word.
>
> Neither shall the flame
> Kindle upon them, nor the fire burn
> A hair of them, for they
> Shall be thy care when it shall come to pass,
> And calling on thy name
> In the hot kilns and ovens, they shall turn
> To thee as it is prophesied, and say,
> *"He shall come down like rain upon mown grass."*

I tell the class, *I think the meaning turns on who "those" are. Let's start with whatever seems straightforward.*

"I'll try. Hecht anticipates 'a later day,' a future time 'when we again are compassed about with foes.' And when 'those . . . whom we do not know'—perhaps because they are future generations, or because they are past generations, souls who have suffered and died—will through their suffering and faith intercede with God for us. In 'the hot kilns and ovens,' they will not be burnt, but will feel God's presence coming 'down like rain.' Evil and persecution will not vanish. But faith provides a balm. That's as far as I can take these stanzas."

That's far.

"I think it's plausible that this 'remnant' is not the remnant of earlier moments in the poem, or even the remnant of Jewish liturgy, but Hecht's own poetic vision of those who have 'call[ed] on thy name / In the hot kilns and ovens' and who, dying, are taken under the wings of God and feel no fire, but something like the blessing of 'rain on mown grass.'"

"I think it's beautiful that Hecht says this 'saved and saving remnant . . . shall be *for us* a nail,'—that they for whom he prays will also have the power to pray for us, to protect and intercede for us."

"Perhaps this gives us a way to read the whole poem: the pious who pray as they die do not pray for intervention. They pray out of love for God and out of the belief that God 'hears.' That hearing does not involve intervention in the world that God has created and set in motion. The task of righting the world is ours."

"The sense of comfort that these stanzas produce is, I think, echoed in aspects of its poetic technique," someone adds. "The final stanzas of Part IV not only alternate long and short lines, as do the five-line stanzas of George Herbert's 'Deniall,' but also add three iambic pentameter lines to each five-line stanza. These concluding lines seem to offer something solid, something you feel you can rely on."

Someone else says, "The rhyme here does the same thing. At first these final stanzas don't seem to rhyme, but if you read them closely, you find that they do rhyme—*abcd abcd* ('pray . . . those . . . grace . . . third'; 'day . . . foes . . . place . . . word'), *efgh efgh* ('flame . . . burn . . . they . . . pass'; 'name . . . turn . . . say . . . grass'). There is a pattern, just not one that's immediately evident. It is something clarified over time. The rhymed words are four lines apart, but they're there. In a way, maybe we could say that that's like not immediately seeing or hearing God's response, but finding that God is there, after all."

Good.

Among the poems by Anthony Hecht that we have read together is another Holocaust poem called "'It Out-Herods Herod. Pray You, Avoid It.'"—its title taken from Hamlet's advice to the Players, where he urges them to eschew emotional excess and bombast, to "use all gently." I ask, *Does Hecht's voice in "Rites and Ceremonies" resemble the father's voice in "'It Out-Herods Herod.'"?*

"The voice in the 'Herod' poem," someone answers, "is a restrained voice that releases its feelings in irony—an irony that, at points, is very pronounced—bitter and comic at the same time—and at other points so suffused with sorrow as to be almost indistinguishable from that sorrow."

And what about "Rites and Ceremonies"? What can we say about its ironic range? Let's find some examples in the four sections of the poem.

Irony in Part I "The Room"

Someone begins, "If irony marks a discrepancy between what should be and what is, then the title 'The Room' is ironic. We think of rooms as familiar places, associated with home and safety. 'Room' is one of the very first nouns we learn as children. But these rooms are death chambers, sealing Jews for gassing, and later storing artifacts taken from the dead. Hecht's title is ironic because it expresses a discrepancy between positive expectation and negative reality."

"I found a different sort of irony in the same section—or, to be more accurate, an irony that is the exact opposite of a positive transformed into a negative. The line, 'Are the vents in the ceiling, Father, to let the spirit depart?' is ironic, not because the speaker is unaware of imminent death. The speaker is fully aware. It is ironic because its innocence and perfect faith abide and turn a horror into a blessing—in the mind of the believer, God's power and love transform the poisonous vents into the spirit's physical path to God."

We are so moved that it's hard to do more than nod.

Someone else goes on. "There is also, in Part I, irony created by literary allusions that reflect what is civilized and noble but that are applied by the author to a reality that is barbaric and base. Immediately after the lines from Ecclesiasticus, there follows not the promise of remembrance but the promise of debasement and disappearance: these dead shall be 'Made into soap'; and after the line from Goethe about the hushed silence of the forest, Hecht writes, 'But for years the screaming continued.'"

"I have another example," someone adds, "but rather than operating by ironic juxtaposition, it operates as an ironic pun. When Hecht writes, 'And the little children were suffered to come along, too,' he's using 'were suffered' in its Gospel sense of 'were allowed.' To suggest that little children's being rounded up for the transports and death camps was a privilege and honor equal to being brought into the presence of Jesus is irony in the form of a bitter joke. And, of course, we hear, behind this, the other meaning of 'to experience suffering.'"

Very good.

"These are ironies that the writer and reader share but that the perpetrators do not hear. If the perpetrators did hear them, they would be too thuggish to grasp or care about the difference between what is noble and what is vile. So could we say that irony is also a way of separating one's sensibility from that of the perpetrators of evil and expressing a superiority to them?"

I think so. We may not have exhausted the ironies of Part I, I continue, *but we've covered a great deal of ground. Let's see what we find in Part II.*

Irony in Part II "The Fire Sermon"

What's a sermon for? What does it do?

"A sermon," someone begins, "is supposed to edify, to bring congregants closer to God."

Good.

"'The Fire Sermon,' taken literally, means that the Church and the Strasbourg mob are edifying the Jews with this message: 'You are powerless before us and will die in agony because you are Jews. For our added pleasure, you will be made in your dying to desecrate your Sabbath and the graves of your ancestors.' The irony of the word 'Sermon' in the title of this section lies in the gross misuse of the term, a misuse that reveals a sick purpose. This irony, compared to some of those in Part I, is an irony that the perpetrators understand."

"Irony can also work through repetition. The three references to 'a judgment' in this section mark an ironic progression from honesty to dishonesty, from primitive belief to political hypocrisy."

Go on.

"The first question that the plague prompts, 'Was it a judgment?' is posed in genuine fear by those who think their sins may have brought about the Black Death. In a movement to self-exculpation, the question becomes rhetorical, 'How could it be a judgment . . . ?' and finally turns into a negation assertion: 'And presently it was found to be / Not a judgment.' And there is irony, of course, in language that suggests the presence of evidentiary proof—'it was found'—when none is present or possible, and when the clear motives for such a statement are political and economic convenience.

The only 'finding' that Jews have poisoned the wells is one extracted under torture."

"The end of Part II, the voice from the flames, touched me perhaps more than anything else in the poem—George Herbert, upon whose poem 'Deniall' Hecht models this sequence, equates his 'broken' rhyme (*ababc*) with his 'broken' spiritual state, a state that only God can mend. Therefore, Herbert's *ababa* fully-rhymed conclusion indicates that God has heard his prayers and answered him. Hecht's final stanza does not end in rhyme, and that heightens the pathos of the final *c* line, 'Out of hearing.' Can pathos be called a form of irony?"

Not exactly, but what you've described I think qualifies as ironic, which always involves a comparison of some sort.

Someone suggests that what also contributes to the emotion we feel is the fact that the speaker is not praying or begging God for himself, as one would expect in dire circumstances, but simply for someone, anyone, some child perhaps. "It is so utterly selfless," someone says, "as to be unbearable and saintly."

Someone adds that, in both "The Room" and "The Fire Sermon," voices, like these, of the dying cry out to us in language that is at once beautiful and resonant of what is most human and most civilized. "And that is profoundly ironic."

We have found, together, a range of ironic moments, some characterized by mockery, others by gentleness.

Irony in Part III "The Dream"

What about irony in Part III? Does it take a different form?

"I think irony here takes the form of false solicitude."

Good.

"Hecht expresses concern for Du Bellay when the proper object of concern should be the Jews made to entertain the Roman mob at the behest of the Pope.

> Du Bellay, poet, take no thought of them;
> And yet they too are exiles . . .
> Still, others have been scourged and buffeted

The insincere suggestion that we can't, after all, worry about everyone is an ironic response to Du Bellay's failure of concern, in which

Du Bellay, like the docent, perhaps like T. S. Eliot himself"—
our glosses for "The Fire Sermon" have alluded to Part III of "The
Wasteland"—"becomes an emblem of the unconcerned aesthete."

Someone notes a smaller irony, one that is almost a joke, as irony
often seems to be—the substitution of 'mirth' for 'whip' in the line,

> Camel and Barbary horse
> Shall feel the general mirth upon their hide.

Someone else has a question. "I don't know whether this is,
strictly speaking, about irony, but it's something that puzzled me
about this section of the poem. It's that, in contrast to the prayers of
the other sections in which the sufferers are given a voice, even if
that voice is mediated through Hecht, here the Jews are mute and
barely mentioned."

A hand goes up. "Perhaps that's the very point. Less attention is
given to the Jews in this passage than to the crowd or the donkeys.
The irony of misplaced focus suggests the reduction to silence of the
Jewish victims. It also suggests that in the view of the mob and its
enabler, the Church, the Jews are less than human. I think you're
right. I think the absence of voice is also a ironic statement."

Irony in Part IV "Words for the Day of Atonement"

What about Part IV? What ironies do you find here?

No hands go up. Then, finally, one. Hesitating, she says, "As far
as I can tell, there's no irony in Part IV."

Does everyone agree?

Heads nod, "Yes."

*Why would Hecht, whose poem is so richly ironic, write such a
conclusion?*

Someone, testing a proposition, begins, "If irony is a way of indicating a discrepancy between what is and what should be, then
maybe it's also a way of criticizing innocence."

How so?

"This is a stretch, but could we say that irony is the opposite of
belief and faith? I mean, irony looks at the world with a kind of sus-
picion, with an expectation that things are not as they are said to
be, or that things will turn out other than expected. Faith does the
opposite. Maybe what happens for those who, like Hecht, look evil

in the face, is that after every irony is explored, faith is left. It abides. Perhaps not even as a permanent possession, but as a state that one, from time to time, experiences. Perhaps that's what the end of this poem represents."

Someone adds, "Hecht includes here an entire prayer from the High Holiday liturgy, beginning with 'The soul is thine,' and then addresses God as 'Father.' You don't speak that way to an entity that you don't believe in."

Someone else joins our effort to define the tone of this final portion. "At the beginning of the poem, Hecht spoke of 'lauds and threnes,' praise and lament; maybe in a sense those two modes of expression are what we hear in Part IV, not as separate elements— now praise, now lament—but fused, joined. And that fusing, perhaps, gives strength even to those in pain and somehow finds its home in faith."

I suggest that this very great poem ends in reconciliation with God, and am immediately corrected.

"It may not be accurate to say that, at the end of the poem, Hecht is reconciled to God because it's possible that he has never not been reconciled."

The sensibility that shapes this poem is hard for us to define. The best we can do is to say that it reflects the response of someone who bears the burden of terrible knowledge but who loves the world and finds beauty in it, in faith, and in the valor and faith of good men.

"In this sense," someone says, "the poem's voice is utterly different from the voice of persecutors, past and future. And that is, perhaps, the greatest irony of all."

.▪ 19 ▪.

Oedipus at Colonus

SOPHOCLES

*In which we consider the effect of ritual
patterns interrupted.*

GRADE 11

We read and briefly discuss Kenneth Burke's definition of literary
form:

> Form in literature is an arousing and fulfillment of desires. A
> work has form in so far as one part of it leads a reader to antici-
> pate another part, to be gratified by the sequence . . .
>
> Or, seen from another angle, form is the creation of an appe-
> tite in the mind of the auditor, and the adequate satisfying of
> that appetite. This satisfaction . . . at times involves a temporary
> set of frustrations [that] in the end . . . make the satisfaction of
> fulfillment more intense.*

I say that we will try to apply Burke's definition to Sophocles' very
great play *Oedipus at Colonus* as I pick up a quarter that I have left
lying on my desk, fiddle with it for a minute, drop it, and let it roll
across the room. My students have been paying close attention, but
are distracted; they can't help but turn to follow the quarter's path
until it clatters to a stop.

"Was that on purpose?" someone asks.

---

*Kenneth Burke, *Counter-Statement*, University of California Press, 1968, pp.
124, 31 (originally published, 1931).

Yes, I confess, I was trying to demonstrate Burke's argument about form and appetite. Something begins, even something as silly and unimportant as a rolling quarter, and our impulse—our need—as human beings is to see it to completion. When we do, tension is released and we can continue with whatever we were about. If an action is suspended mid-performance, its tension remains unresolved and nags at us, even if we don't quite realize it. Oedipus at Colonus, I continue, *contains a remarkable conclusion in which the dramatic tension that Sophocles creates earlier is superbly resolved.* With that we begin our discussion of the prologue.

What action is begun in the prologue?

"Well," someone says, "as the play opens, Oedipus reaches the grove of the Furies and realizes that it is the place where, according to Apollo's prophecy, he is to die, and therefore that this day is to be his death day."

Does he wish to die?

"Yes. He is eager for death."

What happens?

"He enters the grove, and is immediately ordered out of it—first by a peasant and then by a whole Chorus of Athenian Citizens, who demand Oedipus to 'move from where you sit; the place is holy; It is forbidden to walk upon that ground.'"

What question therefore arises?

"How can he fulfill the prophecy, when the precise spot where he must go is forbidden to him?"

And is that the only source of the initial tension—that interrupted action?

"Well, I can't speak for everyone, but the walking scene made me really tense. I couldn't wait for it to be over. He's blind, of course, and as he tries to leave the grove he's so unsure of where to step and where the boundary of the grove is that he asks question after question, and takes a single step with each question, until he finally reaches unhallowed ground. I was so bored."

That's not only an honest response but also, I think, exactly what Sophocles wants us to feel.

"Really? You mean he means it to be boring? and slow? and tense?"

Absolutely. A great playwright doesn't make a mistake of that sort, especially not in an opening scene. Look at how driving the openings of Antigone *and* Oedipus Rex *are.*

"Maybe Sophocles writes it," someone suggests, "to make us conscious of how real Oedipus's blindness is, and how helpless it makes him physically."

"And maybe, by emphasizing Oedipus's physical vulnerability, Sophocles makes Oedipus's strength of mind and will all the more impressive."

Good, both of you, but that may not be his whole purpose. Perhaps something even more important is at work here.

My students look blankly until I add, *What happens at the end of the play?*

"There's lightning and thunder, which are signs from the gods that his time has come, and then blind Oedipus strides, alone and unaided, with bold and sure steps, across the stage to the sacred grove, leading Antigone, Ismene, and Theseus."

Good. And so . . . ?

"Oh! I see—that's why we need that opening scene! as a contrast to this moment! And when we remember the beginning, his terror at each blind step, this moment becomes almost sublime."

Good. Before we look for other examples of Sophocles' use of interrupted action, let's talk for a moment about the Grove of the Furies. Exactly who are the Furies to whom Oedipus prays in the prologue? And what do they punish?

We know about the Erinyes, the Furies, of Aeschylus's *Oresteia*, who pursue and hound Orestes almost to madness after he kills his mother, Clytemnestra, and so someone answers, "They are goddesses, more ancient than the Olympians, who dwell beneath the earth and who punish all who injure or violate blood kin, such as mothers."

"Those who violate mothers," you say?

There is a gasp and a hand is raised. "Oedipus has violated his mother—he has slept with her, and she has become the mother of his sons and daughters. And she has killed herself. If he bears guilt for these actions, as others think he does, the Furies would hardly allow him to enter their grove."

A student takes a deep breath, and then speaks. "Then his entry into the grove in the play's final scene is, in a way, a repetition of his first sin of entry into his mother. And the fact that the Furies not only allow but welcome him—the fact that the earth opens up and he disappears into it—is proof that this king who has been a pariah is now cleansed of all his shame and is made holy."

Precisely.

Someone adds, "There are images in Oedipus's prayer to the Furies that indicate not only that they welcome him, but also that he and they are similar. He calls them 'Ladies whose eyes are terrible.' His own eyes are scarred sockets into which he once drove his mother's golden pins; their eyes ooze pus and blood. He says he does not drink wine, and the libations to the Furies, as we know from the long passage with Ismene, consist only of honey and water."

Excellent.

"And like them," says someone who recalls our discussion of the *Eumenides,* "he, too, will take up permanent residence just outside the city of Athens, to be honored as a protective deity forever. Like the Furies," she continues, "Oedipus has been granted the power to confer blessings on Athens, especially in time of war."

"In fact, we learn that whatever earth receives him is eternally protected. That's why Creon wants to drag him back to Thebes."

Let's go back for a moment to the libations the Furies accept. There is an early scene in which Ismene, just arrived in Colonus to warn her father of the coming of Creon and Polyneices, takes upon herself the rite of propitiation of the Furies for Oedipus's having trod on their grove. How did you like that scene?

One of my students admits, "It felt as tedious as the walking scene in the prologue. But maybe it was important, too?"

Could be. Let's go over what the scene consists of.

She begins, "The citizens want Oedipus to propitiate the Furies for treading on their ground by offering a libation to them. He can't, because he is blind, but his daughter Ismene willingly agrees to do so in his place. But she requires extensive instruction from the Athenians as to how it's to be done. She's given instruction about water and chaplets and sprigs of myrtle and the fleece of young lambs and the way to face when pouring the libations out and how many streams to pour and about including honey and omitting wine and where to place olive branches—it's endless."

It certainly makes us conscious of . . . ?

"Of the great importance of ritual."

Good. And does she do what she's supposed to?

"She tries. But Creon sends his men to kidnap her while she's praying in the grove, in order to use her and her sister Antigone as bait to force Oedipus back to Thebes."

So the ritual, about which we've heard so very much, is interrupted?
"Yes."
Is any other religious ritual interrupted in the play?
"Theseus, who is sacrificing to Poseidon, has to interrupt his worship to rescue the girls."
So Sophocles twice presents interrupted rituals, right?
"Yes."
Do these interruptions have anything in common?
"It's Creon's fault both times."
Exactly. So what does that tell us about Creon—as if we needed confirmation?
"That he's impious, blasphemous."
Excellent. But now let's go further. Is there perhaps an even more important reason that Sophocles draws our attention to these interrupted rituals? Anyone?

We pause for a moment, and then I add again, *Think of the end of the play, the* exodos.

Then someone begins, "The end of the play is all about ritual and its fulfillment. These are not the same rituals as were interrupted before—now they are the rituals of death and mourning—but they are rituals all the same, and they are fulfilled to the letter."

Excellent.

"In fact," someone adds with excitement, "Oedipus does what no man has ever done. Before he dies he performs for himself the washing of the body and the putting on of clean garments—ritual acts that mourners do for their dead."

And Antigone and Ismene? What about them?

"Just after the Messenger brings news of Oedipus's death, he says to the Chorus that Oedipus's children 'are not far away; the sound of weeping/Should tell you now that they are coming.' Antigone enters, saying, "Now may we weep indeed," and for the next 100 or so lines she, Ismene, and the Chorus weep and lament. Then Theseus enters and says, 'Cease lamentation, children.'"

"Is it possible," someone else asks, "that what we witness is an actual ritual of lamentation, performed onstage, in real time?"

That is a stunning question, and very possibly the case. I explain that *while we don't know the exact nature or components of ancient Greek lamentation, death ritual is formal in every culture. This scene contains the following ritual components: (1) a statement that tears and lamentation are appropriate now, (2) a description of the manner of death, (3) a statement of longing for the dead, (4) a promise not to forget the dead, and, finally, (5) a statement that formal mourning is now completed. I end, saying, We may be witnessing not just a dramatized moment of grief but an actual lamentation.*

"If that's the case," the student continues, "then Sophocles has made this moment a kind of answer to all the unreleased tension in the play. Maybe that's partly why, despite our sorrow, we feel such peace at the end of the play."

"Sophocles makes us not just spectators of, but participants in and witnesses to, a hallowed rite."

After a class in which we talk about Oedipus's exquisite speech to Theseus about the mutability of all things, and compare Polyneices to Theseus, we will watch the film of Lee Breuer's production, *The Gospel at Colonus*, perhaps the most brilliant and moving rendition that exists of ancient Greek drama.

.■ 20 .■

The Death of Ivan Ilych

LEO TOLSTOY

*In which we see the genius of Tolstoy's shift
in point of view.*

GRADE 11

In "The Death of Ivan Ilych," Tolstoy achieves the miracle of making readers identify, really identify, with an utterly unprepossessing man whose life has nothing heroic in it and who is not in any expected way "interesting," witty, handsome, or impassioned. My students look upon Ivan Ilych as a model of what they hope they will not become. Tolstoy allows and even encourages us, in the opening portions of the story, to mock and criticize Ilych. Then, without warning, we see Ivan Ilych as Everyman in the journey through life to death. Ilych's destination is not Damnation, as Everyman's was on the medieval stage with its background of a gaping "Hell-mouth." Although Ilych has lived without joy or purpose, his end, amazingly, is bliss, conferred by divine grace, and accessible, this story suggests, to every human being. "The Death of Ivan Ilych" is the oddest of yokings: social satire joined to, indeed made the path of, a tale of salvation. This exquisite novella leads its readers to reappraise every preconception and to respond with enlarged sympathy to weakness and to fear.

At the start of our discussion, many of my students will have disliked the story, some because they find Ivan Ilych superficial and self-pitying, others because Tolstoy's presentation of an illness that is undefined and deadly is frightening.

I begin by asking about the opening of "The Death of Ivan Ilych."
What are we shown?
They answer, "We are at a break during a trial, in a room with lawyers."
And what are those lawyers doing?
"Talking about another trial—engaging in legal gossip."
Good—and then?
"One who's reading a newspaper comes upon Ivan Ilych's death notice."
How do the others react?
"With shock, which quickly passes. Privately they start thinking about what slot has opened up in the judiciary for them."
Do they say those things aloud?
"Of course not [you silly teacher]. What they say aloud is that it's very sad, that the nature of his illness was never explained, that they ought to have visited him, and that they need now to pay a condolence call on his widow, who lives inconveniently far away."
"And that turns into a joking exchange about distances between different parts of the city."
Do we like these fellows?
"No."
Why not? Careful, now.
"Well, they don't care about this man."
And we do?
"No, we don't even know him. But we don't like the fact that they don't care about him."
"And we don't like them because they're caught up in the trivia of their daily lives and push the fact of death aside."
Would we behave differently?
"Well, we'd like to think so—but we might not."
By the way, do we know the name of the city?
"No."
Of other places where Ivan Ilych lives?
"No."
Anybody want guess why Tolstoy withholds that information?
Someone who listens closely but speaks little says, "I'm not sure—to make the characters more remote? or to make them universal?"
Both, perhaps.

Before we look at the rest of the opening, the condolence call paid upon the widow Praskovya Fedorovna and the comedy of the creaking pouffe, we turn to the end of the story. *What happens at the end, and what sort of contrast does it offer to the beginning?*

These questions offer more of a challenge.

"Ivan Ilych dies. In terms of time, the end is a day or so before the newspaper account appears."

Yes. What else? From whose perspective are we told of his death?

"From his own. We're inside the mind of the dying man at the moment of his death—we are, in a sense, where no one except a dying person himself can be."

And what contrast to the point of view at the beginning of the story does this represent?

"Tolstoy starts out narrating at great distance and then gets as close up as you can get—even closer than that, because what he writes is what even a writer can only guess at."

And how does Tolstoy make Ivan Ilych's moment of dying real and intimate?

"I think it's that Tolstoy uses an image that we've never come across before—that of a narrow, deep, black sack, through which Ivan Ilych must thrust himself. It's like in a dream, when there's some physical thing you have to do that's essential to some larger goal, but when you wake up and remember that physical thing, it has no logical connection to that goal. The sack is like that. And yet it's also a perfect image of passing from one state to another. And because it's dreamlike, it's intimate."

Could we say, then, that Tolstoy puts us inside Ivan Ilych's mind and lets us see his dream?

"Yes."

Is there anything else that makes us identify with Ivan Ilych at his moment of death?

"Well, while those around him—his wife, his daughter, his son— hear him screaming, and assume he's in agony, we know what he knows but cannot convey—that he is feeling 'joy.' We're in his head; no one else is."

Another student adds, "Tolstoy seems to show us the thing everybody wonders about—what it's like to die—without telling us that that is what he's doing. In these moments, we become Ivan Ilych— no space separates us."

Someone else has been looking at the text during this discussion, and notices the syntax of the final sentence. Her arm shoots up. "Look at the last sentence, 'He drew in a breath, stopped in the midst of a sigh, stretched out, and died.' The final sentence of the story is also the final moment of his life, and Ivan Ilych is actively doing things, rather than passively feeling things happening to him. It's a huge change. He inhales, stops, stretches out, and dies—and the way Tolstoy writes this makes it sound like Ivan Ilych is finally in control, that he wills and chooses to do these things."

Great. Anything more?

A quiet voice begins, "Well, perhaps what Tolstoy is suggesting here, in the joy of Ivan Ilych's last moments, is that one moment of joy and control, or a lifetime of joy, is just the same. I mean, since we experience things only moment by moment, that each moment is enough." The class is hushed for a moment.

Then we continue. We're ready for the social satire of the "pouffe" scene in which Peter Ivanovich pays a condolence call on Praskovya Fedorovna. *What's funny or incongruous about this scene?* I ask. *What is Tolstoy trying to do?*

We begin reading:

> When they reached the drawing-room, upholstered in pink cretonne and lighted by a dim lamp, they sat down at the table— she on a sofa and Peter Ivanovich on a low pouffe, the springs of which yielded spasmodically under his weight. Praskovya Fedorovna had been on the point of warning him to take another seat, but felt that such a warning was out of keeping with her present condition and so changed her mind. As he sat down on the pouffe Peter Ivanovich recalled how Ivan Ilych had arranged this room and had consulted him regarding this pink cretonne with green leaves. The whole room was full of furniture and knick-knacks, and on her way to the sofa the lace of the widow's black shawl caught on the carved edge of the table. Peter Ivanovich rose to detach it, and the springs of the pouffe, relieved of his weight, rose also and gave him a push. The widow began detaching her shawl herself, and Peter Ivanovich again sat down, suppressing the rebellious springs of the pouffe under him. But the widow had not quite freed herself and Peter Ivanovich got up again, and again the pouffe rebelled and even creaked. When

this was all over she took out a clean cambric handkerchief and began to weep. The episode with the shawl and the struggle with the pouffe had cooled Peter Ivanovich's emotions and he sat there with a sullen look on his face.

"What's funny," someone says, "is that inanimate objects seem to take on a life of their own, like the brooms in *Fantasia*. What Tolstoy is exposing in this comic scene is hypocrisy. There is so little genuine emotion from either the grieving widow or Ivan Ilych's colleague and friend, that the least thing can distract them."

Someone else continues, "And because each feels the need to behave with solemnity for the other's benefit, the creaking pouffe and the caught shawl seem to be the only genuine things in the room."

"Peter Ivanovich is perhaps a tiny bit more appealing than the widow Praskovya, but however decent his intentions, he cannot sustain them for very long."

Let's look a little more closely at Praskovya Fedorovna. Does Tolstoy use her in any additional way to enhance our sympathy for Ivan Ilych?

"Not at first—they're both awful, she and her husband, in different ways—but after a while, yes. Tolstoy makes Ivan Ilych's wife, who's so unsympathetic to his suffering, into an increasingly unappealing character—nagging, selfish, and stupid—so that we don't want to share her reactions, whatever they are, and that brings us a bit closer to Ivan Ilych."

"Tolstoy makes even her best reactions unworthy. There's a moment when she realizes that Ivan Ilych grows irritable at mealtime because his illness is made worse by eating and so she tries to overlook his crankiness, but then, Tolstoy tells us, she immediately commends herself for her self-control. It's always all about her."

"And she's such a hypocrite. Near the end of the story she says to Ilych, who doesn't want to see yet another doctor, something like 'Do it for me.' Tolstoy tells us that that is the sort of circumlocution people concerned for others sometimes indulge in. Everyone, including Ilych, is supposed to understand that it's not really for her sake but for his sake that she is asking that another doctor be sent for—in other words, that she is so selfless that she's letting herself appear selfish for her husband's sake. Then Tolstoy goes on to say that her lie, if understood as an act of solicitude, is indeed a 'lie' because her purpose is really to appear to herself and others as the concerned wife. So the 'lie,' which is presented as a 'white lie,' is an actual lie. She is using her husband's illness to make herself look good. That's disgusting—but I thought Tolstoy's logical twists and turns here were terrific."

We look, briefly, at the arc of Ivan Ilych's learning. *What are the stages in his recognition of what life is about?*

"For as long as he's well, he doesn't question anything. But once he becomes sick and has to see doctors, has to go to them as a kind of petitioner, he finds that they adopt toward him the same demeanor and attitude that he consciously adopts toward petitioners who come before him in legal proceedings."

"He has such recognitions more than once, and while each instance brings him closer to understanding how he has failed in his dealings with others, he can't quite discover what he needs to know until the very end, when his hand falls on the head of his weeping son and he realizes that the 'answer' is love and that he has not yet in his life, until this final moment, loved. And then, at this moment, he can pity not just his son, but also Praskovya."

It's important that literature in the classroom not turn into advocacy of one belief or another, and so I say, *Suppose we don't buy Tolstoy's view of the curative power of love, or his view, if it is his view, that God is love. What still binds us to Ivan Ilych? What about the "Caius" sequence? Do you remember it?*

"Yes. That's where, after Ivan Ilych has overheard his brother-in-law's dire prognosis and is grappling with the fact that he is dying, he remembers his grade school syllogism, 'Caius is a man, men are mortal, therefore Caius is mortal,' and understands that he has understood it only distantly and intellectually—only, as he puts it, as it applies to Caius and to all others, but not as it applies to himself, because he's too real to himself to be able to imagine himself as anything but alive."

Can you find that moment in the text?

"Got it. The text says, tracing Ivan Ilych's thought, that he was 'a creature quite separate from all others. He had been little Vanya . . .'"

Our resident logician, who had just unraveled Praskovya's white lie, takes over. "I think this moment is maybe the most important moment in the story, because whether or not we think God is love, or death is a glorious journey into light, we all know that we think just like Vanya. He believes he is unique and uniquely immune to sickness and change and death, and his belief in that uniqueness is a fallacy that everyone shares. In other words, what he thinks makes him different from everybody else is precisely what makes him just like everybody else."

Now we need to consider what is most frightening in the story—Ivan Ilych's illness. *Can anyone say what makes his accident and its aftermath so distressing?*

"The absence of a clear cause and the inability to pin down the symptoms."

"The fact that he's alone with it, and no one else feels what he feels, or fears what he fears."

"I know this is a little silly, but it's that thing we all do when we feel a pain somewhere in our bodies that scares us—we try to think ourselves into that spot, and can't. And we remember back to when we didn't feel the pain there."

Someone adds, "His illness marks the beginning of the interiorness that culminates in the images of the sack and the light."

What about the serf Gerasim? What's his function in the story?

"We're clearly meant to like him. He's kind, gentle, and patient, and demands nothing in return. He's the only selfless person Ivan Ilych knows."

"Given Gerasim's goodness and poverty, maybe Tolstoy is saying that material goods get in the way of understanding basic things like love and sickness and death—that they get in the way of understanding what we all share."

"That would make sense, since possessions are not things we have in common but things we acquire in order to answer personal needs or appear in some way different from, or better than, others."

Sometimes, I say, at moments of gravity, we have had our attention deflected by the equivalent of creaking pouffes, and many of us, hearing bad news for someone else, may have wondered whether the same event might be useful for ourselves. Tolstoy's tale has not erased our fear of death or our sense of terror at illness. Nothing can do that. But it has told us that Ivan Ilych suffers from the same fears and the same sense of aloneness that come to us all. And, in tone, it has begun in satire and ended in sublimity.

Death in Venice

THOMAS MANN

*In which we assess the protagonist and his love
of the beautiful.*

GRADE 11

We begin our discussion of Thomas Mann's great and enigmatic tale "Death in Venice" with its last sentence: *As "a shocked and respectful world receive[s] the news of his decease," are we, who know Gustave von Aschenbach's story and have seen the manner of his death, to regard him with equivalent "respect"? If so, it must be with respect of a different sort and for a different thing. Does Mann wish us to view him as a fraud? as a dirty old man? as a homosexual who belatedly discovers his nature? as an artist who discovers beauty and sacrifices everything for it? in some other way? Is this a story about erotic desire veiled by claims of aestheticism? Is this a story whose very core is homosexuality, or is homosexuality simply a path to the story's core?* I put these questions to my class, and we find that we have no immediate answers, but that we do have clues.

Someone starts us off. "Mann emphasizes the similarities between Gustave von Aschenbach's appearance and that of the leering old man on board the steamer from Pola, the one pretending to be young but really looking grotesque, fooling no one but himself."

Through what means does Mann suggest their similarity?

"Through physical appearance—through Aschenbach's red necktie, his similarly dyed hair and rouged cheeks and lips—and through the knowing comment of the barber—'now the signore can fall in love as soon as he likes.'"

Another student adds, "And the gondolier, whom Aschenbach asks to follow Tadzio's gondola, 'appeared to have long practice in affairs like these,' which is Mann's way of indicating that Aschenbach's pursuit of Tadzio is as obvious and tawdry as the lascivious old man's attachment to the young clerks, and as self-deceiving."

So, we're satisfied with the parallel?

"Not completely," someone answers.

Why not?

"Maybe because there's so much else about Aschenbach that we know—and because his fascination with Tadzio is so beautiful."

Other hands go up. "And because we've never heard him speak of Tadzio's body in any way linked to lustful action—all we've heard about is the 'shuddering' and the 'rapture' that the sight and contemplation of Tadzio cause him."

If we were satisfied with the parallel to the depraved young-old man on the steamer, what would the story be about?

"About how people criticize others for what they themselves may become—a simple, not very pleasant, moral tale."

Good.

"Or about how gross—or terrifying to the author—homosexual desire is. And that would not be much of a lesson, or would be an embarrassingly personal revelation."

Very good.

"That would make Aschenbach a poster boy for coming out of the closet early. And Aschenbach's not that, of course."

Another hand goes up. "In the scene with the hotel barber, Aschenbach is entirely passive. Sitting in the barber's chair, he allows, rather than requests, cosmetic changes. He lets his presence, rather than his words, speak for him."

And what's the effect of that passivity?

"It shows how obvious his desire is if the barber immediately intuits it without his speaking. On the one hand, it makes us unsympathetic because he's pretending not to be responsible for what he's letting the barber do. On the other, it makes us sympathetic because putting himself into the barber's hands shows how helpless he is in his erotic longing."

Nicely argued. Are there other places in the story where he's passive?

"When he decides to leave Venice because of the sirocco."

Go on.

"He finds that his luggage has been put on the wrong boat, plays the passive victim, and returns to the hotel, which is really what he wants to do and has now found an excuse for doing."

Someone adds, "Both times, he's passive because he's ashamed to take actions that reveal his feelings for Tadzio, even to himself, let alone to others."

Another hand is raised. "There's an earlier instance, also having to do with travel. When he arrives in Venice, the gondolier doesn't follow his instructions. He orders the gondolier to turn back but finds himself in the gondolier's power. And after resisting that power, he submits to it, and while submission and loss of control are not in his nature, he finds it can be pleasant to surrender control."

I'm very glad you mentioned that passage. It's important because it's not specifically related to Tadzio and because lassitude, water, and death are so closely joined in it. The gondola is likened, in its blackness to "a coffin," and, as they head out to sea in the direction opposite to the one Aschenbach has requested, this passage follows:

> Alone on the water with this tongue-tied, obstinate, uncanny man, he saw no way of enforcing his will. And if only he did not excite himself, how pleasantly he might rest! Had he not wished the voyage might last forever? The wisest thing—and how much the pleasantest!—was to let matters take their own course. A spell of indolence was upon him; it came from the chair he sat in—this low, black-upholstered arm-chair, so gently rocked at the hands of the despotic boatman in his rear.

"Maybe we could say that Aschenbach's whole working life, in which he seems to display extreme self-control, is really a matter of his being driven by ambitions and expectations that are external to him. As students, we all feel that sometimes—much of the time, actually. Maybe what looks to him and to the world like self-control and dedication to the writer's art is actually fear of loss of identity, if he were not to 'hold fast.'"

Very good. Let's stay with Aschenbach as writer for a minute and talk about his art and his reputation. It's the last thing to which Mann draws our attention in the sentence, "And before nightfall a shocked and respectful world received the news of his decease." Is this sentence ironic, and if so, why?

"It feels ironic to me. The world's respect, especially the respect of the particular audience that cherishes his work, would diminish if Aschenbach's conduct in Venice were widely known."

Someone casts the situation in thematic terms. "The final sentence is also ironic in that it emphasizes the great divide between the public and private self, and suggests how little the world knows of any individual's inner life."

Excellent. What else? What have Aschenbach's subjects been, and how has he gone about his writing?

"In approaching his art, he has exhibited great discipline—and that's not the sort of freedom we tend to associate with artists. In addition, the heroes of his novels have illustrated the same virtues he has practiced—discipline, tight control of emotion, restraint, and *Durchhalten*, 'holding fast.' In other words, there has been a complete merging of writer and subject."

The passages about what and how he writes are not easy to follow. You've done a really good job of it. Are there any further ironies in the story's final sentence?

"It's ironic that, unknown to 'the shocked and respectful world,' Aschenbach has rejected all that he has written and been."

Excellent. And do we approve of that rejection? Or, to pose the question more clearly, does Mann allow us to approve of Aschenbach's giving priority and precedence to the contemplation of beauty?

"Yes," echoes throughout the room.

"Maybe because the world that Aschenbach sees is so gorgeous, we come to feel that to reject those things would be to forego what is loveliest in life."

Very good.

The class has, the night before, gone through the text to locate lines in which either the physical world or Tadzio is described as beautiful. *What did you find?* I ask.

"We were to assume that Mann's voice is also Aschenbach's in these descriptions, right?"

Right. "Death in Venice" is written in "limited third person," in which what we're hearing is the character's voice or perception, without direct attribution. Let's begin with descriptions of nature.

"I found it beautiful that the sea and sky are described as full of divine energy, throbbing with life and beauty. The text says, 'It was a world possessed, peopled by Pan, that closed round the spellbound man.'"

Good.

Someone else, remembering *The Odyssey* from sixth grade, says, "Aschenbach sees the world with the same immediacy and beauty that Homer does. The standard Homeric epithet, 'rosy-fingered,' for the goddess Dawn becomes, in Aschenbach's hands, the even more exquisite 'At the world's edge began a strewing of roses.'"

Yes, that is gorgeous.

Someone else has chosen the description of Helios driving his chariot across the sky and reads Mann's personification of the moving sun:

> Now daily the naked god with cheeks aflame drove his four fire-breathing steeds through heaven's spaces,

and adds that, "As the passage continues, the beauty of sunlight merges with the beauty of sexual surrender." She continues:

> [F]rom horizon to zenith went great quivering thrusts like golden lances . . . and with flying hoof-beats the steeds of the sun-god mounted the sky. The lonely watcher sat, the splendour of the god shone on him, he closed his eyes and let the glory kiss his lids.

This is, we all agree, the world seen not by a dirty old man but by a very great artist.

We move next to descriptions of Tadzio and find them equally beautiful. "Aschenbach sees in Tadzio," someone says, "a 'chaste perfection of form' and 'a pose of easy grace.'"

Someone has chosen the line, "The head was poised like a flower, in incomparable loveliness," notes that it echoes *The Iliad*, and argues that it gives further classical warrant to Aschenbach's adoration, expressed also in lines such as these:

> [Tadzio] turned and ran back against the water . . . The sight of this living figure . . . beautiful as a tender young god, emerging from the depths of sea and sky, outrunning the element—it was like . . . the birth of form . . . the origin of the gods.

Someone else has chosen one of the most physically intimate descriptions in the story:

> His armpits were still as smooth as a statue's, smooth the glistening hollows behind the knees, where the blue network of veins suggested that the body was formed of some stuff more transparent than mere flesh,

and we discuss for a moment the great tenderness—we can find no other word—that this passage conveys. It concludes:

> What discipline, what precision of thought were expressed by the tense youthful perfection of this form!

and again and again we note that the beauty of the boy is analogized to beauty in its Platonic form, idealized and divine.

We list as many references to mythological figures as we can recall—Tadzio as Hyacinthus, as Narcissus, as the little Phaeacian who loves "change of dress, warm baths and downy beds," as the Spinnario, the bronze statue of the boy with curling locks removing a thorn from his foot—and we decide that, together, these references make Aschenbach's reaction to Tadzio both a lover's response to the beloved and an artist's response to what is transcendently beautiful.

Someone adds, "In all these manifestations, Tadzio is self-absorbed, complete in himself, and thus unattainable."

Great.

"Can we discuss," someone asks, "what the novella suggests happens to erotic desire that is repressed?"

"Repression that is, perhaps, hinted at in Ashenbach's fascination with the old-young man on the boat bursts forth in his terrifying dream in which he is Pentheus, the profoundly repressed king of Thebes in Euripides' *Bacchae*."

Someone who has been in a student production of *The Bacchae* adds that "the spread of cholera in this story, from east to west along the littoral, replicates almost exactly Dionysus's opening description of the advance westward of his cult from Asia to Thebes."

"Spooky," someone replies.

We see how tightly elements of the story are interwoven and decide that our reaction to Aschenbach combines admiration, pity, and perhaps fear of what is hidden in each of us. "On balance," we say, "what 'Death in Venice' does is to embody and describe The Beautiful and the soul's longing for The Beautiful." Classical references, philosophical as well as mythological, move us toward that assessment of Aschenbach. Socrates, Aschenbach recalls, is described in *Phaedrus* as speaking of desire and beauty in terms of

the shuddering and unwonted heat that come upon him whose heart is open, when his eye beholds an image of eternal beauty,

and of saying to Phaedrus, the youth he loves and teaches,

"beauty, my Phaedrus . . . is the sole aspect of the spiritual which we can perceive through our sense, or bear so to perceive . . . So beauty, then, is the beauty-lover's way to the spirit."

We return to the story's end and to the moment of Aschenbach's death, as, seated in the canvas beach chair, he watches Tadzio far out in the water and sees in him the summoning god. Tadzio calls him to eternity, to the realm of forms, the realm of which Plato speaks:

It seemed to him the pale and lovely Summoner out there smiled at him and beckoned as though . . . he pointed outward . . . into an immensity of richest expectation. And, as so often before, he rose to follow.

A hand goes up. "Earlier we were talking about the gondola ride with the surly gondolier, and Aschenbach's reluctant surrender of control. Perhaps in his last moments, surrender and control no longer war with each other. Surrender to Tadzio, 'the Summoner,' is what Aschenbach has chosen, has willed."

A splendid point.

Someone continues, "If that's the case, we can also say that the surrender of will, which Aschenbach has so feared, has become not menacing, but blissful."

"So Aschenbach has given up art for love, and found the exchange a fair one."

"Perhaps," someone adds, "that's what the unattended camera on the beach means—that the artist has abandoned art for something else."

"And maybe," someone else suggests, "the story also says that it doesn't matter how old you are when you feel desire. Suppose you don't feel desire until you're very old, as Aschenbach is? It is still overwhelming, and perhaps then even more so."

Protagonists often learn something. Does Aschenbach? Or, I ask, does posing such a question reduce art to the need to present a moral lesson?

My students decide to address the first question and ignore the second. "The fact that Aschenbach has been passive but makes a conscious choice to remain in Venice and die of cholera, rather than leave Venice and Tadzio, has to count as a strong statement of what Aschenbach has learned, even though he's choosing inaction. I think remaining means that he learns that how he has lived until now—a life of intellect and reason, of self-control and achievement—has been insufficient, that he has not even known what he has missed, and that finding what he has found is so supreme a joy that it is worth death itself."

"Such wisdom comes at great cost but brings him peace and makes his death not sad but joyful."

There is one final comment. "If we return to the question about irony, maybe we should say that the last line of the story is not so ironic after all—we, like the 'world,' respect Aschenbach as an artist who loves what any great artist should love—that which is beautiful."

.∎ 22 ∎.

The Judgment

FRANZ KAFKA

*In which we consider envy, guilt,
and dream narrative.*

GRADE 11

In Kafka's writing, there is always something that eludes us, something that, as in dreams, we almost understand, but cannot quite
hold onto. An event occurs that defies nature or logic but is presented as natural and unremarkable. We know we are in the realm
of unreality, though we feel that just behind that unreality is a reality more profound than any other. Many authors touch us deeply,
but no writer's touch is closer to the bone, more interior, more searing and personal, than Kafka's.

Kafka writes in third person, but we never know more than the
protagonist knows. We discover whatever the protagonist discovers
when he discovers it, no earlier. And the protagonist, like each of us,
grasps only part of what is occurring. The uncomfortable or freeing lesson that students, accustomed to close and full analysis, take
from Kafka is that there are things that are irreducible, ineluctable,
beyond analysis.

I sometimes begin by asking students to think about the features
of dreams. We make a rough list: in dreams objects, persons, and
settings appear out of nowhere, as required by the dream narrative;
we recognize persons we know despite their appearing utterly different; plots merge into other plots; what seems logical in the dream is
revealed upon waking to have been neither logical nor coherent; and

so on. After we agree on some dream elements, we set our list aside and talk for a moment about Freud and his thesis that, in dreaming, images the conscious mind would repress find expression, that in dreams we may be present in several figures at the same time, that settings are sometimes symbolic, and that dreams are highly compressed vehicles of expression in which the same action or object may contain several meanings, even several contradictory meanings.

"The Judgment," I tell my class, was the first piece of writing with which Kafka was entirely satisfied. One way of reading "The Judgment" is as an "oneiric" tale, a dream narrative, that also exists in real time.

The story begins with plodding realism as Georg Bendemann recites his reasons for not having written to his friend in Russia. Then come a series of sudden, dream-like moments—Georg enters a back room in his house, its condition previously unknown; a newspaper somehow finds its way into his father's hand; an edict that lacks all logic and authority is obeyed. We are simultaneously in Georg Bendemann's subconscious mind and in a realm of real events. The two are virtually irreconcilable, yet the story fuses them together.

Georg Bendemann has taken over his father's business, which is now prospering, and has written to a friend in Russia announcing his engagement and inviting the friend to the wedding. These two developments, success in business and a successfully concluded courtship, together seem to define Georg as adult. His friend is unnamed, unmarried, and failing in business—a version of the self apparently altogether different from Georg's. Georg sits in his room at the front of the house he shares with his father, gazing out at the river and thinking of his friend and of what has kept him from telling his friend of his engagement. His reasons do not seem wholly convincing—there are too many of them and something about them rings false.

Then, letter in hand, he enters his father's room at the back of the house. The dirty state of the room and the weakened and unkempt condition of his father fill Georg with guilt. He resolves immediately to repair the damage caused by his inattention. He will even, he tells himself, give his father his own room and move into this one himself.

His father greets Georg's announcement that he has written to his friend with a skepticism that grows increasingly hostile until, carried to bed by Georg and tucked in, he taunts Georg with improbabilities and poses a question that at first seems straightforward and even appreciative: "Am I well covered up now? . . . Am I well covered up?" It is the tucking in, the childlike reductiveness of it, the imposition of control that it represents to Georg's father, that seems the source of the rage that follows. Georg's father suddenly throws off the covers, leaps up with preternatural strength and, "radiant," announces, "I sentence you now to death by drowning." Although the pronouncement seems absurd, Georg feels himself "urged from the room." He rushes to the river, and executes his father's sentence upon himself, while saying, "Dear parents, I have always loved you, all the same." He lets himself drop into the river at the moment when "an unending stream of traffic was just going over the bridge."

Let's begin our discussion with the setting of the second half of the story. What is his father's room like?

"It's dark and stifling, and Georg has not entered it for a very long time."

"And it's in the back of the house."

In the iconography of dreams, I say, *a space that is locked, dark, in the back, or unused is also that place within ourselves where we dare not go—the locus of our unconscious fears and desires.* As Rose says in Kafka's "A Country Doctor" as the doctor opens the small pig shed, out of which two stallions and a groom emerge, "you never know what you're going to find in your own house." *When Georg enters his father's room Kafka suggests, ever so obliquely, that Georg is finally entering his own subconscious mind.* My students find this fascinating and frightening at the same time. Someone says, "That we are in a bedroom further suggests the subconscious because that is the room where we sleep and dream."

"And where," someone adds, "we give expression to our most private urges."

If our reading is correct, whatever Georg finds there, whatever is said to him, is also what he is saying to himself.

We look at the earlier portion of the story and are struck by the sentence, "Georg preferred to write [to his friend in Russia] about things like [engagements of other couples] rather than to confess that he himself had got engaged a month ago to a Fraulein Frieda Brandenfeld, a girl from a well-to-do family."

A hand goes up. "The word 'confess' suggests that he feels he's done something wrong."

"The appositive, 'a girl from a well-to-do family,' also suggests a desire to distance himself from her. It defines Frieda and their relationship in a way that denies any sexuality on his or her part."

"And," the first student adds, "he tries to attribute his feeling of unease to his being sensitive to the loneliness and abandonment his friend may feel on hearing of Georg's engagement. He is less than honest."

"Isn't Georg's coming to his father before posting the letter like asking, 'Am I doing the right thing to marry? Have I your permission?' Georg could simply have posted it."

"Maybe, despite Georg's success in the family business, or because of it, Georg feels guilty that he has displaced his father and thinks that his father hates him for it. And maybe, although he is an adult, Georg, at the back of his mind, regards himself as a child and his father as 'still a giant of a man.'"

Other manifestations of possible subconscious feeling begin to suggest themselves to my class. "Thinking of the way identities fuse in dreams, maybe his father's reaction to Georg's plan to announce to his friend in Russia his engagement to Frieda Brandenfeld really reflects Georg's ambivalence about his engagement—maybe Georg thinks he's not ready, or able, or worthy to assume the role of married man and adult, or sees marriage plans as an overt confession of sexual activity and is embarrassed."

"When his father lifts his nightshirt, 'flutes' his voice, and pretends to be Georg's lascivious fiancé, maybe Georg is projecting his own feelings onto his father. Perhaps Georg is ashamed of his desires and ashamed of being ashamed of them."

Someone then focuses us on the story's resolution. "Does Georg fulfill his father's command because he himself wishes to escape this marriage that he is supposed to want?"

I add that *Frieda's last name, "Brandenfeld," means "burning field" in German, the language in which Kafka wrote, and that just a month before writing "The Judgment" Kafka began to see a woman in what was, even very early on, a relationship about which Kafka was deeply conflicted. Her name,* I continue, *was "Felice Bauer."*

"F. B.—the same initials as Frieda Brandenfeld."

"And water puts out fire," someone says, with excitement. "Maybe that's the reason for the sentence of death by drowning."

Good. But there may be other reasons as well for Georg's fulfilling his father's sentence. Dreams, I remind the class, *are highly compressed, efficient vehicles. What does Georg's suicide do besides end his engagement?*

"Georg's displacement of his father as married man and as head of the family business also ends. By dying, Georg perhaps gets his father to stop hating him."

"You know," someone brightens and adds, "his father calls Georg's friend, who neither marries nor succeeds in business, 'a son after my own heart.' Maybe failure and adolescence are what this father, a competitive and angry man, wants for his son."

"Oh, my god," someone says. "That's awful."

We feel ourselves in the throes of an Oedipal conflict in which the father, rather than the son, is jealous, and in which not the mother but dominance in the household and in business are at stake. The idea of such parental feelings is terrifying to students but we forge on, and I ask, *Are you saying that the father's sentence is meted out to Georg for Georg's having grown up?*

For a moment students laugh, but only for a moment. They can think of no "crime" other than growing up that Georg has committed. Neglect of his father, they agree, is something that Georg regrets and will, he vows, immediately rectify. It certainly is not something that merits suicide. If Georg is guilty of something, that something is nothing more or less than the sin of being, the sin that each of us commits against our parents by becoming ascendant in the natural course of time as our parents grow old and weaken. The alternative is endless dependency, weakness, and scorn of a different sort from one's father for such weakness. This is not an easy story for adolescents to address, and my class is doing exceptionally well.

We turn to the story's conclusion:

> Already, he was grasping at the railings as a starving man
> clutches food. He swung himself over, like the distinguished
> gymnast he had once been in his youth, to his parents' pride.

"Maybe Georg wants to avoid adulthood altogether. Perhaps he wants to be a child again, the 'gymnast' of his youth, the 'pride' of his parents. And since that's not possible, perhaps he thinks that only by dying can he recapture the love he has lost—or has perhaps never had—from his jealous father."

Very good.

"I think he has sentenced himself, but through his father."

"I agree. I mean, how can someone sentence someone else to suicide?"

We look at the penultimate sentence of the story and I ask, *Why does Georg wait until a motor-bus passes to drown out the noise of his fall into the water?*

It seems to the class that his last wish and final impulse are the precise opposites of what has animated him in recent years, the will to make a mark in business, to be a commercial success, to establish himself as a man of substance, a middle-class homeowner, a *pater familias*. Now, they conclude, he would wish none to see, none to mark, none to mourn his passing. The muffling of the sound is the erasure of self, the erasure of ego.

Someone adds, "There's also an internal contradiction here. If Georg dies for love of his parents, for guilt at displacing his father in the natural course of existence, then 'the judgment' ought not to have been carried out because he is not unloving, as his father has charged."

Good.

I add, *There are two religious echoes in the story that I'd like us to consider. At the beginning of the penultimate paragraph, a charwoman comes up the stairway as Georg rushes down. She sees him, covers her face, and cries, "Jesus!" Is she just saying,* I ask, *"Watch where you're going!" or is she expressing shock and alarm because she's seen agony in his face?*

"Or," someone asks, "Has she seen the face of Jesus himself? The story is, after all, set on a Sunday in mid-spring, the day of the week and the time of the year when, according to Christian gospel, Jesus' sacrificial death is fulfilled."

"Then Georg, in an act of love, but an ineffective one, is dying for his father."

There is, I tell them, *one more piece to fit into this puzzle, one more echo. Kafka's diary records that he began "The Judgment" on Saturday night, September 21, 1912, and completed it 12 hours later, in the early hours of Sunday, September 22, 1912. That year, according to the Jewish calendar, the holiday of Yom Kippur, the Day of Atone-*

ment, fell on Saturday, September 21. "The Judgment" is about atonement, and in that sense not unrelated to the day just ended for Kafka, on which Jews fast and beg forgiveness for their sins, and on which God is believed to inscribe in the Book of Life the fate of each person for the coming year. It is the custom of Jews, and would have been a custom observed by the entire Jewish community of the city of Prague where Kafka lived, to perform the ritual of tashlich nine days earlier, on the second day of Rosh HaShanah. The Vltava River flows through the city, and Jews would have gone to the Charles Bridge or to some other, to say a short prayer and symbolically cast their sins into the swift-flowing water, which would then carry away their sins and leave them cleansed.

What Kafka has given us, in both these religious echoes, is the suggestion of the scapegoat, the atoner of inevitable sin. He has given us this in a narrative that fuses dream and reality and that presents to us aspects of ourselves at which we may hesitate to look. "Das Urteil," "The Judgment," is a story of repressed hatred, of wished-for love, of irrational and powerful guilt and fear, and, most tellingly, of the imperfect and indeed impossible resolution of such things.

.▪ 23 ▪.

Waiting for Godot

SAMUEL BECKETT

*In which we see how essential to meaning
stage business can be.*

GRADE 11

Beckett's stage directions in *Waiting for Godot*, as in all of his plays,
are essential to his meaning.

As the lights go up, Gogo (Estragon) is already onstage. That he
does not enter is as important as the fact that, at the play's conclusion, he and Didi (Vladimir) do not leave the stage. The play
ends with:

> VLADIMIR: Well? Shall we go?
> ESTRAGON: Yes, let's go.
> *They do not move.*

Didi and Gogo freeze for a count of about 20. Then the stage dark-
ens and the houselights come on. During that time, Didi and Gogo
stand motionless, staring into space. We as audience wait for something else to happen or for an indication that the play is over. And
then, suddenly, we realize that Beckett is demonstrating that correspondence between word and action is an illusion; or that action and
non-action are interchangeable in their effects; or that these men,
like all of us, only pretend to have a purpose, a direction, a control-
lable future. They do not move because there is nowhere else for
them to go. And if Didi and Gogo stand in for us, then their theatrical space represents our existential reality.

And so, when the play begins Gogo does not enter, but is already onstage. He can wander offstage a bit in one direction or another, but basically he is rooted to this spot.

Beckett is also explicit about what we see: "*A country road. A tree. Evening.*" I ask my class what "road" implies. *What if the stage were entirely bare?*

Someone answers, "A bare stage is anywhere and nowhere. You can play Shakespeare on a bare stage, and it doesn't make anyone nervous. But a road in the middle of a barren landscape is different. It tells us that we are somewhere, but that that 'somewhere' is undefined, perhaps undefinable, unpopulated, and empty."

"A road running from one side of the stage to the other," someone adds, "suggests a terminus on either end, but one that we can't see—and maybe can't get to."

Someone else joins in. "A road also implies travel, so a road implies that we, or the characters, have some hope of leaving this place."

Good comments. By "evening," I add, *Beckett means the time before total darkness, the time of darkening.* And then I ask, *What about the tree?*

"The tree seems to be a real tree," a student says, "but unreal in being solitary. If conditions in nature produce one tree, they produce others in the same place. Where are the others? It makes me uncomfortable."

Onstage Gogo is doing something. A student volunteers to read the stage directions:

> *Estragon, sitting on a low mound, is trying to take off his boot. He pulls at it with both hands, panting. He gives up, exhausted, rests, tries again. As before.*

I ask her to begin again, and this time to stop for as long as it would take for Gogo to "*pull*" seriously at his boot, to pause for a slow count of ten where the text says he "*rests*," during which everyone in class must be absolutely silent, and then to replace "*As before*" with the actual stage directions she has already read. We treat all stage directions in the same way. What am I up to? even my most patient students wonder.

Chekhov writes silences into his plays, but they are silences filled with sighs, silences that signify a breakdown of conversation or an incapacity for action; their purpose is characterization. Beckett's silences are existential, absolute; their purpose is not to character-ize but to represent the essence of existence. The longer we wait, and the more often we wait, the more conscious we become of exist-ing in a void. Nothing is more essential to reading Beckett than this waiting. Slowly, gradually, we begin to grasp what Didi and Gogo recognize—that we exist in time and space, endless and empty, dra-matized as "waiting" for Godot.

In fact, the very subject of the play is time. And only when we are forced to share moments of silence with Beckett's characters can we sense what otherwise, at all other times and places in our lives, are only intellectual abstractions—emptiness and eternity. Because action exists only in time, we tend to think that action is a signifier of time, but the truth is otherwise: action makes us forget time.

We discuss the initial stage business, the pulling at the boot, fol-lowed by Didi's examination of his hat. *How do you like the play so far?* I ask my students. *Be honest.*

A brave student answers, "I sort of feel like the audience's time is being wasted—after all, nothing is happening. Someone's just pull-ing at a boot, and doesn't even get it off."

"There's no plot, and no dialogue."

I agree with my students that we are looking at something that seems pointless, waiting for meaning to unfold. Waiting for a plot. Waiting for characterization. We don't realize that the play has indeed begun in earnest and that Beckett is engaging us in its cen-tral action—the "waiting" of the title—the hope for meaning, the hope for release from the present and its limitations.

A few moments later Didi says, "This is getting alarming." The comment is one of several that break the fourth wall. We, as audi-ence, hear in "This is getting alarming" what we are now thinking: perhaps coming to the theatre tonight was a mistake. We go to the-atre expecting action on stage, but we define action to ourselves as something other than watching someone put on and take off a boot or a hat, something other than watching someone eat a car-rot or a radish. By placing these actions front, center, and in actual time, Beckett makes his audience think about what it is that we do expect—action directed to some overall end or purpose. But what if the very idea of an overall purpose is folly?

"This is getting alarming" also and equally applies to Didi and Gogo—they must fill the time or they shall go mad. What is "alarming" for them is that they have no immediate topic, no riff, until Didi comes up with "One of the thieves was saved." Rather than being a *non sequitur*, it is quite the opposite. What is spoken of matters less than the act of speech. Like the lyrical sequences in Act Two:

> Like leaves.
> Like sand.
> Like leaves.

and

> Rather they whisper.
> They rustle.
> They murmur.
> They rustle.

Didi's Gospel reference is an attempt to fill the void. Riffs relieve us as much as they relieve Didi and Gogo; otherwise, we all are made conscious of the void.

Equally central to the play as Beckett's dramatization of time is his dramatization of the search for meaning, and a chief means of this dramatization is Lucky's speech in Act One. Lucky, the carrier for Pozzo, enters midway through the act with a rope about his neck like a pack animal. He is mute until he is ordered to "think"; then he launches himself into an unstoppable monologue of over 600 words. This monologue, like the set and the silences, properly falls into the category of stage business rather than into the category of stage speech. As speech, it is unintelligible. It hints constantly at meaning, but never releases that meaning other than as a cry of woe. It is unpunctuated and rambling, full of unresolved conditionals, sudden shifts in register, qualifiers that promise an idea is on its way or has just been presented ("with some exceptions," "but time will tell," "for reasons unknown," "if that continues," "and who can doubt it will," "is better than nothing," "but not so fast," "what is more"), full of syntactic units that constantly uncouple. Premises keep slipping away from us until we finally give up the quest for meaning.

My students, believers in meaning, serious, trained to analyze closely, assume we are encountering an encrypted message. They suggest that if we skip certain phrases, we are left with a coherent opening premise awaiting its apodosis: "Given the existence . . . of a personal God . . . outside time . . . who from the heights of divine apathia divine athambia divine aphasia loves us dearly . . . ," yet no resolution follows:

> Given the existence as uttered forth in the public works of Puncher and Wattmann of a personal God quaquaquaqua with white beard outside time without extension who from the heights of divine apathia divine athambia divine aphasia loves us dearly with some exceptions for reasons unknown but time will tell and suffers like the divine Miranda with those who for reasons unknown but time will tell are plunged in torment plunged in fire whose fire flames if that continues and who can doubt it will fire the firmament that is to say blast hell to heaven so blue still and calm so calm with a calm which even though intermittent is better than nothing but not so fast and considering what is more that as a result of the labors left unfinished crowned by the Aca-cacademy of Anthropopopometry of Essy-in-Possy of Testew and Cunard it is established beyond all doubt all other doubt than that which clings to the labors of men . . .

As my students attempt to fathom Lucky's speech, they realize how central to being human is the need to understand. In this way, too, Beckett makes us share Didi and Gogo's situation as they wait for Godot and for the release that his arrival is to bring. I tell my class that when the play was first produced, in Paris in 1952, Beckett asked that the director begin rehearsals with Lucky's speech. Like the play itself, it is a "tragicomedy." Should we laugh or weep at it? Its tone is sad, but its delivery is slapstick—Lucky's monologue ends with a pratfall and the snatching off of Lucky's "thinking cap," a child's joke turned into a theatrical reality. Its message, we decide, is that there is no message.

Why, I ask, *must the play have two acts?* (Our library owns a copy of the never-surpassed 1961 Burgess Meredith, Zero Mostel, Kurt Kasznar, Alvin Epstein production, the only drawback of which is that just Act Two was filmed. The only comparable performance of *Waiting for Godot* that I have ever seen was one performed in Yiddish by the New Yiddish Rep in New York in the fall of 2013, and later transferred to the Enniskillan Beckett Festival in Ireland.) After we read Act One closely, we watch the film. Then we study Act Two, and, if the class wishes, we watch the film a second time.

My students say that, by means of a second act that essentially replays the first, Beckett is telling us that waiting for meaning, existing in a void, is the inescapable condition of man. That Act Two is described as "*Next day. Same time. Same place,*" that Lucky and Pozzo enter again, claiming not to have encountered Didi and Gogo the day before, that a Boy enters, looking exactly like the Boy in Act One, but saying he is that Boy's brother and has not come the day before, are essential if we are to understand that what we are seeing is not an isolated moment or a single day, but life itself. Such, also, is the function of Didi's circular song at the beginning of Act Two, which Burgess Meredith sings in character and to perfection.

VLADIMIR: A dog came in—
> *Having begun too high he stops, clear his throat, resumes:*
>> A dog came in the kitchen
>> And stole a crust of bread,
>> Then cook up with a ladle
>> And beat him till he was dead.
>>
>> Then all the dogs came running
>> And dug the dog a tomb—
> *He stops, broods, resumes:*
>> Then all the dogs came running
>> And dug the dog a tomb
>> And wrote upon the tombstone
>> For the eyes of dogs to come:
>>
>> A dog came in the kitchen
>> And stole a crust of bread.
>> Then cook up with a ladle
>> And beat him till he was dead.
>>
>> Then all the dogs came running
>> And dug the dog a tomb—
> *He stops, broods. Softly.*
>> And dug the dog a tomb.
> *He remains a moment silent and emotionless.*

The song's most remarkable feature is its circularity, by which it, too, becomes an emblem of the play.

I ask my class to set the words aside at first, and to consider only what we hear—a moment of song, unaccompanied, not particularly melodic, thin in the great space that it tries to fill. But song, nonetheless—an emblem of the human spirit. His tune CCCAGGF, CCCFED, a repeated descending line of close intervals, is neither happy nor sad, a replication of the larger patterns of the play.

We talk about the lyrics. They are both silly and serious, for who cares about a dog or a cook's temper? *Do the dogs represent rescue that is tardy and ineffective? What of the epitaph?—are action and history, rather than feeling or thought, our essence? and are lives defined by random acts and happenstance? Do epitaphs matter and, if so, why?*

"Perhaps," someone suggests, "the dog's epitaph is not unrelated to what Didi says in answer to the Boy's question, 'What am I to tell Mr. Godot, Sir?'"

Tell him . . . tell him you saw me and that . . . that you saw me . . . You're sure you saw me, you won't come and tell me tomorrow that you never saw me!

I was here, you saw me—this is Didi's epitaph. The Boy does not reply, but simply runs off. *Will anything be told to Godot?* I ask. *Is there even a Godot to tell something to? Will Didi be even less remembered than the dog he sings of?*

Beckett's meaning and staging are one. If Shakespeare's plays are transferred to a different time and place, something is lost but usually not something essential. But everything is lost when Beckett's staging is altered. If, for example, the country road and the tree are replaced by a New Orleans rooftop with Hurricane Katrina waters rising on all sides, as was the case in a recent production, the constricted rather than expanding playing space and the specificity of place, time, and political context strip from the play its core. Gogo and Didi's uncertainty about what day of the week it is, the question about time raised in their minds by the tree that today is leaved and yesterday was bare, the reference to "a million years ago, in the nineties," all these things create a temporal dislocation essential for the play's universality. *Waiting for Godot* is not about "waiting" for a rescue boat that might arrive.

By the time we have completed a close study of the play the class realizes that it is really not about waiting at all. Waiting is merely its emblem, not its end. The play is about our essential condition, our existence in a void, our seeking of meaning, and our finding that the actions we take are no more than stopgaps against the terror of eternity.

We also find that knowing those things makes us both absurd and noble. "Pull on your trousers," Didi says to Gogo, who has removed the cord holding his pants up to test whether that cord is long and strong enough for them to hang themselves with. It isn't, and so *"He pulls up his trousers"* and continues to wait, with as much dignity as he can muster, as the play ends.

▪▎24▐▪

Man and Wife

ROBERT LOWELL

*In which we find in rhyme pattern
a clue to the whole.*

GRADE 12

MAN AND WIFE

Tamed by *Miltown*, we lie on Mother's bed;
the rising sun in war paint dyes us red;
in broad daylight her golden bed-posts shine,
abandoned, almost Dionysian.
At last the trees are green on Marlborough Street,
blossoms on our magnolia ignite
the morning with their murderous five days' white.
All night I've held your hand,
as if you had
10 a fourth time faced the kingdom of the mad—
its hackneyed speech, its homicidal eye—
and dragged me home alive. . . . Oh my *Petite,*
clearest of all God's creatures, still all air and nerve:
you were in your twenties, and I,
once hand on glass
and heart in mouth,
outdrank the Rahvs in the heat
of Greenwich Village, fainting at your feet—
too boiled and shy

20   and poker-faced to make a pass
      while the shrill verve
      of your invective scorched the traditional South.

      Now twelve years later, you turn your back.
      Sleepless, you hold
      your pillow to your hollows like a child;
      your old-fashioned tirade—
      loving, rapid, merciless—
      breaks like the Atlantic Ocean on my head.

The challenges of the Lowell poem are also its virtues. It rewards the close attention that it requires, and its appeal is that what at first seems opaque becomes clear, and what seems solely confessional is also universal. We begin, as with a puzzle, by looking at whatever is obvious—here, the title, "Man and Wife," a phrase from the marriage service, tells us that the poem may be a portrait of a marriage.

I present only the most essential background for this reading: Lowell's dates (1917–1977), the fact that his wife was from the south, his history of hospitalizations for mental illness. We define unfamiliar terms like the anti-depressant "Miltown," "Marlborough Street" in Boston, with its line of magnolia trees, "the Rahvs," "Dionysian," and "the traditional South," and I discover how quickly slang becomes obsolete—my students no longer know "heart in mouth," "boiled," or even "poker-faced." To a list of words that includes "invective" and "tirade," I find I need to add "abandoned" in the sense of "unrestrained, self-destructive," since my class thinks the only meaning of "abandoned" is "left behind."

We read "Man and Wife" a second time, a little more confidently, but we're still shaky. *What,* I ask, *is the most elementary poetic device thing we can think of?*

"Rhyme."

Good. Let's start with that.

Students hear rhyme but see no pattern. The poem has two stanzas, one of twenty-two lines, one of six. At its beginning, Lowell makes us conscious of rhyme through two introductory couplets, "bed . . . red" and "shine . . . Dionysian." Thereafter, the couplet pattern, the rhyme pattern of tightest alignment, breaks down. "Street" comes next, in line 5, and stands out, unrhymed, unmated, disturbing us as breakdowns of patterns always disturb us, but then we find another couplet, "ignite . . . white." Then, two unrhymed lines in a row ("hand . . . had") and we're thrown off again; then the poem seems to change its mind and "mad" follows, rhyming with "had." We think, well, okay, the pattern *is* one of couplets, except that between each couplet there may be an unrhymed line. We are flexible. Then things begin to go awry and all order begins to disintegrate. As we move through the poem we find that "Street" rhymes with "*Petite*," but only after a gap of seven lines. There is too much separation between units that ought to be joined. We don't hear the "eet" rhyme, but we see it if we search for it. It's there, just not easily found. And slowly we begin to reflect upon content—are we finding in the rhyme something like what we are meant to see in this marriage?—ties that exist but have become tenuous, connections that are desired but too hard to maintain? We emerge from our rhyme exploration of stanza one with this pattern, using successive letters of the alphabet for successive rhymes: *aa bb c dd e ff g c h g i j cc g i h j.*

The spaces between the two parts of a rhyming pair have widened.

Someone points out that line 8, "All night I've held your hand," is unrhymed. It shouldn't be—it's an expression of reaching out, of joining. And yet there it remains, separate, isolated.

Someone else points to the fact that there is no rhyme at all in stanza two. What we have is "back . . . hold . . . child . . . tirade . . . merciless . . . head."

A close reader corrects us and says that "head" rhymes with "bed" and "red," the end words of the opening couplet.

So we discover, through something as basic and unflashy as rhyme, the essence of the poem. A disintegrating marriage, connections still felt, still there, but tenuous, irregular. The connection between the end line and the opening lines, between the then and the now, exists, but its music is not heard, just as this marriage's happiness is a memory, and just as the marriage is half what it was.

We decide, since we've spent so much time on one formal aspect of the verse line, that we might as well look at another. Everyone, even those who can't quite recall terms like "trochee," "spondee," or "tetrameter," knows "iambic pentameter." We look at the opening lines and beat out the rhythm. It is somewhat irregular but close enough to iambic pentameter to be so designated—ten syllables, five beats, unstressed syllable alternating with stressed. But then, at that same unrhymed eighth line, the pattern breaks. "All night I've held your hand" has only three metric feet. It is trimeter, not pentameter. We expect two more measures; we hear absence, silence.

Slowly we are discovering that if we take time to look, things that appear to be almost impenetrable can become clear.

We go on to "voice."

To whom is the speaker speaking?

He and his wife are lying on a bed and his wife is turned away from him. "Now . . . you turn your back./Sleepless, you hold your pillow to your hollows like a child." She is, he intuits, awake, but pretending to sleep. The speaker is, then, saying these things not to her but to himself as he lies beside her. And our discovery that this is an interior monologue makes "Oh my *Petite,*/clearest of all God's creatures, still all air and nerve" and his memories of their meeting, of his shyness, and of her appealing sharpness become all the more filled with sorrow and pathos.

We move now to the chief images of the poem. They are assaultive and unpleasant, and it's important to say so. The best literary analysis begins not with fancy terms but with a gut reaction and then with an exploration, however hesitant, of the sources of that reaction. *What makes the images feel assaultive?*

We begin with whatever strikes us as most obvious. Any word that doesn't quite fit its context, that shocks us in some way, is a clue. "Scorched" is one such word. And we discover that there are other images of fire in the poem, all of them odd and unexpected. Magnolia blossoms "ignite" the morning; her language burns him. The image of fire reappears in Lowell's description of the "the rising sun," itself fire, that "in war paint dyes us red"—and that line introduces, at the poem's beginning, the idea of bloody battle.

What, I ask, puts out fire?

"Water," I am told.

And is there water in this poem?

"Yes, but not the sort of water we seek. He's 'boiled' and the whole ocean 'breaks' on his head."

Water then, is no remedy; it's as heated or as violent and destructive as that which it is supposed to tame. Lowell's use of these two most elemental images in this poem, not in opposition but in combination, suggests that there is succor nowhere, assault everywhere.

We are left with the feeling that there is no place to go, no way to repair this marriage, nothing, as Beckett says, to be done.

We return, as one always should, to the beginning of the poem, and rediscover not only the meanings of "abandoned" but also the inability to function that not arising, when one is awake, conveys. There is, of course, much more that might be done, but we have made a beginning. The tone of "Man and Wife" is of anguished reflection, and yet, in Lowell's hands, an acutely personal narrative has expanded from something about one person and one marriage to things applicable to all of us—relationships gone wrong, regret, longing, and guilt, in a lethal mix and in a superb poem.

.∎ *25* ∎.

Once More to the Lake

E. B. WHITE

*In which we address temporality and its
grammatical markers.*

GRADE 12

In E. B. White's essay "Once More to the Lake," everything turns on
the final sentence—turns, in fact, on the prepositional phrase that
ends that sentence. It is a remarkable place for an essay's epiphany.

White describes his return to the summer "camp" of his youth,
accompanied by his young son. I confide to my students that the
longing he expresses increases with age—the longing to recapture
the past, a past so alive in one's memory and imagination as to seem
impossible to be lost, impossible to recede into immateriality. It does
recede, of course, but for as long as White's essay lasts, until its
final, knowing conclusion, we are complicit in White's deliberate
and lovely self-delusion that nothing has changed, that, despite all
he knows and believes, the past can be recaptured, that "there had
been no years."

He knows, of course, as we do, that it's folly. The camp has
changed a little—there is "an unfamiliar nervous sound of outboard
motors," "more Coca-Cola and not so much Moxie and root beer and
birch beer and sarsaparilla," and the waitresses have begun to wash
their hair, but that's about it; the balances, heavily weighted in the
scale of non-change, remain steady throughout the essay, until the
pans swing suddenly, radically, and irretrievably, and tell us that the
past is not recapturable.

The essay's title itself teeters between promise and closure. Does "once more" mean "yet again," or "just this last time"? At the essay's end we know it is the latter. The hope of holding onto the past, of being able to return to it and retrieve it, has quietly dissolved. Were White to go back "once more" to the lake, his next trip would be merely a journey to a place, not a journey to a time.

As ideally suited to White's telling as the title and the ending is his phrase describing the physical and emotional essence of the spot, "the placidity of a lake in the woods." Inland lakes in Maine are just like that—the phrase is perfect—but beyond the accuracy of description, there is, I tell my students, something else: the lake and camp are the *locus amoenus*, the pleasant place, the Eden of White's longing.

"A 'placid' lake," someone says, "is an emblem of something unmoving, unchanging; and a lake that is both 'placid' and surrounded by 'woods' is sheltered from incursion and from change, sheltered from time."

Excellent.

Someone else notices that "Like so much else in this essay, the lake is unnamed. Even the smallest bodies of water have names—so-and-so's pond, the such-and such creek—but without a name White's lake is the lake of anyone's childhood, while also remaining so privately and intimately his that he need not name it."

As White speaks of traveling to Maine with his son, he jokes that the boy "had never had any fresh water up his nose" and "had seen lily pads only from train windows." The marvelously tactile quality of this writing, engaging all our senses, begins. By the essay's second paragraph we are immersed in what Wordsworth would call "the beauty of the morning." We experience it in what we see, hear, smell, and touch. It is through such sensual description that the lake is brought forward to us, into present time.

> I guess I remembered clearest of all the early morning, when
> the lake was cool and motionless, remembered how the bed-
> room smelled of the lumber it was made of and of the wet woods
> whose scent entered through the screen. The partitions in the
> camp were thin and did not extend clear to the top of the rooms,
> and as I was always the first up I would dress softly so as not to
> wake the others, and sneak out into the sweet outdoors and start

out in the canoe, keeping close along the shore in the long shadows of the pines. I remembered being very careful never to rub
my paddle against the gunwale for fear of disturbing the stillness
of the cathedral.

We talk about White's style in this early passage and decide that
it's both colloquial and lyrical.

Someone notices the four "and's" in the second sentence, and
stresses them as she reads,

> The partitions in the camp were thin and did not extend clear
> to the top of the rooms, and as I was always the first up I would
> dress softly so as not to wake the others, and sneak out into the
> sweet outdoors and start out in the canoe.

"The 'and's,'" she says, "create a sense of ongoing action, of continuity through time."

Someone says, "The anaphora, with phrase after phrase beginning 'remembered,' is an additional way of suggesting continuity."
She points to other initial repetitions as well.

Another student adds, "His sentences are often constructed with
appositives, not just single appositives, but two or three in a row,
and both anaphora and appositives are, in a sense, backward turning: they deepen and clarify the original term." We find an example,
almost at random:

> this unique, this holy spot—the coves and streams, the hills that
> the sun set behind, the camps and the paths behind the camps.

How, in other ways, does White make time stand still?

Someone answers that "Because verbs are the parts of speech
that convey time as well as action and duration, we ought to look at
the verbs."

"Or at their absence," a friend adds, and reads a sentence, or what
passes for a sentence, with no verbs at all:

> Summertime, oh summertime, pattern of life indelible, the fade-
> proof lake, the woods unshatterable, the pasture with the sweet-
> fern and the juniper forever and ever, summer without end.

And another:

> The shouts and cries of the other campers when they saw you,
> and the trunks to be unpacked, to give up their rich burden.

"Here's a sentence," someone else says, "full of participles instead of main verbs. And it's long—the participles and the length make it feel like these actions go on forever, like the whole scene is eternal." She reads the passage describing the aftermath of the summer storm, when the sun comes out again:

> Afterward the calm, the rain steadily rustling in the calm lake, the return of light and hope and spirits, and the campers running out in joy and relief to go swimming in the rain, their bright cries perpetuating the deathless joke about how they were getting simply drenched, and the children screaming with delight at the new sensation of bathing in the rain, and the joke about getting drenched linking the generations in a strong indestructible chain. And the comedian who waded in carrying an umbrella.

"And," our "and" expert notes, "look at all those 'and's.'"

Pleased with our discovery about participles, we address subjunctives, those signifiers of habitual action not limited to a particular moment in time. Someone points out, "There are lots of sentences with 'would.' For example, when White describes his and his son's routine at the camp he says,

> We would be tired at night . . . the breeze would stir . . . Sleep would come easily . . . the red squirrel would be on the roof . . . After breakfast we would go . . . we would walk . . . the pop would backfire."

We move on from verb constructions to other syntactic features. What about White's use of definite and indefinite articles—of "the" instead of "a"?

A hand goes up. "There's 'the dragonfly.' White uses the definite article 'the' when it would be more natural to use 'a.' He does it as if to say that the dragonfly he sees now land on his fishing pole is 'the' dragonfly he once knew. He does the same thing when he talks about 'the' comedian who 'waded in carrying an umbrella.'

Someone adds, "White uses demonstratives such as 'this' in the same way. He says, there's 'this person with the cake of soap, this cultist,' who had been at the lake 'over the years' and 'here he was. There had been no years.' And he says, 'The waitresses were the same country girls . . . still fifteen; their hair had been washed, that was the only difference—they had been to the movies and seen the pretty girls with the clean hair.'"

Great. What about names? Are there proper names in the essay?

"Well," someone begins, "I think the only things that are named are brands like 'Coca-Cola' and 'Moxie'—commercial names that are, or were, virtually universal. But the lake is unnamed, as we said, and even more importantly, his son is unnamed. White calls him 'the boy' or sometimes 'my boy,' but never by his name."

Why not?

"If he named his son, his imaginative merging with the boy, the chief device through which White recaptures his own past, would be impeded. Omitting a name lets identities fuse and flow into each other."

Excellent.

Another hand goes up. "This isn't exactly a technical thing, but it's part of the fusing of identities, and I think just as important. When, 'lying in bed the first morning, smelling the bedroom,' White hears 'the boy sneak quietly out and go off along the shore in a boat,' he says that he 'began to sustain the illusion that he was I, and therefore, by simple transposition, that I was my father.' In asserting that he is also his own father, and his son is White, White asserts that all things are as they once were and that generations, as markers of time, can be erased. He plays with identity and time, half comically, half seriously."

The discussion is moving in all sorts of directions, and someone notices that "There's something very interesting about how White draws our attention to time. At the beginning of the essay he writes that when the wind 'blows across the afternoon and into the evening' he feels a longing to return to the lake. And, arriving at the lake, he says, 'we settled into the kind of summertime I had known.' In both sentences we expect a physical place or thing to be the object of the prepositions 'across' and 'into'—'blows across *the water*,' for example, or 'settled into *our cabin*'—but instead we get a time of day or year."

That's great. What's going on?

"White has made time palpable, turned it into something he can express, if he chooses, in concrete or lyrical, rather than literal, terms. Maybe those metaphors—if they are metaphors—prepare us, since they come very early on, for the playfulness about time that marks the whole essay. Because, really, he knows as well as we do that all his assertions about there being 'no years' are just wishes, not reality."

Very good.

White's essay is not hard for students to accept intellectually, but difficult to appreciate emotionally. They are too young to feel their youth as anything but eternally present, or to feel that they are awaiting "the chill of death." Therefore, we try to come at the tone of "Once More to the Lake" technically rather than emotionally. Until the last word of the last sentence, White has successfully merged father with son: "Everywhere we went I had trouble making out which was I, the one walking at my side, the one walking in my pants." At the essay's conclusion White, suddenly relentless in forcing the harsh truth upon himself, uses precisely the same trope of merged identity to destroy that trope. After the storm,

> When the others went swimming my son said he was going in too. He pulled his dripping trunks from the line where they had hung all through the shower, and wrung them out. Languidly, and with no thought of going in, I watched him, his hard little body, skinny and bare, saw him wince slightly as he pulled up around his vitals the small, soggy, icy garment. As he buckled the swollen belt suddenly my groin felt the chill of death.

"What we expect," someone explains, "instead of 'my groin felt the chill of death,' is something like 'my groin felt the chill of the same icy trunks I used to pull up as a boy after those same afternoon thundershowers. There were no years.' What we get is not sameness, but difference. The boy feels only the 'chill' of the bathing suit, but White, his father, feels time and the 'chill of death.'"

At that moment, the illusion breaks, the literal becomes figurative, and real knowledge forces itself through—what awaits White, soon perhaps, or perhaps not soon, but certainly, is death. If we miss this final, subtle, sudden turn, we miss the entire essay—it becomes nothing more than an account of a nostalgic trip back to the place he spent summers when he was his son's age. What the essay truly is, we suddenly realize, is an examination of mortality.

"Nostalgia," someone says, "can become sentimentality. But White's tone is not at all sentimental. And I think that's because he has a sense of humor and is so down-to-earth. Any essay," she continues, "that begins with getting water up your nose can never become pompous or sappy, can never 'overdo it.'"

"And," someone adds, "an author who can write *The Elements of Style* and then end the first paragraph of his essay in a way that draws particular attention to the violation of one of the principles of parallel structure that he espouses, combining a prepositional phrase with an infinitive—

> A few weeks ago this feeling got so strong I bought myself a couple of bass hooks and a spinner and returned to the lake where we used to go, for a week's fishing and to revisit old haunts—

can never be someone who falls into the trap of taking himself too seriously, or of losing control of tone."

∎ 26 ∎

Notes of a Native Son

JAMES BALDWIN

*In which we admire Baldwin's brilliant analysis
of the sources of hate and bias.*

GRADE 12

I ask my students how they've liked James Baldwin's "Notes of a Native Son." They respond with immediate and uniform praise. "Baldwin is really smart and really honest." "It's about a lot of things and yet it hangs together." "The ending was overwhelming."

In a sense Baldwin is doing what they, more haltingly but most sincerely, want to do—thinking deeply about feelings, his own and other people's, and trying to be impartial in his conclusions.

Would someone, before we begin discussion, summarize the essay as concisely as you can? Summaries can be very difficult. They require the mature ability to step back from a piece of writing and see what is central, what is secondary, and what the underlying structure is. *Suppose,* I press them, *you had to say everything in one sentence?*

One senior begins, "Then I'd say, 'Baldwin takes the occasion of his father's death to think about how his father looked at the world and about what he, his father's son, thought he knew and didn't really know.' How's that?"

Pretty good. Anyone else want to give it a try?

Another hand goes up. "I'd say, '"Notes of a Native Son" moves back and forth between two things implied in its title'—my sentence has a colon here!—'Baldwin as a "native son" of America, believing in the American promise of justice and dignity and experiencing assaults of bias against those Americans, like himself, who are black, and Baldwin as the "son" of his father, sharing, without fully realizing it until his father's death, his father's sensibilities and burdens.' How's that?"

Not bad. Someone else? Groans all around.

"I'll give it a try. If I were to summarize the essay I'd borrow the phrase about moving back and forth between two things, but I'd say, '. . . those two things are Baldwin's personal life and the public and political context of that life.' Good, huh?"

Pretty good.

"This will put every other sentence to shame. 'The essay is, in the final analysis, a tribute to his father, a reevaluation of both of them, and an application of what he learns about himself to human conduct in general.'"

"That's fairly impressive," someone teases, but also means it.

"I offer a completely mundane sentence," someone else says. "I mean, someone has to. 'Baldwin begins and ends with his father's funeral, which occurs on Baldwin's birthday, and in between describes a kindly white teacher, his father's resentment and fear of her, his own first encounter with racism working in a war plant in New Jersey, what that encounter did to him, the fear and anger just below the surface in Harlem before black soldiers are shipped out, his dying father in the hospital, the funeral and sermon, his memories, the Bradford Hotel riots, his father's own sermons, and his resolve about how he must live his own life.'"

That was actually helpful. Now try it in about 20 words.

"'The essay, which seems to be about family and about race, is really about hatred, its sources and its effects, personal and general.'"

The class applauds, someone grouses, "I think that was 23 words," and we move on.

Let's see, I say, *if we can discover why we like Baldwin's essay. What in it moves or impresses us? If we had to name a distinguishing feature of Baldwin's prose, what might that be?*

"Maybe that he analyzes things from every possible angle."

"He doesn't think in stereotypes or speak in platitudes. He looks at himself and sees honestly what motivates him, and applies that same honesty to others."

Can you give us an example?

"I think that maybe one of the best examples comes in Part 2 where Baldwin speaks of his father in the hospital:

The moment I saw him I knew why I had put off this visit
so long. I had told my mother that I did not want to see him
because I hated him. But this was not true. It was only that I *had*
hated him and I wanted to hold on to this hatred. I did not want
to look on him as a ruin: it was not a ruin I had hated. I imagine
that one of the reasons people cling to their hates so stubbornly
is because they sense, once hate is gone, that they will be forced
to deal with pain."

Someone else raises her hand. "That says it all."

Another hand goes up. "The essay is about being the black son
of a black father, but it's also about just being a son, and the difficult relationship between any parent and child, the missed and
mixed signals, the communication that always goes awry—all the
things that, at some point, when perhaps, as here, the parent dies,
fill us with grief. In other words, together with all that this essay
says about being a 'Negro'—Baldwin's term, not mine—in America,
the essay is also about something universal—about how we react
and relate to our families, and why."

Excellent.

Someone else adds, "That combination appears with special power
in the passage we just read about visiting his dying father in the hospital."

Another hand is raised. "What that passage also shows is that
however unflattering and painful an admission may be, Baldwin
doesn't shy away from it. Like Hamlet, he moves constantly from
the particular to the general, and back again."

"I have another example. When Baldwin describes the rumors
that precipitate the Harlem riot the evening of his father's funeral,
he says that a 'Negro soldier, in the lobby of the Hotel Braddock, got
into a fight with a white policeman over a Negro girl' and that the
fight 'ended with the shooting of the soldier.'

Rumor, flowing immediately to the streets outside, stated that
the soldier had been shot in the back, an instantaneous and
revealing invention, and that the soldier had died protecting a
Negro woman. The facts were somewhat different, but no one
was interested in the facts. They preferred the invention because
this invention expressed and corroborated their hates and fears

so perfectly. It is just as well to remember that people are always doing this.

We all do this," she adds. "We are the people in those crowds."

"We also all clash with our parents, and if we're able, though few of us are as smart as Baldwin or can take our thinking as far, we try to discover what our feelings and motivations really are, and sometimes we even try to imagine what things are like for our parents. Both those things are hard, as hard as letting go of anger, so this essay feels very personal."

Someone else joins in. "Can I add a confession to the one we've just heard?"

Of course.

"Baldwin speaks of 'endeavoring to feel a sorrow for [his father] which never, quite, came true,' and I know what that's like—wanting to feel something you think you should feel, but can't."

I think we all do. Remember Peter Ivanovich and the pouffe in Tolstoy's "The Death of Ivan Ilych"?

Someone else plucks up her courage and adds, "When he senses his father's timidity in front of the white schoolteacher and the white waitress's timidity in the fancy restaurant, those shows of weakness, rather than making Baldwin back off, fuel his rage. I'm ashamed to admit it, but I know what that's like, too, and I've done that."

"I have, too," someone else says.

Another hand goes up. "My comment is about racism."

Go ahead.

"Articles and essays and books about racism that I've read assert its great evil, talk about how it tears apart the body politic, and attribute it, as Mark Twain does in the case of Huck's father, to fear and ignorance, or to capitalism, or to something quite broad. Baldwin's focus is almost unique. He writes not so much about its causes as about what dealing with racism does, might do, and must not do, to the black man. That's so different. Maybe it's not even politically correct, but I think it's important and powerful."

That's great.

"This is another characteristic of Baldwin's prose. He admits that sometimes he can't figure things out, that he doesn't know something, or can't quite pin it down, or that he didn't know something at the time when he would have needed most to know it."

Excellent.

"Maybe," someone else ventures, "it's this exploratory quality, combined with his self-criticism, that convinces us that we can trust what he says he *does* know."

Now, I say, *let's look more closely at the text to see how the very syntax of Baldwin's sentences reflects these things.** We begin with a sentence from paragraph three where Baldwin, speaking of himself and his father, writes:

> We had got on badly, partly because we shared, in our different fashions, the vice of stubborn pride.

What's the first thing he does in this sentence?
"Admits that he and his father didn't get along."
Good. And then what follows?
"A partial explanation or excuse in the phrase beginning, 'partly because we shared . . .'"

What if the phrases were arranged differently? Suppose the sentence read, "Partly because we shared, in our different fashions, the vice of stubborn pride, we had got on badly." What would be different?

The class pauses for a moment and then a hand goes up. "Baldwin admits, at the very outset, something that people don't usually like to admit about themselves and their parents—'we had got on badly.' He's very 'out there.' Your change makes it sound like he's apologizing or excusing himself before even telling us what he's guilty of— like he's taking less responsibility."

Someone snickers, "That's what politicians do."

"Beginning with 'Because' would also make Baldwin sound like he's showing us how perceptive he is. Some people turn apologies into boasts. Mr. Collins in *Pride and Prejudice* does that all the time, but Baldwin never does. And because Baldwin is personally truthful we are inclined to find his analyses valid also."

Another hand goes up. "How Baldwin ends his sentence is important, too. In 'Partly because we shared, in our different fashions, the

---

*The effect of where, within a sentence, a grammatical qualifier or a subordinate clause is placed is discussed in an excellent essay by John F. Fleischauer entitled "James Baldwin's Style: A Prospectus for the Classroom." It appeared in *College Composition and Communication*, vol. 26, no. 2 (May, 1975), pp. 141–48, and is available on JSTOR.org. I am indebted to this article for many of the insights about the sentence under discussion.

vice of stubborn pride, we had got on badly,' you've moved the word 'pride' from its emphatic position at the end of the sentence and buried it in the middle, where its confessional force is diminished."

Excellent.

Another student adds, "There's something else. Baldwin begins with a fact—'We had got on badly'—and then presents an explanation—'partly because . . .' His sentence reproduces actual experience, in that first something happens, and then we analyze it, in life just as in this sentence."

Great, all of you.

We discuss a few other sentences, and then move on.

Before we conclude for today, I say, *let's talk about music—about symphonies, for instance.*

"Symphonies?"

What are the essential components of a symphony?

"Different movements."

"Theme and development."

"Length."

"Different instruments playing at the same time?"

"Why are we doing this?"

Are there any obvious references to music in this essay? I ask.

"There's the word 'Notes' in the title. I've thought of it as 'jottings,' and what we've said about the exploratory quality of the essay supports that, but 'Notes' can of course also mean musical notes. And Baldwin does use musical terms such as 'dissonant' and 'coda.'"

"And he divides the essay into three parts—three movements, we could say—and labels each part."

Someone's face lights up and she says, "There's a change in tone within the funeral sequence, the trigger for which is actual music. When 'someone began singing one of my father's favorite songs,' Baldwin writes, 'abruptly, I was with him, sitting on his knee, in the hot, enormous, crowded church which was the first church we attended.' And then Baldwin remembers moments of sweetness from his father when Baldwin was very young. The tone changes to something we could call mellow and maybe *lento,* and is triggered by music."

Excellent.

Another hand goes up. "In the ride to the cemetery, we hear a sudden and different motif—deep toned and majestic, like the final chords of a great symphony—in which verses from Joshua that both he and his father preached come into his mind. The text italicizes them:

> *And if it seem evil unto you to serve the Lord, choose you this day whom you will serve; whether the gods which your fathers served that were on the other side of the flood, or the gods of the Amorites, in whose land ye dwell: but as for me and my house, we will serve the Lord.*

From this memory, Baldwin takes the lesson, as if his father were there speaking to him, that,

> It was necessary to hold onto the things that mattered. The dead man mattered, the new life mattered; blackness and whiteness did not matter: to believe that they did was to acquiesce in one's own destruction. Hatred, which could destroy so much, never failed to destroy the man who hated and this was an immutable law."

She continues, "To 'serve the Lord' is to make the hard choice not to hate, to live with the paradox, as Baldwin says, of accepting 'life as it is, and men as they are,' while at the same time never accepting 'injustices as commonplace.'"

Another hand is raised. "We could say that the concluding 'notes' of this essay return us, in a sense, to the title. Baldwin says, 'I wished that he had been beside me so that I could have searched his face for the answers which only the future would give me now.' So what he's suggesting is that these words that he's written—the whole essay—are 'notes' in both senses, parts of a symphonic whole and thoughts that need further development. Despite the enormous insights in the essay, 'notes' suggests that the full answers are ones that only life itself can yield."

Beautiful. I assume that nothing further can be said, but I am wrong.

"As I read part three, and heard these final 'chords,'" someone adds, "I realized, suddenly, that not what the preacher says, but this essay, written years after his father's death in 1943, is the real eulogy for his father.—'"

"Wow," someone else responds, "That's great."

"—It does what the preacher's eulogy doesn't do: it presents his father as he really was, his weaknesses and his strengths. And it moves from harsh assessment, to forgiveness, to love. The title could be 'Eulogy for My Father' but that would anticipate the essay's conclusion. 'Notes of a Native Son,' of a son who resembles his father and is, for better or worse, also a son of his country, is the perfect title."

◼ 27 ◼

Old China

CHARLES LAMB

*In which we find loss and aging presented with
lightness and grace.*

GRADE 12

"Old China," perhaps the finest of all Charles Lamb's *Essays of Elia,*
opens out like a series of nested Russian dolls and insists, through
its title and its framing action, that it is not in the least serious—
that it is about china teacups and idiosyncratic pleasures. The ideas
in "Old China" unfold so quietly, gently, and gradually that Lamb's
essay seems as delicate and weightless as old china itself.

Lamb begins by affirming a predilection for old china that began
so early in his life that he cannot recall a time when he did not love
those "little, lawless, azure-tinctured" figures on teacups and china
jars and saucers. "When I go to see any great house," he says, in a
reversal of the priorities of most touring visitors, "I inquire for the
china-closet and next for the picture-gallery." In part, what he loves
about the blue figures is that they are set in a "world before perspective." "Here," he tells the reader, "is a young and courtly Mandarin,
handing tea to a lady from a salver—two miles off." When Lamb,
or more precisely, his narrative double "Elia," says "Here," we do
not know whether we are agreeing about teacup scenes in general,
peering with him into the china closet of a great house, or glanc-
ing down at a particular teacup that he holds in his hand. We do
know that the wall between writer and reader is permeable. He has

drawn us into his presence and made us part of an intimate, polite conversation.

Nor are we alone. Someone named Bridget is here as well, and she is not happy. This "set of extraordinary old blue china" that he is "now for the first time" using becomes the catalyst for Bridget's complaint that they were much happier in the days before they could make such purchases with ease. She recalls instance after instance of the pleasure they once felt in buying or enjoying something modest that they had scrimped and saved for: a dish of strawberries; peas early in the season; a Leonardo print; "a folio Beaumont and Fletcher"; being given a seat and tablecloth in a country inn where the hostess allowed them to unwrap their own lunch and purchase only a single ale; sitting in the topmost gallery seats to see "Rosalind in Arden or . . . Viola at the Court of Illyria"; or tallying accounts together on New Year's Eve and resolving to spend less in the coming year.

What, I ask, does Lamb's topic seem to be at this point?

"Not antique china anymore, but wealth and poverty," they say.

And what's Bridget saying to Elia about wealth and poverty?

"That wealth brings less joy than poverty brings, since when you're poor every purchase is invested with meaning and every decision with intensity."

Elia remains so quiet during Bridget's long and leisurely disquisition that we are lulled into thinking that nothing can be offered in reply. When Bridget finishes, Elia says, with indulgent kindness, "Bridget is so sparing of her speech on most occasions, that when she gets into a rhetorical vein, I am careful how I interrupt it." And then he answers. Elia tells his cousin, with the mildest irony, "I am afraid we must put up with the excess, for if we were to shake the superflux into the sea, we should not much mend ourselves."

How does Elia give weight to Bridget's argument before he rejects it and tries to wean her from it?

"Elia says that there is nothing he would not give to have those days again, with all the attendant struggles, but now he and she are old and must live more comfortably and must, indeed, be thankful that they can live comfortably. In a long sentence of lovely rhythms and deep feeling, a sentence that he does not want to let go of and so extends and extends, pushing its conclusion off for as long as he can, he says:

Yet could those days return, could you and I once more walk
our thirty miles a day, could Bannister and Mrs. Bland again be
young, and you and I be young to see them, could the good old
one shilling gallery days return—they are dreams, my cousin,
now—but could you and I at this moment, instead of this quiet
argument, by our well-carpeted fireside, sitting on this luxurious
sofa—be once more struggling up those inconvenient staircases,
pushed about and squeezed, and elbowed by the poorest rabble
of poor gallery scramblers—could I once more hear those anxious shrieks of yours, and the delicious *Thank God, we are safe*,
which always followed, when the topmost stair, conquered, let in
the first light of the whole cheerful theatre down beneath us—I
do not know the fathom line that ever touched a descent so deep
as I would be willing to bury more wealth in than Croesus had,
or the great Jew R— is supposed to have, to purchase it."

What's the essay's topic now?—wealth versus poverty?
"Not anymore," they answer. "It's about youth versus age."
"I think it's about time passing, and about longing for the days of
one's youth."
"And about the fact that we can't recapture the past or be young
again."
There's a final sentence, I say, *and an interesting absence of transi-
tion to it.*

And now do just look at that merry little Chinese waiter holding
an umbrella, big enough for a bed-tester, over the head of that
pretty insipid half-Madonna-ish chit of a lady in that very blue
summer-house.

Why is there no transition? I ask.
"Maybe because there's nothing more that can be said. One must
just hold certain feelings in, and carry on."
And how might we describe Elia's tone here?
"It's very gentle."
We have read Francis Bacon and agree that, unlike Bacon's tone
in "Of Studies," Lamb's is anything but authoritative.
Is the essay still about the wish to recover one's youth?
"No. The topic has expanded again, like those nested dolls that
open out. It's no longer about longing for what is impossible, but

about fortitude and acceptance of limitations, and about finding joy and cheer in what is available."

Excellent.

"The essay is saying that material possessions offer pleasure, and that loving material things is not necessarily bad."

Yes. That, too.

"We could," someone adds, "call the act of collecting china-ware a frivolous pursuit, so maybe Lamb is suggesting that it's all right to be frivolous, even more than all right. Being frivolous is sometimes good for the soul and spirit."

"Or maybe he's saying that what appears to be frivolous may not be at all frivolous."

"I think Lamb is suggesting that childhood pleasures don't have to disappear when childhood disappears, as Elia's delight in the tiny two-dimensional figures demonstrates—and that such pleasures keep us young."

We begin to talk about method. We reread the last sentence and mention what's obvious—that Lamb uses old china to frame the essay. With the essay's larger topics now in mind, we look back at the opening. Paragraph two talks about figures that "float about, uncircumscribed by any element, in that world before perspective— a china tea-cup."

A hand shoots up. "He says '*before* perspective,' not '*without* perspective.' Maybe that's because he's thinking about being freed from the constraints not just of space, but also of time."

Nice.

"And," a supporting voice adds, "the essay's first paragraph ends with another suggestion of timelessness: Elia says, 'I am not conscious of a time when china jars and saucers were introduced to my imagination.'"

"A few paragraphs down, describing the scene on the teacup, Elia speaks of 'a young and courtly Mandarin, handing tea to a lady from a salver,' and that's just what actually happens at the end of the essay—Elia hands Bridget a painted teacup—maybe the very one of the 'young and courtly Mandarin,' the lady, and the teacup."

Another voice pipes up appreciatively, "That's great. And I wanted to say something else. Old china is fragile. It can be so easily broken, and yet Lamb speaks of it as something that withstands time. I think that's such a nice irony."

Another hand has been up for a long time. The essay's conclusion reminds her of the end of Elizabeth Bishop's poem "Poem." We go back and read Lamb's line one more time:

> And now do just look at that merry little Chinese waiter holding
> an umbrella, big enough for a bed-tester, over the head of that
> pretty insipid half-Madonna-ish chit of a lady in that very blue
> summer-house.

In "Poem," Bishop is gazing at a tiny painting "about the size of a old-style dollar bill" by a now-dead uncle. He has painted a rural Nova Scotia scene that Bishop knows and suddenly recognizes. The poem concludes in this way:

> dim, on a piece of Bristol board,
> dim, but how live, how touching in detail
> —the little that we get for free,
> the little of our earthly trust. Not much.
> About the size of our abidance
> along with theirs: the munching cows,
> the iris, crisp and shivering, the water
> still standing from spring freshets,
> the yet-to-be-dismantled elms, the geese.

"'Old China,' too," my student says, "is about 'the size of our abidance.'"

.■ 28 ■.

Hamlet

WILLIAM SHAKESPEARE

*In which tracing images of war takes us
to the play's center.*

GRADE 12

Are there many references to war and fighting in Hamlet? *I ask.*
"Not many."
The class's answer is understandable. After all, there is no blood
in the play, and there are no battles of the sort that we find in the
Henrys or in *Macbeth*. Undeterred, I press on. *Let's see what, if any-
thing, we can find. For example, how does the play begin?*
"With Barnardo and Francisco on guard duty on the ramparts of
the palace."
And what do they fear?
"A ghost."
Yes, but why are they on guard?
"Because Denmark expects an invasion—a Norwegian army of
'lawless resolutes' led by young Fortinbras."
Yes. What about Barnardo's language? Anything military in it?
"Well, when he tells Horatio about the Ghost,

> Sit down awhile
> And let us once again assail your ears,
> That are so fortified against our story,

he uses the military terms, "assail" and "fortify.""
Good. And why might Shakespeare introduce those metaphors?

222

"It's almost a bit of comic characterization—people tend to use the language of their professions in other situations—but it also might be a way of establishing, ever so lightly, a war-like context."

And what about the Ghost when he appears? Anything military there?

"Of course [you silly teacher]. He's wearing full battle dress—armed 'from head to foot.'"

"And described as moving with 'martial stalk.'"

Why is Horatio able to recognize the King in full armor?

"Because, according to Horatio, King Hamlet wore the same armor 'When he the ambitious Norway combated' and when 'He smote the sledded Polacks on the ice.'"

So the dead king is presented, from the beginning, as a warrior of courage and prowess who protected his kingdom?

"Yes."

How does Hamlet feel about himself in comparison with this mighty father?

"In his first soliloquy, he says that Claudius 'is no more like my father/Than I to Hercules.' Among other things, Hamlet is saying that he regards himself as cowardly."

Does Hamlet ever speak of "taking arms"?

A hand shoots up. "Only in 'To be or not to be.' There Hamlet speaks of 'the slings and arrows of outrageous fortune,' and of 'tak[ing] arms against a sea of troubles.'"

Good.

Enthusiasm for the topic grows, and someone else offers an additional reference. "Before 'To be or not to be,' Hamlet asks the Player to recite lines about the fall of Troy in which Pyrrhus wears armor, 'black as his purpose' and encrusted with blood. The speech describes Pyrrhus's slaughter of King Priam by the walls of Troy."

Yes. And is anyone in the play like Pyrrhus?

"Maybe Claudius, in that he has killed a king."

"Maybe Hamlet, in that his father has charged him to kill another king—Claudius."

"Hamlet requests the speech about Pyrrhus, right?"

Right.

"Well, maybe Hamlet requests it not only because he longs for his mother to feel the grief that the widowed Hecuba feels, but also because he's kind of 'trying it on'—thinking about the bloodiness of what he is charged with doing and about how it may transform him, how it may make him as monstrous as Pyrrhus."

Good. So is the military imagery in the Pyrrhus scene related to the larger situation of the play?

"Absolutely," my class responds.

Is there other military imagery in the play?

"In Act IV, Fortinbras's army crosses the stage. And someone identified as 'Captain' stops to talk with Hamlet."

"There are cannons going off all the time—'implements of war.'"

The cannon are extremely important, but let's hold off on them for a moment. Anything else?

"I don't know if this counts, but there's a duel at the end of the play."

Let's talk about it and see where it takes us. Who, for example, delivers the invitation to the duel?

"Osric, the 'waterfly,' a most unlikely messenger of anything serious. He invites Hamlet to an exhibition match with Laertes, in which Claudius claims to be wagering on Hamlet's side."

How long is the scene with Osric?

"Long."

What makes it so?

"Hamlet stretches it out. He toys with Osric about Osric's hat and the weather and about Osric's inflated language."

"And Osric goes on and on about the weaponry that will be used."

Do you remember the riff on the term "carriages"? Can you find it for us?

"Osric says, 'Three of the carriages, in faith, are very dear to fancy, very responsive to the hilts, most delicate carriages, and of very liberal conceit'—whatever that means. Then Hamlet, amused, asks, 'What call you the carriages?' and Osric answers, 'The carriages, sir, are the hangers.' Hamlet replies, 'The phrase would be more germane to the matter if we could carry a cannon by our sides. I would it might be hangers till then. But on! Six Barbary horses, their assigns, and three liberal-conceited carriages.'"

Good. Here's a tough question. Do these references to "carriages" echo anything earlier?

Sometimes with my help, sometimes without it, we turn back to the beginning of the play and to Horatio's description of King Hamlet's battle with the King of Norway. The two fight in single combat, and the winner takes title to the lands of the loser. This is an heroic, one-on-one battle by kings to save their subject soldiers from slaughter. The terms of battle are presented in language that is highly legalistic and, for Shakespeare, unusually repetitive. King Fortinbras agrees to

> . . . forfeit, with his life, all those his lands
> Which he stood seized of, to the conqueror;
> Against the which a moiety competent
> Was gaged by our King, which had returned
> To the inheritance of Fortinbras,
> Had he been vanquisher, as, by the same comart
> And carriage of the article designed,
> His fell to Fortinbras.

"Carriage," I say, *is a word easy to pass over in this opening scene, but perhaps we should attend to it, since the word appears, although with a different meaning, so insistently in the Osric scene.*

The class is silent for a moment or two, and then someone says, "This is crazy, but what Hamlet is about to do at the end of the play—engage in one-to-one combat with Laertes—is like what his father is described as having done at the beginning of the play."

That's excellent.

"Maybe the repetition of 'carriages' is an almost unconscious reflex on Shakespeare's part linking these moments."

"And both scenes are introduced with very full and fairly boring language about the terms of the wager."

Great. We've noted similarities between these two scenes. What about essential differences?

"Both combatants, King Fortinbras and King Hamlet, knew that they were fighting to the death, and fighting for something important, and both were brave. Hamlet and Laertes are also fighting to the death, but this time one of the two, Hamlet, doesn't know it and Laertes doesn't think it will apply to him."

Very good. King Hamlet is described as "valiant." Is Hamlet valiant?

"He doesn't seem so, but he is. Just before the duel, when he's alone in the hall with Horatio, Horatio is worried for him and says, 'You will lose this wager, my lord.' Hamlet replies,

> I do not think so. Since he went into France I have been in continual practice. I shall win at the odds. But thou wouldst not think how ill all's here about my heart. But it is no matter.

Horatio, still worried, responds, 'Nay, good my lord—,' and Hamlet interrupts him and dismisses his own fear, saying, 'It is but foolery, but it is such a sort of gaingiving as would perhaps trouble a woman.' Horatio says, 'If your mind dislike anything, obey it. I will forestall their repair hither and say you are not fit.'"

And then?

"Then Hamlet says,

> Not a whit, we defy augury. There is special providence in the
> fall of a sparrow. If it be now, 'tis not to come; if it be not to
> come, it will be now; if it be not now, yet it will come. The read-
> iness is all. Since no man of aught he leaves knows, what is't to
> leave betimes? Let be.'"

Let's talk about this speech. It's a culminating moment of the play, not only in its beauty of expression and assertion of divine providence, but also in what it tells us about Hamlet's character.

"I'll try. Hamlet senses something and yet sets his misgivings aside. If he sensed nothing and went blindly into the duel, there would be nothing brave about his action. Now there is. And if he could guess at Laertes and Claudius's precise plan, he would, in moral terms, be no better than they. So this speech represents a perfect balance of bravery and intelligence."

"What he knows is that death may come at any time. Death is the 'it' of his 'augury' speech. But what he also knows, or has learned, is that one must live and act in whatever time one has."

Excellent, both of you. So how does Hamlet measure up against his father?

Someone else takes up the challenge. "Perhaps these military echoes and parallels prove that Hamlet is now, having become so in the course of the play, every bit of what his father was—that his valor, although not strictly speaking battle valor, is kingly—and that he is as much to be admired as he admired his father."

Bravo.

We have one further military image to look at, I tell the class—*the one we set aside earlier: the cannon. With whom and with what are cannon associated throughout the play?*

"With Claudius and drunken revelry."

And how are we supposed to feel about Claudius's use of cannon to announce his drinking?

"Disgusted."

"That it is yet another form of Claudius's usurpation—not of the throne but of 'implements of war.'"

Good.

"At best, it's a gross misuse of the 'implements of war.' At worst, it's blasphemous in that Claudius, at the end of the coronation scene, orders that,

> No jocund health that Denmark drinks today,
> But the great cannon to the clouds shall tell,
> And the King's rouse the heaven shall bruit again,
> Respeaking earthly thunder,

reducing 'heaven' to his echo."

"Unlike the hero king he has murdered, Claudius is without dignity or restraint. He appropriates to himself what is not rightly his."

"Trumpets often mark entrances of royalty in Shakespeare's plays, but Claudius insists on kettledrums and trumpets and cannon, constantly. When Hamlet chastises Gertrude, he speaks of 'the bloat' king. This, too, is a kind of bloatedness."

"The cannon are finally associated with poison, Claudius's preferred method of killing kings. Claudius calls for cannon to be shot off when he drops the 'union,' the poisoned pearl, into the wine cup he sets aside for Hamlet."

Read that passage to us.

"He says, as Hamlet and Laertes prepare to duel,

> Give me the cups.
> And let the kettle to the trumpet speak,
> The trumpet to the cannoneer without,
> The cannons to the heavens, the heaven to earth,
> 'Now the King drinks to Hamlet.'

So the cannon become associated not only with 'bray[ing]' drunkenness, beast-like behavior, but also with murder."

And is that the final reference to cannon in the play?

"Yes," the class says, sure that they've finished their work. Then there is a moment of wariness and the thought that perhaps there is something else—or why the leading question?

A cautious hand goes up. "Is 'a peal of ordnance . . .'?

Yes!

We slow down, so that everyone can follow what's happening. "Is the 'peal of ordnance' that is heard at the very end of the play, after all the bodies, and last of all Hamlet's, are carried off, a cannon shot?"

It is.

"Then the cannon and the sounds of war have now become associated with Hamlet, to whom Fortinbras assigns full military honors. Perhaps we could say that the prior association of cannon with Claudius—and Claudius himself—has been obliterated."

Bravo! Let's read Fortinbras's lines, and that concluding stage direction.

> Let four captains
> Bear Hamlet like a soldier to the stage,
> For he was likely, had he been put on,
> To have proved most royal; and for his passage
> The soldiers' music and the rite of war
> Speak loudly for him. . . .
> Go, bid the soldiers shoot.
> > *Exeunt marching, after which a peal of ordnance is shot off.*

Imagine, I tell the class, what this is like onstage. Everyone has gone off. The stage is bare. But the play is not over. We wait, and then, from offstage we hear the sound of cannon being shot off, perhaps again and again, the equivalent of a 21-gun salute. For whom, I ask, other than for a soldier is such an honor always reserved?

"For the commander-in-chief—for the king."

And is Hamlet king?

The class pauses. They have not considered this. And then someone says, "Yes. He must be. In that short space between Claudius's death and his own. Even though there's no coronation."

And what kingly thing does he do in those moments?

One hand after another goes up, and someone answers, "Hamlet says of Fortinbras, 'He has my dying voice.' In other words, he passes on his kingdom to one whom he thinks worthy to rule it. He ensures an orderly succession."

Bravo, again. And so what can we say of this prince who has idealized his father and found himself wanting?

"That he, too, is kingly."

"And that the military imagery of the play has told us so."

.∎ 29 ∎.

The Iliad

HOMER

Antony and Cleopatra

WILLIAM SHAKESPEARE

*In which we contemplate deaths that convey
a sense of the sublime.*

GRADE 12

This chapter, like the next, reflects the work of spring tutorials in twelfth grade—classes in which students read and discuss literary works without the obligation to write analytically about them. In this tutorial, we studied Homer's *The Iliad* and Shakespeare's *Antony and Cleopatra* and posed to ourselves the question of what makes a literary work "sublime"? What initially puzzled us as we tried to define sublimity is that *The Iliad* and *Antony and Cleopatra* present death in radically different ways.

Death in The Iliad

Death, *The Iliad* tells us, is the inescapable condition of our lives; no one avoids it. What *The Iliad* does, and what gives it its power

---

All *Iliad* quotations are from Helaine L. Smith, *Homer and the Homeric Hymns: Mythology for Reading and Composition* (University Press of America, 2011). Numbers in parentheses after each quotation refer to Book and line numbers.

and beauty, we decide, is to face, squarely and constantly, the reality of death. The only thing that approximates immortality, and a weak substitute for it, is fame—being remembered in song after one dies—and that, Achilles tells Odysseus, is cold comfort. The only comfort living men have is the knowledge that death is our common lot. The great warrior Diomedes asks the Lycian fighter Glaukos who he is that he dares confront Diomedes in battle, and Glaukos responds,

> Son of Tydeus, great of soul, why ask from whom I am descended?
> Like the leaves, so are men.
> The wind blows the leaves to the earth, but the wood,
> Blooming again, sends forth fresh leaves in spring.
> So it is with men—a new generation appears and another dies.
> (6.145–149)

All heroes know that life is short and that, before and after them, there have been and will be others who likewise must die. This is the wisdom that *The Iliad* offers, again and again.

We locate examples of this sensibility throughout the text. When Lycaon begs Achilles to spare him, Achilles answers that now, with Patroclus dead, he spares no man. "Fool," Achilles begins, "offer me no ransom, nor plead with me." Before Patroclus died, Achilles says, "I spared many Trojans," but now not one shall escape death. He continues,

> So, friend, you too must die. Why plead about it, weeping?
> Patroclus died, and he was a far better man than you.
> Do you not see what sort of man I am, beautiful and huge,
> My father a king, a goddess the mother who bore me?
> Yet, even over me hang my death and my harsh destiny.
> There will come a morning, or an evening, or a mid-day
> When some man will take my life from me in battle
> With a spear or an arrow from a bowstring.   (21.106–113)

"What is so moving here," someone says, "is not only that Achilles knows his death will come as it comes to all of us, unannounced and on a specific day at a specific hour, but also that he moves, within six lines, from addressing Lycaon as "fool" to addressing him as "friend."

And why is that significant?

"Because Lycaon is indeed a 'fool' to think that death can be avoided, but a 'friend' in that all men go to the same doom and in that Achilles sees himself even in Lycaon, just as we see our destiny in that of these heroes."

Good.

We discover, too, that every deed of honor in *The Iliad* is performed with the full awareness that death awaits the hero. In answer to Diomedes, Glaukos adds,

> My father Hippolochus begat me and of him I am sprung.
> He sent me to Troy and charged me
> Always to stand with the bravest, and to strive to be best,
> That I may never shame the race of my fathers, who were in
>   their time
> The greatest men in all the land of Lycia.   (6.206–210)

And later, Glaukos's comrade, the hero Sarpedon, says to him, as they stand in the front ranks of the fighting,

> Glaukos, why are we honored above all others
> In Lycia, with seats of honor and the finest meats and full
>   wine cups? . . .
> And why are we given the richest lands by the banks of the
>   river Xanthos,
> Orchards, and vineyards, and ploughlands for wheat?
> These honors oblige us to stand in the front ranks
> Of the Lycians, in the hard fighting.   (12.310–316)

There are many moments in *The Iliad* in which a hero faces his own death, knowing it is not in his power to prevent death, for that power belongs solely to the gods. This is what the greatest of men, Sarpedon and Glaukos, Achilles and Aias, know, and they are determined at least to remain aware of what is in store.

"One such moment," someone says, "is Aias's prayer to Zeus. It is a speech of greatness, of piety, and of courage.

> Father Zeus, only release from darkness the sons of the Achaeans,
> Make the air clear, and give our eyes sight again; in bright
> Daylight destroy us, if now that is your pleasure.   (17.645–647)

The Greeks and Trojans have been fighting so furiously that dust clouds now block out the sun. Everything is in darkness. The Greeks are suffering great losses and the hero Aias understands, suddenly, that he and the Greeks fighting beside him will die—indeed, that it is Zeus's will that they die, since Zeus controls all things.

"And so," my student continues, "Aias prays, not for mercy, since the will of the gods is insuperable, but for sunlight—'make bright the air'—that he may go to his death 'in shining daylight,' seeing, conscious until the very end."

Excellent.

We note that even the gods, Zeus and Thetis, mourn before the event for their mortal children who will die, and that when Zeus speaks of Troy, his beloved city, as that which will shortly fall, we are in the realm of truth—and of sorrow.

"Because much of *The Iliad* is filled not simply with death, but with grieving," a student adds, "we know that we are not alone in our own personal griefs. It may be this, as much as anything else, that joins comfort to sorrow and makes *The Iliad* sublime."

Someone adds, "What affects us as much as grief for those who have fallen is grief for those still living who know that they too will fall and who grieve for those who have."

Excellent.

We note just a few such examples, each different, each heart-rending: Cassandra's cry to the city when she sees the body of her brother brought back from Achilles' tent for burial:

> Come, Trojan men and women: see Hector
> If ever when he was alive and returned home from battle
> You were joyful,
> For he was the joy of the city and all its people—   (24.700–706);

Andromache's grief that she will never have a final word from Hector to keep with her all her days; Thetis, whom Iris finds in her hollow cave at the bottom of the sea, wearing the same dark blue robe that Demeter wears in her anguished search for her child, and surrounded by all the sea goddesses, grieving for the fate that she knows will soon befall her son Achilles; and great Zeus himself, commanding that when his son Sarpedon shall fall in battle, Apollo is to cleanse the dark blood from the body, wash Sarpedon in a running stream, anoint him with ambrosia, put immortal robes on him, and give him to the twin brothers, Sleep and Death, to carry to the

land of Lycia for burial. Grief and death in *The Iliad*, we find, are
everywhere.

"And yet," someone adds, "the prospect of death never inhibits action. There is a sublimity of courage here also."

Exactly.

Death in Antony and Cleopatra

Despite *The Iliad*'s epic grandeur and distance in time, death in *The
Iliad*, my class points out with some amazement, is actually far more
realistic than death in *Antony and Cleopatra*.

An excellent insight, I respond.

We note that as Antony and Cleopatra approach death, each
speaks of death as continuation rather than cessation, as union, as
enlargement, and as an arena for the expression of love and courage.

Someone tries to explain how fantasy and reality are reconciled.
"When Cleopatra calls out to Antony, 'Husband, I come,' she is in
the realm of fantasy but a fantasy so grand and so fine that we,
moved by the most beautiful language Shakespeare has ever written, believe for the space of the play in that same sublime fantasy."

"Antony shares her fantasies," someone adds. "When he receives
the false report of Cleopatra's death, which is her attempt to soften
Antony's anger towards her for twice abandoning him in battle, he
is filled with grief. In a world without Cleopatra, death becomes for
him the desired end to 'the long day's task.' And as Antony prepares
to die, he imagines he is joining Cleopatra in Elysium 'where souls
do couch on flowers' and where he and she will walk 'hand in hand'

> And with our sprightly port make the ghosts gaze.
> Dido and her Aeneas shall want troops,
> And all the haunt be ours."

"Neither lover perceives death as dissolution and nothingness.
When Cleopatra says,

> O see, my women,
> The crown o'th' earth doth melt . . .

she chooses 'doth melt,' perhaps because 'doth die' is both too common a thing for him, and inaccurate; in her vision, Antony 'melt[s]'

into the earth and sky, fills it, becomes one with it, and enlarges it. He is not, thus, ever really gone."

Great.

"The idea of life continuing into eternity," another student suggests, "is also expressed in the line, 'O withered is the garland of the war.' To Cleopatra, Antony both is and wears the garland of victory, and we hear in her mourning phrase an echo of her earlier farewell when Antony sailed to Rome:

> Upon your sword
> Sit laurel victory, and smooth success
> Be strewed before your feet.

These images of life, of 'garlands' and 'crowns,' become the images of death; nothing is lost and nothing of value, both lovers assert, really changes."

Very good.

Someone offers a similar example. "Cleopatra's words, as Iras and Charmian dress her in 'royal robes' for death, are 'Yare, yare, good Iras!'—a reliving of the moment on the barge, made even more explicit when she says, 'I am again for Cydnus / To meet Mark Antony.' Death will replay, in more exquisite terms and without the world's 'snare,' the progress of their love."

"It's really impossible to speak or hear these lines and feel that death for both of them is other than a sublime joy. If there is to be no more change, since death 'shackles accidents and bolts up change,' then their love, as each insists, will go on forever."

Are there any other values associated with death in Antony and Cleopatra?

"Death brings to fulfillment every aspect of Cleopatra's womanliness," someone notes, and we list those aspects together.

"She is 'a lass unparalleled.'"

"'The maid that milks and does the meanest chares.'"

"Wife to Antony who is now and forever her 'husband' and not Fulvia's or Octavia's."

"A nursing mother whose last words to the weeping Charmian are,

> Peace, peace!
> Dost thou not see my baby at my breast
> That sucks the nurse asleep!"

Someone adds that "Death comes to Cleopatra, by her own reckoning, 'as sweet as balm, as soft as air.'"

Is there anything else about death that we want to mention that contributes to our sense of sublimity here?

"Hamlet dies with something left unsaid, some knowledge to which we will never be privy—'O, I could tell you—But let it be,' while Cleopatra dies asking, 'What should I stay—,' and Charmian easily completes her mistress's sentence with 'in this vile world?' There is nothing left unfinished, not even a final sentence."

"I think it's important that death is willed in *Antony and Cleopatra*. Every major figure—Enobarbus, Eros, Antony, Iras, Cleopatra, and Charmian—dies by choice, death in each case being an expression of love or personal loyalty."

"But in *The Iliad*," someone points out, "no one seeks death. Life and action are one, and as long as one remains alive, one feels ties of the deepest necessity to one's comrades, one's family, one's city, and one's people; the 'long day's task' of the hero is never done. And yet, there, too, we feel ourselves in the presence of the sublime."

That's an excellent comparison.

"Maybe," someone adds, "because Antony and Cleopatra define death as the state in which they can be together forever, when each dies the sadness we feel is not for them, who see themselves as gaining eternity, but for ourselves, who are losing their company—their vitality and valor."

"And their deaths are so different from anything we can imagine, so different from what is possible for us, that those deaths do not make us feel, as death does in *The Iliad*, that we, too, must die."

Nice.

Our discussion turns to thoughts of infinitude and constriction.

"The real world," someone notes, "is, for such figures, confining; death is seen as a release from that confinement, as an entry into boundlessness. In their lives the world has been too small for each of them—at the very beginning of the play we learn that they "must . . . needs find out new heaven, new earth."

"The world of *The Iliad*, unlike the world of *Antony and Cleopatra*, is actually one of constriction—action is played out in the finite space between the Greek ships and the ramparts of Troy. *Antony and Cleopatra*, on the other hand, spans the whole world, from Alexandria to Rome to Sicily to Parthia, and onward, and Antony and Cleopatra are themselves fluid in the roles they play."

If being unbounded is what imbues the deaths of Antony and Cleopatra with beauty and sublimity, it is also, paradoxically, the opposite sense of being bound and limited that imbues with sublimity the death of *Iliadic* heroes. We have read two sublime texts, but know only that sublimity comes in many guises.

.▪ 30 ▪.

An Imaginary Life

DAVID MALOUF

The Parnas

SILVANO ARIETI

*In which we discuss the generous endings
imagined for real protagonists.*

GRADE 12

In the spring, senior English classes are replaced by tutorials for
which no grades are given; small numbers of students meet weekly
with a teacher to read and discuss literature not previously studied,
or to view and discuss films, or to do some creative writing. In this
case, we combined all three: we examined two texts that fuse fiction
and nonfiction, noted comparable moments in film, and ended with
a creative writing exercise.

In *An Imaginary Life*, the Australian novelist David Malouf re-
creates, with hints from Ovid's own writing, the poet's 12-year exile
and death on the coast of the Black Sea. In *The Parnas*, the Italian-
American psychiatrist Silvano Arieti reconstructs the final hours of
Giuseppe Pardo Roques, the lay leader of the Jewish community of
Pisa whom Arieti knew and admired, and who was murdered by the
Nazis in his home on August 1, 1944. Both writers ascribe to their
subjects—the Latin poet Ovid and the Italian Jew Pardo Roques—
in different but extraordinary ways deaths imbued with grace, end-

ings that are gifts. It is this particular aspect of authorial response that we attempted to explore and then incorporate into creative writing assignments of our own at the end of the course.

An Imaginary Life

My students thoroughly enjoyed reading *An Imaginary Life*, and when I asked what they liked most, they said, "the interior voice of Ovid, speaking of his early memories on his father's farm, of his imagined playmate, and of his dreams of the wild and barren steppes"; "a sense of how intimate and lyrical first-person narration can actually be"; "Malouf's vision of Ovid"—this from a Latin student—"as only belatedly understanding the truths behind his great poem, *The Metamorphoses*"; "the suggestion that early Roman virtues ceased to exist in imperial Rome, but were present in a primitive outpost— the price of sophistication"; "the extraordinary conclusion, in which Ovid and the wild child set off across the tundra, and in which both Ovid and the child express what must be called love: cosmopolitan Ovid journeying into a vast and barren land to save the child from the villagers once the headman had died, and the child finding and masticating food, as the child has seen animals do for their young, when Ovid becomes too weak to do so himself."

Someone adds, "I was particularly taken by the ending where Ovid says, 'The notion of a destination no longer seems necessary to me,' and then sees the child in the distance gathering food and, at a certain point, letting the snails he has gathered fall from his hand. As the child continues into the distance alone, across the pools of water, I found myself wondering if the child knows, mid-gathering, as Ovid did of his brother, that death has come and that he must move on alone." She continues by quoting Ovid's words at the moment of his death:

> "He is walking on the water's light. And as I watch, he takes the first step off it, moving slowly away now in the deepest distance, above the earth, above the water, on air . . .
>
> I am immeasurably, unbearably happy. I am three years old. I am sixty, I am six.
>
> I am there.

I thought that was overwhelming," my student says.

The Parnas

The Parnas is less lyrical than *An Imaginary Life* and requires more initial patience from students, who find their patience fully rewarded at the novel's end. As "parnas," the word Sephardic congregations use to denote the synagogue's lay leader, Giuseppe Pardo Roques was a man of great learning, dignity, and faith, a benefactor of Christians and Jews alike, but subject all his life to a fear of animals—a fear so great that it prevented him from going outdoors except to the synagogue half a block away, lest he be set upon by dogs. When the Nazis took Pisa north of the Arno, virtually all Jews fled to the Allied southern portion of the city. Pardo remained because his phobia precluded travel of even that short distance.

I ask my students what has struck them most about *The Parnas*, and they reply, "Not the brutality of the Germans, as recorded by Arieti in his 1960s interviews with Pardo's neighbors, but the neighbors' hearing Pardo cry out again and again, as his friends and servants are murdered and as he is blinded and beaten to death, "You are the animals, you are the animals."

A Comparison

How does a writer with necessarily limited knowledge of his or her biographical subject move beyond that knowledge and yet convey a sense of truth? To what extent is the ability to do that dependent upon loving or coming to love the person who has become the subject of the fictive biography?

Seeking to unlock ideas and clarify thoughts, I say, *Let's take any significant aspect of either* An Imaginary Life *or* The Parnas, *and see what comparisons we can make.*

Someone starts us off with a point of central importance. "Ovid's story is, first and foremost, a story of exile, but it's also in a sense about returning."

Excellent. Explain what you mean by "returning."

"He returns in memory to his childhood, to feelings never resolved, to longings never explored. And eventually he returns to the civic virtues of early Rome—to the things that his father advocated and that he regarded, once, as old-fashioned. There's a moment where he says,

> As a Roman citizen of the knightly order . . . I scoffed at such
> old-fashioned notions as duty, patriotism, the military virtues.
> And here I am, aged fifty, standing on guard at the very edge of
> the known world.

A classmate agrees and adds, "He also says, speaking of the hand-
iwork of the women of Tomis, and comparing it as a model to his
own life,

> What they sew has good strong seams but not a stitch that is fan-
> ciful . . . Everything I ever valued before this was valuable only
> because it was useless.

The critical phrase, 'before this,' implies that Ovid is engaged in a
reevaluation. So here's a further example of a return to early Roman
virtue and a reassessment of his life."

A third student enters the discussion. "I think the child also represents a return—not only to Ovid's young fantasies, but also to
the self before it is civilized, when the self knows the world only
'through the senses'—before the distinctions and separations that
language and place impose. Ovid even says that, without language
in Tomis, he must discover 'the world as a small child does.'"

Another hand goes up. "Perhaps the most obvious return is one we
haven't yet mentioned because it is so basic. It's never stated outright,
but we are meant to understand that what Ovid returns to is also his
own great poem, *The Metamorphoses*, but in a way that is deeper and
fuller than he ever imagined. That return makes *The Metamorphoses*
not a piece of entertainment, but a vision of life itself."

Excellent comments, all of you.

What about The Parnas? *I ask. Is there a sense of return there as
well? Or, if not, why not?*

"Well, being very literal, we could say that Pardo and his guests
and neighbors hope for a return to the Italy they knew before Mus-
solini and Hitler."

Yes.

Encouraged, she goes on. "The literal return hoped for in *The Parnas* is not of place, as it is initially in *An Imaginary Life* when Ovid
yearns for Rome, but of time—a return to an earlier time or to a
future time that will resemble the past and perhaps be even better."

Excellent.

A friend says, "I think that's a really good assessment. Pardo carries inside himself his learning, his faith in God, and his love of man. He does not 'return' to those things, in the way that Ovid returns to earlier values, because he has never set them aside or broken with his past or felt a sense of their loss."

Someone who has been sitting quietly but thinking deeply raises her hand. "Maybe what Pardo always is aware of and what Ovid learns are almost the same thing: a sense of shared humanity. Pardo's sense of shared humanity is apparent in his relationship with Christians as well as with Jews, with neighbors who come to draw water from his well, with his household servants, with the poor of Pisa who come every Friday to his house for food or coupons for restaurants, or money for doctors or for trips to the hospital to visit the bedside of sick relatives. His sense of shared humanity is also apparent in his belief in the essential goodness of people. In Ovid, we see that same sense of shared humanity grow from a feeling of complete alienation to esteem and admiration for the headman and to love for the child, who is barely human. The sense of shared humanity that Ovid comes to feel does not even require, in Ovid's final days with the child, the bond of language."

An outstanding comparison.

Based on this argument about Pardo's always knowing things and Ovid's learning them, could we say something about the different shape of the two narratives? Or is their shape essentially the same?

"Maybe it is fair to say that, while *An Imaginary Life* traces Ovid's arc of learning, *The Parnas* presents Pardo as already in possession of essential knowledge."

An objection is raised. "I disagree. What's most important to Pardo is something that he does not know—where his phobia comes from or how to free himself of it. His learning that, not over time but in a sudden epiphany, is what makes *The Parnas* so beautiful."

"Maybe we can all agree," someone else adds, "that another way of looking at the 'shape' of these two texts might be to say that Pardo's epiphany comes at the moment of death, and Ovid's is a process of many years."

Good.

"Is paradox a principle of narrative construction?" someone asks.

What do you have in mind?

"Well, Ovid is at first completely isolated. He cannot understand anything that is said and finds nothing familiar in his surroundings or in the habits and beliefs of those around him. At the end of the novel, he is, by all rational measures, more isolated than ever. He and the child, who has no language, are traversing a barren, endless landscape. Paradoxically, though, he doesn't feel isolated at all."

And Pardo?

"Pardo, by all rational measures, is isolated, even though he is in his own home and in the city he has lived in all his life. It is also paradoxical that he doesn't feel isolated, surrounded as he is by servants and friends who love him and linked as he is to the world through books, worship, and deeds of kindness."

Isolation is then a relative thing, at least in these works we are discussing?

My class seems to think so.

Another hand is raised. "If we talk of paradox and isolation in *The Parnas*, perhaps we should talk of the scene in the dark at the end, and the isolation of each German soldier within himself, for brutes such as they, at bottom, are isolated from every human feeling and from other human beings, even from other brutes. The self that feels nothing is, I'm pretty sure, an isolated self."

"And a self," someone adds, "which must pretend to feel a sense of community through drunkenness that dulls feeling, such as Pardo's neighbors reported hearing in the soldiers' singing after the killing was over. An act like that, of false camaraderie, is itself a kind of paradox."

A hand goes up. "There's another paradox in *The Parnas* that we haven't mentioned—it's not about isolation, but it is, I think, interesting: it's that a man beset by imaginary fears can also act with great courage when faced with real danger. The neighbors attested to having heard him ask the soldiers for the lives of those in the house, and then, as he was beaten to death, call out boldly, again and again, 'You are the animals, you are the animals.'"

The mention of animals brings us to the center of both stories.

"Should we talk about the significance of animals in the two stories?" someone asks.

We must.

"In *An Imaginary Life*, Ovid dreams repeatedly of animals. There is the centaur dream that begins in terror but ends in something very different:

> Suddenly . . . out of the swirling sky, a horde of forms came thundering towards me—men, yes, horses, yes, . . . the centaurs. But these were not the tamed creatures of our pastoral myths. They were gigantic, and their power . . . was terrible . . . I stood silent in the center of the plain and they began to wheel in great circles about me, uttering cries—not of malice, I thought, but of mourning. *Let us into your world*, they seemed to be saying . . . *Let us into your lives, believe in us. Believe.*

And animals appear again in Ovid's dream of the wolves:

> I venture out beyond the stubbled fields into the desolate plain beyond, into the grasslands beyond the edge of the world . . . I fall to my knees and begin digging . . . Sometimes wolves come, and they claw at the earth beside me. Howling . . . whatever it is they are scratching after, I must discover before them, or I am lost. So I dig harder, faster, sweating . . . I know what it is we are looking for. It is the grave of the poet Ovid—Publius Ovidius Naso, Roman of the equestrian order, poet. In all this desolation, no one knows where he lies.

Both dreams are set on the endless steppes beyond the village fields," she continues, "both are in a sense prophetic, and perhaps most importantly, in both, the border between man and animal is fluid, permeable—if that's the right word—and that fluidity, the merging of man and beast, is somehow a path to one's inner self. Ovid is full of joy when he becomes one with the insects and grass shoots he sees in the earth, the birds whose calls he can imitate, the child who spans both worlds."

And in The Parnas?

Her friend takes up the challenge. "In *The Parnas*, it's just the opposite. For Pardo, animals are terrifying. Arieti's thesis, which Pardo's final words bear out, is that Pardo, as a young man, becomes aware of the unspeakable deeds of evil of which men are capable in their dealings with other men. His conscious mind finds such knowledge unbearable and displaces that evil onto animals, which he shuns. The phobic transference of evil to animals allows Pardo to believe in the goodness of man. The screams that neighbors attest they heard late that morning—'You are the animals, animals, animals'—mark the moment in which Pardo sees before him, in the soldiers, the wolves he has feared and is suddenly free of his phobia. Animals become just animals; they are no longer merged with men. It is, paradoxically, the moment of his torture and death, but it is also the moment of his freedom and joy."

Excellent. And since what you've said has brought us to the endings of both stories, what might we say those endings share? What do both authors imagine for their characters?

A hand goes up. "Deaths that are, in a sense, good."

There is immediate objection. "How can we call Pardo's death 'good'? He is beaten and blinded, his house is ransacked, and those he has tried to protect are killed. His death is not even quick. His torture lasts for hours."

"But it's good in the sense that his mind is freed of its phobia—he no longer displaces his fear about the evil of man onto animals. He sees the German soldiers as actual animals, with 'a snout, fur, four claws, and a tail,' and knows himself blessed by God in these last moments of his life. And he acts with courage. What Arieti as author has done is to give to Giuseppe Pardo Roques, whom he loves and admires, a death marked by freedom, power, and understanding. Arieti's years of working with psychiatric patients have shown him that such a transformation in a moment of great pressure or crisis is possible, and the neighbors' report seems to confirm Arieti's thesis. Pardo's epiphanic death is a gift of love from author to subject."

And what about Ovid's death? Can we also call that a good ending—of his life and of his story?

"He is out on the plain, with the wild child, and feels a oneness with the child and nature that, Malouf suggests, is precisely what Ovid has written about glibly, tongue-in-cheek, with a sophisticate's wink, in *The Metamorphoses*, but which these final moments reveal to be sacred mysteries that have lain behind Ovid's fables and prompted them. Ovid has now touched those mysteries, touched the roots of life and being, and feels transformed. What could be better than that? So his death, unmarked by the world in which he strove to be famous, is also a good death—a gift from the author to a subject the author has come to love."

Congratulations, everyone. You have touched upon all the things that I hoped our discussion would cover—and then some.

We agreed that after our discussions of *An Imaginary Life* and *The Parnas*, we would spend some time viewing and talking about films in which fictional material is added to supposedly "real" stories, in the way that Malouf and Arieti add to the biographies of Ovid and Pardo.

Someone suggests the 1993 film *Point of No Return*, and we begin with that. While no one is averse to seeing Bridget Fonda and Gabriel Byrne, what draws us to the film is a short sequence in which Fonda, playing Maggie/Claudia, a government operative, nearly reveals her true identity to her unsuspecting boyfriend. Byrne, as Bob, the government handler, is also present and creates, on the spot, as protective cover for Maggie, an episode from her supposed childhood in which she rides a horse that bucks, but holds on and never lets go. The fictive backstory he devises is, of course, different from the endings that Arieti and Malouf devise, since Bob, too, is a character in the story, but like their fictions, his is also a gift of grace. As we watch the movie, we realize that it is, in addition, a confession of love.

> BOB: She was born in Kansas City but raised in Chicago . . . I used to see her during the summers on this farm that my uncle owned. You didn't know she spent summers on a farm, did you? Well, she did. I remember, I remember one summer . . . the local kids . . . the kids' family owned this mare—black as a raven's wing, completely wild—remember?—they called it Beauty. She was trained as a trotter but she never really had been ridden. Anyway, the kids told Claudia that she had to ride Beauty, that it was like an initiation kind of thing that they all had to do. One day I remember, about noon, it was really, really hot. We heard this scream. And we went outside and there was Claudia—Claudia, bareback on this wild horse. Well, the horse went completely crazy, bucked, reared. She hung on. She gritted her teeth, dug her heels in, and then she hung on and, by God, she rode that horse. I guess that's how I remember her really—a slip of a girl on a wild black horse. She was so beautiful. She was so beautiful that she gleamed.

Another student suggests the 2007 film *Atonement*. We talk briefly about the plot, in which Briony, an adolescent girl with a crush on the estate gardener, finds him with her sister and, full of jealous fury, falsely testifies to his having sexually assaulted a houseguest. That testimony sends him to prison, from which he is released on condition that he serve as a combat soldier in World War II. He dies in France. Briony's sister cannot bear to remain at home among those who have falsely accused him, and she is killed in a bombing attack in London. As an adult, Briony becomes a famous novelist, eventually understands the magnitude of what she has done, and believes, by writing a novel in which her sister and Robbie are happily reunited after the war, that she has "atoned" for her deed.

Here, as in *Point of No Return*, we note that a character endows another supposedly real character with the "gift" of something better than life itself provided.

But more interesting to us is the critical difference between what Bob and Briony do. Briony's "gift" to her sister and to Robbie is not a gift to them but to herself, an attempt to seek absolution, and therefore a further misuse of the very characters she has wronged. Briony offers her "gift" out of self-interest; Bob and, more importantly, Arieti and Malouf offer theirs out of love.

We move on to the final part of our spring tutorial—creative writing. I ask my students to select an historical or literary figure and, with the aid of hints culled from some background research, to write a story of anywhere from 10 to 25 pages, imagining either the death of that figure or an unknown portion of the life of that figure that is in some way linked to what their research has revealed. We read and talk about this writing as it progresses, and some students continue their stories beyond the time of the tutorial itself.

Credits

About the Author

For forty years, HELAINE L. SMITH has taught English to students in grades 6 through 12 at Hunter College High School and at The Brearley School in Manhattan. For ten years she was a Reader of English Composition Essays and AP Essays in Language and in Literature for The College Board. She is the author of two volumes for high school and college English and Humanities instruction: *Masterpieces of Classic Greek Drama* (2005) and *Homer and the Homeric Hymns: Mythology for Reading and Composition* (2011), has written articles for *Arion, Semicerchio, The Classical Journal, Style,* and *Literary Matters,* and recently completed eight adaptations of Aristophanes' comedies for middle school. She received the Sandra Lea Marshall Award at Brearley in 2005, and teaches Brearley's senior Shakespeare elective.